Great Pretenders

Crime & Society
Series Editor John Hagan
University of North Carolina–Chapel Hill
Editorial Advisory Board
John Braithwaite, Robert J. Bursik, Kathleen Daly, Malcolm M. Feeley,
Jack Katz, Martha A. Myers, Robert J. Sampson, and Wesley G. Skogan

---

Great Pretenders: Pursuits and Careers of Persistent Thieves, Neal Shover

Rape and Society: Readings on the Problems of Sexual Assault,
edited by Patricia Searles and Ronald J. Berger

Alternatives to Imprisonment: Intentions and Reality, Ulla V. Bondeson

Inequality, Crime, and Social Control,
edited by George S. Bridges and Martha A. Myers

FORTHCOMING

Poverty, Ethnicity, and Violent Crime, James F. Short

Youth and Social Justice: Toward the Twenty-First Century,
Nanette J. Davis and Suzanne E. Hatty

Crime, Justice, and Revolution in Eastern Europe, Joachim J. Savelsberg

Crime, Justice, and Public Opinion, Julian Roberts and Loretta Stalens

The White-Collar Offender, Michael Benson and Francis T. Cullen

Great Pretenders

Pursuits and Careers
of Persistent Thieves

Neal Shover

WestviewPress

A Division of HarperCollins*Publishers*

Copyright © 1996 by Westview Press, Inc., A Division of HarperCollins Publishers, Inc.

Published in 1996 in the United States of America by Westview Press, Inc., 5500 Central Avenue, Boulder, Colorado 80301-2877, and in the United Kingdom by Westview Press, 12 Hid's Copse Road, Cumnor Hill, Oxford OX2 9JJ

Library of Congress Cataloging-in-Publication Data
Shover, Neal.
    Great pretenders : pursuits and careers of persistent thieves /
Neal Shover.
        p.   cm. — (Crime and society)
    Includes bibliographical references and index.
    ISBN 0-8133-8730-2 (hc.) — ISBN 0-8133-2811-X (pbk.)
    1. Burglary—United States—Case studies.   2. Thieves—United
States.   I. Title.   II. Series: Crime and society (Boulder, Colo.)
    HV6658.S54   1996
    364.1'62—dc20   96-464
                                                                      CIP

The paper used in this publication meets the requirements of the American National Standard for Permanence of Paper for Printed Library Materials Z39.48–1984.

10   9   8   7   6   5   4   3   2   1

To the memory of my parents,
and to Joe Newman,
who never dreamed it would come to this

Contents

Preface

In the late evening of December 5, 1980, Michael Halberstam, a nationally known cardiologist and author, and his spouse returned to their Washington, D.C., home after spending the evening out. Inside their home the couple encountered a burglar, who shot Mr. Halberstam and then fled from the house. Accompanied by his wife and seriously wounded, Dr. Halberstam left the house, took the wheel of their automobile, and began driving to a nearby hospital. En route he saw the burglar on foot, intentionally struck him with the automobile and continued on. Dr. Halberstam died on the operating table later that evening. The injured burglar was captured by police, convicted of homicide, and sentenced to a lengthy prison term.[1]

The Halberstam burglary and homicide received extensive media coverage, not only because the victims were socially prominent and the crime played out many citizens' worst fears about street crime but also because of what subsequently was learned about the burglar, Bernard Welch. While incarcerated for burglary in a New York prison several years earlier, Welch escaped, resumed his criminal pursuits, and accumulated a substantial personal fortune in the process. He owned a home in an upscale suburb of the District of Columbia, a vacation home in Minnesota, and several luxury automobiles. He had driven a Mercedes to the Halberstams' neighborhood on the evening of the ill-fated burglary.[2] When Welch's Virginia home was searched, police found "a million dollars worth of furs, silverware and other valuables believed to have been stolen" by him.[3] Media accounts of the degree and trappings of his success were splashed before the public for weeks. Although dozens of residential burglaries were reported to Washington, D.C., police on the day the Halberstams were victimized, the city's newspapers carried no account of others. The reasons doubtless include the fact that most burglars, their exploits, and their victims are not nearly so newsworthy as Bernard Welch and the Halberstams.

In the contemporary world, most states prohibit or regulate literally thousands of behaviors, but eight crimes and those individuals suspected or convicted of them are at the core of criminology textbooks and undergraduate criminology courses. Called Index crimes by the Federal Bureau of Investigation's uniform crime reporting program, they are murder and nonnegligent manslaughter, forcible rape, aggravated assault, arson, robbery, burglary, larceny-theft, and motor vehicle theft. Collectively, the last four are a majority of Index crimes annually reported to the police in the United States. In 1992, for example, the nearly 12.5 million robberies, burglaries, larcenies, and vehicle thefts reported to local police represented 91 percent of all reported Index crimes.[4] Police made nearly 2.5 million arrests for Index offenses, but arrests for these four crimes were 77 percent of the total.[5]

Index property crimes (including robbery) and those who commit them, in fact, are a large part of the workload of the entire criminal justice apparatus. Of all persons confined in U.S. state prisons in 1991, nearly four in ten were serving sentences for robbery, burglary, or other property crimes.[6] These crimes rank high in the concerns of many citizens. Odds are high, for example, that today's urban resident in the United States has been or knows a victim of burglary. Little wonder that Index offenders, particularly thieves, receive so much attention from academic criminologists, from the criminal justice enterprise, and from policymakers.

Few thieves commit crime with Bernard Welch's degree of craft, monetary success, and good luck. Whereas he carefully scrutinized victims' jewelry and other valuables, most household burglars content themselves with cash or items, seized hastily, that can be disposed of easily in their home neighborhood and circle of contacts.[7] Whereas his victims typically were residents of upscale neighborhoods, the bulk of those arrested and confined for household burglary are far more likely to victimize working-class households. Welch's crimes were not committed close on the heels of leisure time interactional dynamics in which alcohol or other drugs were consumed and where this and interpersonal forces often distort judgment and decisionmaking. There is no evidence he was under the influence of alcohol or any other drug. Nor did his crimes, as do many of those committed by his peers, spring from financially desperate circumstances. Welch melted down much of his stolen jewelry into gold bars, purchased real estate, invested some of his criminal proceeds, and when arrested, had substantial wealth. Most offenders, by contrast, spend their meager criminal proceeds on high living or on pressing financial exigencies and when arrested, as most eventually are, have little or no resources beyond whatever sum of money is in their pockets at the time. In the words of one, "Whatever they've got, they've got it in their ass pocket."[8] Many, perhaps a majority, of thieves steal and hustle with others, an operating style that leaves them vulnerable to their partners' failings and misfortunes. Welch had no co-offenders and no one, therefore, whose mistakes or loose tongue could rebound to harm him.

Persistent thieves, the subjects of the analysis presented in this book, are distinguished by persistence at common-law property crimes despite their, at best, ordinary level of success. All have at least one adult conviction for robbery, burglary, or theft but return to further crime commission afterward. Many of them commit crime over several years and serve multiple jail or prison terms in the process. In a word, they are men who failed to learn their lesson. The crimes they commit are those that invariably and immediately come to mind when the subject of crime is raised in conversation or featured in the media. Their crimes victimize large numbers of ordinary citizens but receive little media attention. The sociological origins, activities, and criminal careers of these unsuccessful persistent thieves are the focus of my attention in this book.

The men whose lives underpin it are fitting subjects for the label *career criminal*. Although "career criminals" have been depicted as little more than domestic enemies, the suggestion that most are "ordinary folk . . . caught being ordinary once too often"[9] also captures an important truth about them and their lives. The label *pretenders* is apt; most pursue criminal gains despite knowing, in reflective moments, that a time of reckoning almost certainly will follow. My principal analytic objective is to present through their eyes a description of their activities and consequential contingencies at different points in the life course. It is grounded in a variety of data, principally ethnographic in nature, which are explicated in some detail in the Appendix. Although I have tried to present an accurate, if broadly sketched, description of these garden-variety thieves and hustlers, still I am talking about a range of temperament and style that ranges from benign hunter-gatherers to mean-spirited, rapacious thugs. I hope the picture presented does not obscure this variation too severely. For those inclined to theory and projects of crime control, whether as academics, policymakers, or apparatchiks, the materials presented here are a portrait of your adversary and your bread and butter.

Thieves whose involvement in crime is limited to their juvenile years or another brief period of their lives are outside the focus of analysis.[10] Nor does the book depict the experiences of "professional thieves," offenders who, since Edwin Sutherland's pioneering study,[11] have been the focus of recurring sociological interest and investigation.[12] It is not difficult to see why professional criminals have attracted interest. They commit crime with some degree of skill, earn reasonably well from their crimes, and despite stealing over long periods of time, spend rather little time in jails or prisons. They are unusual both in their degree of success and in their comparatively small numbers. The analysis presented here is limited also by its exclusive focus on the experiences of males. The crimes, careers, and perspectives of female offenders are beyond my research experiences and expertise. Despite past ethnographic inattention to them, available evidence suggests women's motivations for crime, its subjective meaning, and the roles they play in criminal incidents may differ considerably from men's.[13] Although analyses of women offenders similar to this study are sorely needed, they must be done by investigators who are far better informed and knowledgeable than I. Readers will note also that little is said about the women whose lives are intertwined with the men who are the principal focus. Suffice it to say that the world of persistent thieves generally is an extremely partriarchal one in which women are relegated to subordinate roles.[14] Exploited or treated with indifference by their male partners, women lead lives that too often are miserable and difficult. Routinely it is they who are left to cope with the consequences of men's unsuccessful escapades and the incarceration these can bring.

Notes

1. *Washington Post,* "Intruder kills Dr. Halberstam," December 6, 1980, p. A1.

2. Barbara Kleban Mills, "Up Front," *People* 15(January 19, 1981), pp. 30–33.

3. *New York Times,* "Authorities search a home of suspect" (December 10, 1980), p. 21.

4. Federal Bureau of Investigation, *Crime in the United States, Uniform Crime Reports, 1992* (Washington, D.C.: U.S. Government Printing Office, 1993), p. 208.

5. Federal Bureau of Investigation, *Crime in the United States, Uniform Crime Reports, 1992* (Washington, D.C.: U.S. Government Printing Office, 1993).

6. Bureau of Justice Statistics, *Survey of State Prison Inmates, 1991* (Washington, D.C.: U.S. Department of Justice, 1993), p. 4.

7. See, for example, Paul F. Cromwell, James N. Olson, and D'Aunn Wester Avary, *Breaking and Entering* (Newbury Park, Calif.: Sage, 1991); and Richard T. Wright and Scott Decker, *Burglars on the Job* (Boston: Northeastern University Press, 1994).

8. Bruce Jackson, *A Thief's Primer* (New York: Macmillan, 1969), p. 133.

9. James Leo Phelan, *Criminals in Real Life* (London: Burke, 1956), p. 55.

10. See, for example, Norman Greenberg, *The Man with a Steel Guitar* (Hanover, N.H.: University Press of New England, 1980).

11. Edwin H. Sutherland, *The Professional Thief* (Chicago: University of Chicago Press, 1937).

12. Interest in professional thieves certainly is not limited to U.S. academics. Examples of research on this type of offender in other countries include John A. Mack, "The able criminal," *British Journal of Criminology* 12(1972), pp. 44–54; and Malin Akerstrom, *Crooks and Squares* (New Brunswick, N.J.: Transaction, 1985). A useful anthology of work on professional criminals is Dick Hobbs, editor, *Professional Criminals* (Aldershot, U.K.: Dartmouth, 1995).

13. Scott Decker, Richard Wright, Allison Redfern, and Dietrich Smith, "A woman's place is in the home: Females and residential burglary," *Justice Quarterly* 10(1993), pp. 143–162.

14. These matters are explored in Darrell Steffensmeier and Robert M. Terry, "Institutional sexism in the underworld: A view from the inside," *Sociological Inquiry* 56(1986), pp. 304–323.

Acknowledgments

I am pleased to thank publicly some of the persons and organizations who in countless ways contributed to completion of this project. For her love, boundless good cheer, and just plain hard work, I am profoundly indebted to Jeanie Shover. For more than twenty-five years, while I have snooped around the worlds and lives of thieves and completed the studies outlined in the Appendix, Jeanie has been a constant source of support and help. There is no other whose contributions have been so singularly critical for this and all my projects. My indebtedness and gratitude to the dozens of offenders and ex-offenders who tolerated my presence and my inquisitiveness are enormous as well. Should any of them chance to read this book, I hope they find it passes the "member test" of validity. Research assistance provided by Ruth Duncan, Hildy Saizow, and Jim Sulton facilitated my early research on thieves. David Honaker and Kenneth Tunnell, my research assistants on the Desistance Project, merit special praise for the many hours they devoted to data collection. As the manuscript for this book neared completion, Belinda Henderson and Heith Copes chased down statistical data and many obscure references. Jeanie Shover, Sandy Maples, Kay King, Letitea Johnson, and Elizabeth Vodra patiently and expertly transcribed the tape-recorded interviews and materials from offender autobiographies that represent the lion's share of data for the book. The opportunity to tackle seriously analysis and interpretation of data from the Desistance Project was provided by three months as visiting scholar at the Centre for Socio-Legal Studies, Wolfson College, Oxford. During this period, I benefited enormously from reactions to a colloquium I presented that eventually became the heart of Chapter 4. I appreciate very much the contributions made by Paul Fenn, Keith Hawkins, and other colleagues in the Centre. In their role as project monitors for the National Institute of Justice, Patrick Langan and Winifred Reed provided unflagging support and a bottomless store of patience. The Inter-University Consortium for Political and Social Research (ICPSR) and the Rand Corporation kindly provided data sets: respectively, the Rand Inmate Survey and the Rand follow-up study of prison inmates. Staff at ICPSR also provided data from the University of Massachusetts survey of 1,982 convicted felons serving time in U.S. state prisons. I am grateful for the cooperation of both organizations.

Joel Best, John Irwin, and Darrell Steffensmeier kindly read and offered comments on an early draft of the manuscript. Their criticisms and suggestions are reflected in many places in the writing. To the extent there is a discernible theme or story line here, they are largely responsible. Other colleagues likewise read, offered suggestions on, and thereby improved selected chapters of the developing manuscript. Robert Bursik read and offered useful comments on Chapter 3. The observations of Derek Cornish, Richard T. Wright, Paul Cromwell, and David Honaker were helpful in Chapter 4. Mike Maguire, Werner Einstadter, and Michael Levi also made useful comments and suggestions on Chapter 4. Paul Rock kindly read the finished manuscript and offered detailed, sound suggestions for improving it. I only regret that the publication schedule left me little time to take account of them. Neither he nor any of the other readers are responsible for anything confusing, far-fetched, or simply incorrect remaining in these pages.

I thank Richard Quinney for his last-minute help in cover design. The cover photograph is his. I am grateful also to John Hagan for encouraging and supporting this project and to Dean Birkenkamp and his colleagues at Westview Press for publishing it. My debt to Jill Rothenberg, Westview associate editor, stands out. As editor, Jill earned my gratitude not only for competently managing the entire project but also for her encouraging, upbeat style and fine sense of humor. I have worked with other editors, but she is the best. The materials presented here draw substantially upon research supported by grants #80-IJ-CX-0047 and #86-IJ-CX-0068 from the U.S. Department of Justice, National Institute of Justice (Neal Shover, Principal Investigator). Points of view or opinions expressed here do not necessarily reflect the official position or policies of the Department of Justice.

Neal Shover

1

Pathways of Persistent Thieves

The years since 1970 have brought dramatic change in the way elite academicians and policymakers talk about crime and what should be done about it. In the place of labeling theory, which had enjoyed considerable support for a decade or more, economists and cognitive psychologists along with many in the criminological mainstream began to advance an interpretation of crime as *choice*. The fundamental assumption of this approach is that criminal acts are products of decisionmaking in which the individual examines and assesses available options and their potential net payoffs, paying attention particularly to the possibility of arrest.[1] In this view, crime unambiguously is *chosen*, purposeful behavior.

The rise of crime-as-choice theory was accompanied by a new focus on "career criminals," men who commit a disproportionately large share of street crime. Although some commentators have taken a rather bleak view of prospects for reversing their pattern of crime, there is good reason to contest this. In contrast to the contention that most career criminals commit crime over many years, there is little doubt that criminal participation by many persistent thieves is intermittent and that they eventually stop committing the kinds of crimes they committed when younger. A study by Daniel Glaser and his students is instructive. They interviewed several hundred federal prison inmates and followed up with additional interviews in the first nine months after the inmates were released. Their research showed that men generally do not devote their energies exclusively to crime for long periods of time. Instead, they "follow a zig-zag path . . . [going] from noncrime to crime and to noncrime again. Sometimes this sequence is repeated many times, but sometimes they clearly go to crime only once; sometimes these shifts are for long duration or even permanent, and sometimes they are short lived."[2] Viewed one way, Glaser's research sensitizes us to scrutinize points in the lives of persistent thieves when seemingly they choose either to engage in crime or to avoid it. In short, the notion that most offenders follow a zig-zag path of criminal participation compels us to be sensitive to *turning points* in criminal careers and the reasons for changes in direction at these junctures.

Significant turning points as well as changes in the frequency of crime commission and crime preference are evident in the six biographical sketches that comprise this chapter. We see in them short-term movement into and out of crime as well as long-term changes in the intensity and quality of offending. Notice that most of the men were products of the lower reaches of the working class, a simple fact of origin that both limits and distorts their perceived legitimate options. Inevitably, this constrains their decisionmaking. Notice also that several of these men found attractive and were drawn to some aspects of crime or hustling. Last, pay attention to how their interests, their commitments, and their willingness to risk imprisonment change over the life course.

I met the men described here under varying circumstances, although most were participants in research projects described in the Appendix.[3] I spent no more than a few hours with most of the men, but I have had occasional contact with others over two decades. This in part explains variation in the detail provided in the biographical sketches. Further adding to this variation is the fact that for some of the men, I had access to correctional records and rap sheets, but for others the only materials I could draw from were interviews.

Carl Horton

A rather passive, quiet man in his mid-50s, Carl Horton was on federal mandatory release when I interviewed him. When asked how many calendar years he spent in confinement, Carl Horton responded like nearly all men who have served multiple prison sentences: "I haven't figured it up." He could only estimate: "I kind of guess, I think maybe about 17 years."[4]

Born in rural North Carolina, Carl is the youngest of five children. His parents separated when he was approximately 12 years old. Carl remained with his father before rejoining his mother and siblings, who since had migrated to Washington, D.C. There was very little family cohesion, and Carl, being the youngest, was left to fend for himself much of the time:

> It was Depression time, and my mother had her thing. I guess she was young and wanted her own life, or something, I don't know. And I had so many different—what would you call them?—stepfathers, or so forth and so on, you know. Mixed me up a lot of times. I was too young to understand, and it would just break my heart, you know. Sometimes she would disappear or something and they would put me with my grandmother and stuff. I was kind of a mixed-up kid.

Although he had no involvement in delinquency, Carl began drinking heavily by age 21 and his entire life has had a problem with alcohol.

Carl was first incarcerated at age 19, when he served six months for robbery. As he describes the incident today:

> I was drinking in an alley with some people, and this guy supposedly had been robbed. Or something like that. And they locked me and this girl— Mary something, I can't think of her name—concerning it. He claimed he was robbed of, I don't know how much money, but I didn't have a penny on me, nothing. And it wind up where they broke it down to a misdemeanor. . . . Anyway, I entered a plea and they gave me six months.

While incarcerated he "met people and got to know guys in there." He was fascinated and captivated by their accounts of criminal activities:

> I listened to them talk about how to make money, big money. . . . And I got to thinking I was kinda smart then. Tryin' to figure ways to make money illegally, you know, without working too hard for it.
> Q: You wanted to be a good hustler, huh?
> A: I wanted to, yes.

Carl never realized his criminal ambitions because "I figure I didn't have the intelligence or something, the know-how or whatever. . . . I never had any luck." Although he committed rather little crime, Carl served multiple prison sentences.

Carl attributes nearly all his criminality to the combined effects of momentary need for money and the influence of alcohol. He says that when pressured for cash and intoxicated, he is easily led and also tends to do "stupid" things. Carl never has robbed anyone and estimates that he had committed no more than 10 burglaries in his entire life. They were unskilled and yielded little return; he notes that he never made more than $200 from any of the crimes he committed. Lack of criminal sophistication is evident in this description of two burglaries:

> I was living on P Street, I think, and I got behind in my rent and everything. . . . And I broke a window in a place and pulled some stuff out of there to sell. And I got caught, and I think I got four years in Lorton [then the District of Columbia reformatory].
> I got arrested in '74, I think. There's a place near where I was living called Lee's, some kind of auto place. A friend of mine had busted the window in the place and told me what he got out of there. Says, "It's still open." So, I went down there and got the rest. Put it on one of those push carts that you get in the Safeway and stuff. And I'm pushing it up the street at 4 o'clock in the morning, and the police grabbed me.

Of the prison sentences he has served, Carl says that eventually he reached a point where "I didn't have the fear, you know. I say, 'well, hell, it's a place to eat and a place to sleep, and there's no pressure on me. I can get my mind clear.' It lifted my brain of worry, so it was kinda easy."

Carl once worked for nearly four years as a baker, but it has been many years since he last held steady employment. Today he has few occupational and social resources from which he can draw. He never married but did father a child by a girlfriend some years ago. He has no contact with either of them today. His siblings live in another city, but so long as his fortunes are down, Carl avoids contact with them, primarily because of the embarrassment it would cause him.

Carl believes that he wasted many years of life, and indeed he tends to speak about it in the past tense: "I had dreams of doing better for myself and making life better for myself, you know. I had dreams. And I kept dreaming and dreaming and dreaming, but they never quite came true."

Carl Horton seems overwhelmed by the downward turns his life has taken. Most of his youthful dreams, both legitimate and illegitimate, have vanished. Asked to describe a typical day, he said:

> Well, I get up about 5:30. I shave and wash up. I come out and if my friend, William, don't have any jobs, I go down to, go catch the bus to Georgia and Alaska—that's the District [of Columbia] line—and stand around and wait for somebody to dig footings or pour concrete or something like that. . . . And I would stay there until about 9:30. If I don't catch out [get day labor] by 9:30, I hitchhike a ride back downtown. If I got money, I catch the bus. But if I don't have money, I'd hitchhike a ride. And I come downtown and stop around two or three places where the guys hang around. They drinkin' wine and stuff like that. Somebody always got something. We drink some wine or, you know, whatever. And if I got anything at home, I go home and eat me a sandwich or something like that. If not, I'll go around to one of these places where they give away free food. They got about three or four places around here where you can go and all you have to do is line up and go in and eat. . . . That keeps you holdin' together, in physical condition, you know. That's about it.

Although he is dissatisfied with his present life, Carl knows that his advancing age makes it unlikely that he will be able to secure work and a steady income.

Brian Biluszek

An only child, Brian Biluszek was born in Michigan to an accounting clerk and his wife. The parents divorced when Brian was a small child, leaving him with no significant childhood memories of his mother. After the divorce, the father and Brian returned to live with the former's parents. When Brian was six years old, his father took employment as a clerk in the aircraft industry, and he and Brian moved to the state of Washington. Although Brian's father subsequently married a woman who had a child by a previous husband, relations between her and Brian were not good. For this reason, Brian returned to Michigan and lived with his paternal grandparents for approximately one year before returning to his father's home.

As he approached adolescence, relations between Brian and his father deteriorated, in part because the latter "did not show his emotions" easily and Brian, as he puts it today, was a "smart ass." Although Brian began stealing candy and other small items from stores before age 10, he did not begin serious stealing until he reached adolescence. While his family was on vacation, their home was burglarized, an experience that angered and upset his father. The police investigation that followed struck Brian as extremely cursory, "a farce." He drew the lessons that burglary not only is safe but also that it could be a vehicle for getting back at this father:

> I started stealing, I really believe I started stealing, you know, for psychological reasons, wanting to get even with somebody. . . . The only thing I can think of is that I had so much, such a great deal of hatred and contempt for my father that, you know, that if I'm stealing something I'm doing something to hurt him, I'm getting back at him, I'm getting even.

Although Brian had no official juvenile record, at age 15 he began breaking into homes in the neighborhood where he lived. He describes himself as a person who always has had difficulty relating easily with others, and stealing gained him acceptance with other boys who also were committing crimes: "I wasn't stealing with them, we were just a group that knew that each other were stealing, kind of a little group of 'hoodlums' in the school." Although most of his crimes were committed alone, Brian and a neighbor boy collaborated on some break-ins while he was in high school. Asked how he learned to steal, Brian said it was "through trial and error, TV and picture shows, stuff like that. Trial and error mostly." In addition to the money he garnered from break-ins, they were "*awful* exciting, a big rush."

Brian enlisted in the army at age 18, but he did not wear the yoke of authority well. He was AWOL on several occasions, spent several days in the stockade, and was discharged after only seven months. Today he says that when he enlisted he was promised training that he did not receive, and this only embittered him: "I think I had unreasonable expectations of it. I swallowed the line, you know—'I'm going to learn a trade.' And the recruiter, I felt that the recruiter had promised me certain training that I didn't get. And I thought they'd lied to me." After his discharge, he returned to Michigan and lived with an aunt and uncle.

Brian's periods of stealing were intermittent; on at least one occasion he went for a year or more without doing any break-ins. This was true while he was in the military and for nearly one year after his discharge. He says that "when I'd get in an emotionally stressful situation, I would start back with that pattern of burglarizing." At age 20, Brian followed a girlfriend to Georgia, where she planned to attend school. Before leaving town, however, he stole money from a former employer that he believed was rightfully his. He explains: "He wouldn't give me my last paycheck, because I had created some liability that he would have to take care of." Once in Georgia, however, Brian resumed his old pattern:

> I wanted money, I needed money, and I knew I could get it that way. . . . I didn't want to look for a job. It's not the fact that I didn't want to work, . . . it's the fear, it was the fear of going out and having to ask for work, you know, look for a job. It wasn't the actual working.

The reasons he stole had changed since his adolescent days:

> In the beginning, I didn't have to worry about a place to stay, you know. I was living at home, I was getting fed, I didn't need any money. I think, back then, I'd take liquor and guns and jewelry and money, if it was there. It didn't really matter. Right at the end, I was stealing to support myself, so I was into stuff I could sell. And I always checked the freezer and refrigerator before I left a house, to take meat, you know. If there was steaks or something, I would take food.

Asked what he did with the things he stole, Brian replied, "that was a big problem, because I was afraid to try to pawn anything and, mostly then, I took, I just took money, credit cards, and handguns, you know. When I got popped [arrested] I had, like, forty pieces in the house . . . that I didn't know what to do with, and . . . I was too scared to try to sell them. . . . I was kind of naive." He says today that "if I knew then what I know now, I probably could have been making three or four times as much money as I did."

Although the great majority of Brian's burglaries victimized households, when he did break into a business it yielded a larger sum of cash than he ever had gotten from his previous household burglaries: "I did one [burglary], it was an insurance company, and I found, I got about five or six hundred dollars in cash. And I'd never gotten that before out of a house, and I was just *thrilled* with businesses." Consequently, he decided to continue business break-ins. One night, he was interrupted as he was preparing to break into a business that he believed was empty at the time.

Q: How'd they catch you?
A: I'm not real sure if it was, I really believe there was someone in—it was a restaurant I was trying to break into—and I believe there was someone inside the building. And they called the cops. They heard me outside.
Q: They caught you dead bang?
A: Uh, I was trying to break open the door, and I heard a noise that sounded an awful lot like the hammer on a revolver being pulled back. And I left. And I'd parked my car, probably a quarter of a mile down the road, and I went down the railroad tracks and crossed the ditch and got back in my car. And I started to drive away, and when I started to drive away, you know, there were blue lights everywhere.

After his arrest the police found considerable stolen goods in Brian's apartment. He was offered an 11-year sentence in return for a guilty plea, declined, and eventually settled for 6–10 years. As he says today:

Looking back on it, I mean, I had been down there probably three or four months in Georgia, and I still spoke like someone from up North and had absolutely no family down there. And with all of the wealthier people that I had offended in a small southern community, I was very lucky.

After his first year of prison confinement, Brian discovered that doing time "got easy," and he settled into "the dull routine of it." He spent approximately 36 months in prison.

When he was paroled, Brian was "real scared" and didn't know what he wanted to do. "I was scared of having to deal with people," largely because he always has been "introverted." He says that "I knew I didn't want to work, 'cause I was scared of working. . . . People really terrified me, free-world people. I couldn't handle it for some reason, I don't know." He enrolled at a nearby university and, several months later, resumed committing burglary. Again, some aspects of his crimes had changed:

Q: Before you went to the joint, were you usually drunk when you broke into a place?
A: Oh, I never drank. I mean, I'd been drunk a few times, but I didn't drink on a regular basis.
Q: So drinking didn't have anything to do with you breaking into places?
A: No, I had plenty of nerve before I got arrested. Too much. I was pretty cocky.

Now he usually drank before stealing "because of the tremendous amount of fear that I felt":

> I was, I still am, terrified of having to go back to prison. I was afraid being out here, and I was afraid of going back. When I was doing these burglaries, I think I was wanting to go back, because being out here was really more terrifying than being in there.
> Q: What was terrifying about being out here?
> A: I've got to make my own way, make my own decisions, work, function in society. I don't have to do that in the joint.
> Q: Were you afraid when you were stealing?
> A: Not when I was drunk, no. God's own drunk, fearless man! I'd do crazy things when I was drunk. Seemed like I didn't care. . . . I would do crazy shit that I didn't think about would send me back [to prison] until after I'd already done it. So I got into the school thing. And I just kind of hung in there because it was nice and easy.

While attending school, Brian lived in an old house near campus that had been subdivided into efficiency apartments. His tuition was paid from a state program, and he also held part-time employment in a campus cafeteria, which gave him access to free food. He estimates that after resuming burglaries he broke into "five or six, probably less than ten, houses or apartments." One day he was surprised by returning residents while in their home:

> I had a bag full of shit, I don't even know what it was—I was drunk. The thought crossed my mind when I went in the house—because I kind of went in the back, through a broken window, a small window or something—that if someone came in I wouldn't be able to get out. And they came in the front door, and I just went blank. I was just terrified, I guess. I didn't know what to do, and hell, I stuck my hand in my pocket and stuck my finger out like you see in the movies. And I stepped out where they could see me and told them both to get back away from the door. And they moved back away from the door, and I hit the door, running. . . . I didn't sleep any that night. I was just physically shaking, until well into the next afternoon.

He cannot recall with certainty, but Brian believes this was his final burglary. Two years later, he received a B.S. degree and immediately found employment in his chosen field. After this, as he puts it, "I was making good money, I didn't need anything."

As is true of nearly everyone who has committed a large number of crimes over a period of years, Brian has only the crudest estimate of how many burglaries he has committed. Initially, he said "300 to 400." Later, he said "I once figured out that I served about two days in prison for every [burglary] I committed." This would place the number of his burglaries at approximately 550. In addition to burglaries, over a period of several years Brian also stole three automobiles. He and a neighbor boy stole one car when they discovered keys in the ignition. They "took it down to an old quarry and hot-rodded it and just tore it up." In that same period they also chanced upon a car with the keys in it, took the keys, and returned later and stole the car. They drove the car to another city and abandoned it. Brian stole another car by duplicating the keys after its owner left the car to be serviced at his place of employment. The car "had a good set of tires, and I needed a set of tires." He later took the car from the owner's driveway, removed the wheels, and left town.

Brian smoked marijuana for many years and occasionally used psychedelic drugs when he was younger, but he never used "hard drugs." After his parole, however, he began drinking heavily, a practice he continued for many years. As he says today, "things got pretty foggy there, I don't remember much of the 80s. . . . I abused alcohol and drugs that bad. There are a few high points that stick out, and that's about it." During that time he also served two short jail terms following convictions for driving while intoxicated. Although he has worked for many years and has committed no burglaries during this time, Brian still has "those thought patterns today, I mean it's just like an automatic reflex with me, you know. If I see something, some little gear clicks, you know—well, I could get into *that*. Or I could steal that. That's as far as it goes these days." Brian has been married twice, the first time before he went to prison. Both marriages ended in divorce, in part because he describes himself as a person who is hard to get along with: "I'm egotistical, and I like my own way, and I want what I want when I want it." He has no children.

Brian began attending Alcoholics Anonymous more than two years ago, has managed to stop drinking, and at age 45 says he is happier than at any time in his life: "This last year of my life, since I've been going to AA and trying to work this AA program and everything, this probably has been the only happy year I've enjoyed in my life. I'm having fun, I'm really enjoying it." I asked Brian how widely it is known that he is an ex-convict:

Q: Do people where you work know that you were locked up?
A: Yeah.
Q: How long was it before they knew, before you told anyone?
A: Well, see, I don't know who knows and who doesn't know, but I really haven't been making a secret of it lately. But I don't bring it up in conversation either. I guess I was probably, I've been with this company, I guess, four or five years, and they probably knew that I was an ex-con before they offered me a job.
Q: What you're telling me is that you actually don't remember ever *telling* anyone?

A: Yeah, it's one of those things, you know, it's information that just gets out and just kind of drifts through the office.

Q: Do you ever talk to anyone about it at work?

A: Not at work. No one's ever asked me though, either.

Q: Do you feel bad about being an ex-con?

A: Not now.

Q: Why?

A: It's just something that happened, that I did, and I was responsible for doing, you know. It's over. I can't do anything about it. . . . I've been out almost 20 years.

Brian has two half brothers by his mother's later marriage to another man, but he has almost no contact with his father or other relatives today: "I have absolutely no desire. . . . My mother's sister calls me every now and then, but I don't make any effort to contact her, I don't make any effort to contact any of my family." Although he is not afraid of prison, he does not want to return there. There is one exception: "If I was in my 60s and homeless, I'd commit a robbery and wait for them to arrest me."

Robert Timmons

Robert Timmons was reared by his mother in Washington, D.C., as an only child. Her regular employment left him with little supervision, and as he tells it, "I ran in the streets. I was a street child, really." Robert first came to the attention of officials at the age of nine, charged with being incorrigible. A report from that time states that he is "constantly truant from school, stays out late, lies, and steals." Released on probation, he also was placed in a boarding school. Because of misconduct and running away, a few months later Robert was committed to the District of Columbia's Industrial Home School, at Blue Plains, Virginia, then a racially segregated institution for delinquent boys.

Robert was before the juvenile court again at age 13 for taking a bicycle and at age 15 for housebreaking. He was placed on probation both times. When he appeared in court again two years later charged with unlawful entry and escape from the detention home, Robert was committed to the Federal Bureau of Prisons' National Training School for Boys (NTS). He subsequently escaped from NTS on three occasions and, during one of them, assaulted a woman with an iron bar and attempted raping her. At age 16, because according to Robert "they couldn't handle me there," he was transferred from NTS to the federal reformatory at Chillicothe, Ohio. He was confined there when Pearl Harbor was bombed, and he recalls later when inmate volunteers were sought to clean up rubble from German bombing of British cities. Robert remained in Chillicothe for two years before returning to NTS and a parole two months later. He quickly resumed his earlier pattern of street life and crime. As Robert interprets it today:

> The thing was to make it big, to get in the rackets, sell whiskey. (There wasn't no drugs then but whiskey and gambling, see.) And these were the people I looked up to. I can remember very clearly now, there was a man named Mr. Leon in our neighborhood who had two cars and several homes. People looked up to him because . . . most people was poor. I liked to dress good because those in our community that made it big, I wanted to be them. I wanted to be like Mr. Leon. Yeah, I wanted to be all of that. And I would get with a gang, a group of fellas, and go out and rob and, you know, go uptown, 'cause it was mostly white, where we'd go to and burglarize. [We'd] take their money and all their goods and whatnot, see. This is the only thing I'd ever known prior to the time I went to the penitentiary.

Less than two months after release from the National Training School, Robert was convicted of attempted housebreaking and received a 60-day sentence. Less than one year later he was sentenced to 6–18 months on a charge of assault with a deadly weapon. As he describes the incident today:

> I went to Lorton for shooting somebody. I got in an argument.
> Q: Did you kill him?
> A: No, I didn't kill him. I shot him, oh, must have been twice, three times. I tried to shoot him a fourth time, but the gun hung up. His name was Roosevelt, got in an argument with him. He called me a lot of names and offered me outside. And I had my .25 pistol, and he pulled a knife. Nicked me, tried to cut me all up with a switchblade. [He] backed me against the wall, and I had trouble getting my gun out. And when I did get it out, I started shooting, and I was trying to kill him.

Reflecting on this period in his life, Robert says "I was *terrible!* Even among my peers, I was considered terrible. They called me 'Black Robert,' say, 'don't mess with Black Robert.'"

Within weeks of his release from Lorton, Robert was convicted on multiple charges of carrying a deadly weapon, unlawful entry, and larceny and was sentenced to 15 months. Within months of his release, he was convicted of robbery and sentenced to concurrent terms of 1–3 years and 2–7 years at Lorton. Following a knife fight with another inmate and the loss of 200 days "good time," Robert was transferred to the U.S. penitentiary at Atlanta, Georgia. After serving nearly six years, he was discharged via conditional release. Six months later, he and another man were arrested shortly after robbing a cleaners. Convicted on multiple counts of armed robbery, Robert was returned to Atlanta with a sentence of 9–27 years. As in the past, he proved to be a problem for prison officials:

> When I was in Atlanta, they didn't like the way I talked. They, uh, wanted me to do something a certain way, I did not do it. I did it my way. So this brought on hardship. They would, every occasion they'd get, they would pick on me. Slightest error I made, they'd bring it to my attention. They was on me all the time. . . . They had "incorrigible" stamped on my record.

Robert was a Muslim for many years and openly acknowledged this during his periods of incarceration. Along with his refusal or inability to kowtow to correctional personnel, his religious beliefs and his insistence on practicing them openly added substantially to the problems he encountered from the correctional establishment. As he explained to me, "See, now, I was defiant. And for a black person to be defiant in an institution, he's asking for trouble." During his stay at Atlanta, Robert was accused of proselytizing and of holding a "cult meeting" on the prison yard. While confined in "the hole" in Atlanta, Robert says he was visited by the director of the Bureau of Prisons and told "we got a place for you. Don't worry, we'll take care of you." Shortly thereafter, Robert was recommended for transfer to the U.S. penitentiary at Alcatraz Island, California. The report that recommended transfer charged that "he is a rabid racial agitator and is constantly trying to stir up trouble in that connection." It claimed, further, that "he is a definite menace to the morale and good order of the institution." Apparently convinced of his dangerousness, the Bureau of Prisons transferred Robert Timmons to Alcatraz.

During the nine years he spent on Alcatraz, Robert held a variety of work assignments, including a lengthy stint in the barbershop. He continued practicing his religion—a report notes that he is "very faithful" to it—and was seen by the prison staff as "race conscious." Although he was not a serious disciplinary problem, he did receive misconduct reports for fighting, fighting in the dining room, insolence, and refusal to obey orders. Despite the ominous tones of official reports, Robert began to change himself while at Alcatraz. He was denied parole but claims "by that time I had rehabilitated myself. They didn't rehabilitate me, I rehabilitated myself, really."

In 1963, when the Bureau of Prisons closed Alcatraz, Robert was returned to Atlanta. The move made him feel "fantastic" and "for the first time I felt free." He remained at Atlanta for six years and continued the process of self-change that began during his days on Alcatraz. By the time he appeared before the parole board again, according to Robert, "I had changed my whole outlook, really." His final release from confinement occurred 14 years before I met and interviewed him. He was arrested approximately one year after release:

> I was picked up downtown. It was a mistaken identity, and I had a roust with the police and detectives. We got into it, and they busted my nose. I never did get it reset. And I went to the district jail, and the D.A. dismissed the case because he didn't want it, he didn't want to try it.

The incident occurred in 1970, and Robert has had no contact with the criminal justice system since.

When I met and interviewed Robert Timmons, I was struck by the contrast between the person described in his correctional records and the man I interviewed. I found him to be pleasant, almost ebullient, and interested in my research. He had been employed for nearly 13 years as a hospital technician. He enjoyed his work, as evidenced by the way he talked about it. He also did side work using skills he acquired while in prison:

> I can tailor, I do upholstery work, chairs. Whenever I feel like doing a chair or doing some antique furniture for somebody, I let them know I'm ready. "I'll take care of you now." Or whenever somebody wants their hair cut in the hospital, they know I'll do that. I'll take my equipment to the hospital tomorrow and cut a guy's hair. I say "always give me a notice a day in advance." I'll always be able to make a living. I'll never sell my equipment.

There is little about Robert Timmons or his demeanor to suggest that he was largely "state-raised" and had spent nearly half of his life in correctional institutions. Unlike some of the state-raised, who internalize the reasons for their failures, Robert Timmons has externalized them and, consequently, has few regrets about his past. As he explained it:

> You must remember I didn't have no way or means of making no money or anything when I was young. So, consequently, I resorted to crimes. Not that I had the natural tendency to do so. It was conditions that forced me to. I had no other choice. I had worked at jobs. I worked at construction and all that, but I mean as far as having a regular job and getting a salary, no.

Robert married after his final release from prison, although he was separated from his wife when I met him. He resided in an apartment located in a suburb of Washington, D.C. He was unhappy with himself for being too deeply in debt but otherwise expressed happiness and contentment with his life. He was no longer active in Islam because his pattern of casual involvement with women conflicted with its teachings, and he did not want to be a "hypocrite." Until several years before I met and interviewed him, Robert believed he had no living relatives. When his mother passed away, however, he was contacted by a woman and learned she is his aunt. Through her he learned that he also has several step-siblings. The discovery of these family ties meant a great deal to Robert. He visited his family often and obviously enjoyed the warmth of these contacts. Although his relatives did not know about his prison record, he was planning someday to tell them about it. As he put it, "I would like them to know that I haven't always been the nice person I am today." Reflecting on the years he spent stealing and in prison, Robert says, "I thought I was right. But I was wrong, like two left shoes. . . . I don't want that kind of life no more. I know what it was. It's terrible."

Roger Morton

One of four children, Roger Morton was born and reared in eastern Kentucky, the son of a painter and a full-time homemaker. Asked if there was conflict or problems in the parental family, he says "no" and also that he "was very lucky and had a close-knit family." Discipline, however, was both strict and corporal:

> My dad used to whup on me *severely*. I mean, I should have known better. He was strict on us. I don't want to say [I was] "beat" though, he just whipped me with a belt, a switch or something like that. Then, I thought he was just bein' too hard, 'cause I'd see other folks that just let their kids get away with everything. But now that I look back, he was right about it, he was trying to teach me better, he meant well with what he was doin'. I respect him a whole lot. I get along great with my dad now.

As Roger and his siblings got older, "we had our own ways to go, I guess." Like Roger, one of his brothers later served a sentence in the penitentiary. Roger says that "me and him are the black sheep in the family."

Roger began working at age 10: "I'd get out and work on the farm, work in the garden, raise stuff to eat, mow yards around the place to get me a little extra spending money, haul hay, cut tobacco." His youth was not free of involvement in delinquency. In one incident, he and several other boys were out running around late at night and ended up committing acts of vandalism. Today he attributes his delinquency to spending time with the wrong crowd, "doin' what they do and trying to fit in. . . . [We'd] go out, see somebody do something, get to laughing about it or something, and the next thing you know, *you're* doin' it!" In another incident, he and his brother were squirrel hunting when they encountered and joined up with another person. The three then chanced upon a house they did not know about and decided to break into it. They stole old coins, fishing tackle boxes, and other items. Both these episodes of delinquency were disposed of with sentences to probation and orders to make restitution.

Roger graduated from high school and enlisted in the U.S. Marine Corps a few weeks later. Although there were juvenile charges pending against him at the time, he did not enlist because he was given an ultimatum. He says instead that "they suggested that I needed to do *something*." Trained as a truck driver and diesel engine mechanic, Roger enjoyed the time he spent in the Marine Corps, during which he was stationed in several countries. Before shipping out, he also committed approximately 15 business burglaries. Most of these burglaries occurred following bouts of heavy drinking while Roger was accompanied by friends. Typically, they would "just be out riding around. 'There's a place, let's see what we can get out of it.' Something like that." He refers to this period of time and his activities as a "spree" and notes that none of them were arrested for the burglaries they committed.

Eventually, Roger was posted to Okinawa, where he was involved in an incident that ended his military career. Describing it today, he says:

> We went out drinkin', partying one night, me and my best friend. We'd been stationed in North Carolina together, we were in the same unit over there. We were just runnin' buddies, we knew each other well. . . . And we ran into a coupla fellas . . . and we got to partying with them. They were buying drinks, and we were about out of money. They kept buyin', so we kept drinkin'. So we got ready to head back to base, we got a taxi . . . [The driver] took us to the back main gate, and it was open. . . . I had $20, so I told them, I said "I'll pay for the ride," a three-dollar taxi ride. I gave him the $20, and he tried to give me change for a five-dollar bill. . . . I was drunk, but I wasn't that drunk. My friend—he was sittin' in the front seat—I was standing outside the driver's door, tryin' to get my money back. He was tryin' to pull off, and I was just holdin' his arm, trying to keep him from driving off. My friend hit him in the nose. I opened the door and [the driver] fell out. I reached in—well, I had the two dollars he give me—and got 15 more dollars. Me and John turned around and left, didn't think no more about it. I thought the other two guys just got out and went on their way.

Two days later, however, Roger and his buddy were questioned by military police about the incident. As it turned out, after the two left the taxi driver, "the boys that were in the backseat, both of them robbed him [the taxi driver], I mean beat him up severely and robbed him. I guess by John hitting him in the nose it fired them up, and they wanted to get redneck." When one of the assailants was caught, he told on the three others. All four men were turned over to Japanese authorities, and all were convicted of assault and robbery. "Their logic behind it was that if I would have just let the guy took my $15, he never would have been beat up, he never would have been robbed." Roger received a sentence of four years. The experience embittered him, primarily because military authorities offered him little assistance and, he believes, abandoned him despite knowing there was little substance to the charges against him. After he learned that he would be going to prison, Roger and another soldier stole automobiles and used them for joyriding on the island. Roger was a disciplinary problem for Japanese prison authorities and earned no good-time reduction of his sentence. He eventually served a total of 49 months.

After his release, Roger returned to eastern Kentucky and lived with his parents for a few months. He then moved to Atlanta, began doing construction work, and later became assistant manager of a nightclub. As he notes today, "I had all that good free liquor so I took advantage of it. And that's where I started goin' downhill." When the nightclub eventually closed, Roger returned to construction work. He earned high wages, most of which he received in cash and were not reported. He spent his free time drinking. He also accumulated several minor criminal charges related to excessive drinking and served approximately 4–5 months in a halfway house after conviction for failing to pay for gasoline at a service station. Commenting on this period of his life, Roger says that he remained bitter over his treatment by military and Japanese-justice officials. This found expression in

> a state of mind you get into. You say, "what the fuck." You don't care. About anything. "I've been to prison. So what." They have to *catch* me. I can go out here and steal something, they have to *catch* me. I've been in prison before. I really did think like that—"I've done that before, I'm not afraid." The fear was gone then, I'd already broken it in over there in Japan. You know, you're taught when you're a small kid, you don't never want to go to prison. You're supposed to fear those places. It was already gone. I had a lot of bitterness in me, for them doin' me like that. I was in a state of mind where I didn't care no more.

Although Roger was living in Atlanta, he frequently traveled back and forth to Chattanooga, Tennessee, where his widower father then resided. There he met and began dating a divorced woman with two children. When the couple later married, they set up housekeeping in north Georgia. Roger continued his heavy drinking. Although he has experimented with many types of illicit drugs, alcohol has been his problem. After the marriage, relations between Roger and his wife were stormy, in part because of finances.

Me and her was having problems, so I knew, somehow or other I was gonna leave. And I wasn't gonna be a schmuck and leave her with all those bills that me and her had made. So I went out and done the only thing that I could think of at the time, did something idiotic. I went out and stole money to pay the bills up, and then I was gonna take off.

One night, he "went out, just riding around lookin' for something to steal and sell." I asked him, "What kind of mood were you in?" He replied, "I was drinkin'. The mood was desperate, that's what mood I was in. I had to have some money. Most definitely. The lights was gonna be turned off, all kind of bad things was gonna happen if I didn't have the money." Roger stopped in a grocery store to buy some snacks and ended up robbing the clerk:

There was an older lady in there, she bought some little necessity items. . . . [She] come up 23 cents short, or something like that. And she was standin' in line, there was five or six people in there. And this [clerk] was gonna make her take and put something back and re-ring everything up. And it just embarrassed the lady right there in front of everybody—"You ain't got enough money to pay for it!" Degraded her. And I just stepped around all of them and throwed a quarter up there and told her she didn't have to put nothing back. There wasn't any need of going any further with it. And the little old lady just thanked me and left, she didn't even wanna look at me. I had [some items] and I set them down, went and got my car, drove it around, and filled it up with gas. . . . I just knew what I was gonna do. I filled the tank up, went back in there, and let all those people leave, went back in there and started talking to the lady. I *knew* I was gonna do it, but I wasn't giving it much thought, as far as takin' her money or anything. I was just generally gonna let her know that what she done was screwed up. And she started gettin' mouthy with me about it. I told her, "you shouldn't have embarrassed that old lady." And I said, "now that you mention it, if the quarter meant so much to you, give me the rest of your damn money." I never put my hands on her. They called it strong-arm robbery, . . . [but] I just told her, "give me your money." . . . She give me the money. I said, "you got a back room or something, you better be gettin' into it." She went and locked herself in the bathroom, and I got in the car and left.

A few days later, Roger heard that his brother had been misidentified as the perpetrator. To prevent his brother's arrest, Roger decided to turn himself in. En route to jail, he drank a fifth of vodka in order to work up the nerve to surrender. (Roger says that drinking of this magnitude "was normal for me then.") He stopped in a convenience store to get a soft drink, but entering the store he became "dizzy and almost passed out."

Apparently his behavior alarmed the clerk. She pulled a pistol, they struggled over it, a shot was fired, Roger took the proceeds from the cash register, ran, and was apprehended almost immediately. He subsequently learned that the store he "robbed" was owned by a police official, which he believes was a major determinant of the 35-year sentence he received. Two days after pleading guilty, Roger was in the penitentiary.

As he tried to settle into doing time, Roger found it difficult because of "bein' married and missin' my wife and things like that. I just told her to quit writin' after a while. It was hard to keep up with them and do time, too. So I had to either do one or the other. I think they understood, finally, and they went on with what they had to do." His wife divorced him and Roger did his time. Looking back on it today, he says that "I just, I growed up a lot." Roger served seven years, was paroled in 1991, and returned to live and work with his father.

A few months after his release, Roger looked up his former wife, and eventually they remarried. Their relationship continues to be tumultuous. Roger's persistence at it he attributes to the fact that he loves his wife. Roger, his wife, and their two teenaged children now reside near Nashville, Tennessee, where he works as a painter. Because of the nature of his employment, the family's economic fortunes are subject to seasonal fluctuation. When I met and interviewed him, he and his wife recently had filed for chapter 13 bankruptcy protection. Roger has curtailed his drinking and foresees little chance he ever again will be incarcerated:

> Think about it, I started goin' to the joint when I was a juvenile. And I spent most of my young life, all the good years of my life there. My grandfather told me that "youth is wasted on the young." And mine was wasted in the joint. I figured if I could get out, turn my life around somehow, and have some things in life that I missed while I was in there, then maybe I hadn't wasted my whole life. Anyway, I give them enough of my life. . . . I don't like bein' in a cage, lookin' through bars. . . . Prison's not my place.

He describes himself today as "a laid-back country boy" who has learned how to steer around trouble. He does, however, express regret that he did not make greater use of his athletic abilities while younger and also that his bad-conduct discharge from the Marine Corps has made him ineligible for veteran's benefits.

Michael Preston

Michael Preston was born in rural Virginia but grew up in one of the poorest neighborhoods of Washington, D.C. His family disintegrated while

Michael was a boy, and thereafter he was shunted between the homes of various relatives. He began running in the streets at an early age and began committing acts of petty stealing and delinquency while very young. As a result of chronic school truancy and petty stealing, at age 12 he was committed to the Industrial Home School, where he remained for approximately four months. Quickly resuming his earlier pattern of truancy and delinquency, Michael was recommitted to the same institution, this time remaining there for more than one year. Following his release, Michael and other boys began a pattern of purse snatching, which quickly led to his re-arrest and a commitment to the National Training School for Boys. He remained there for 18 months before being paroled to the home of an aunt and uncle.

Michael says he was not an "exploiter" of other boys, but he learned how to "take care of myself" during his juvenile confinement. This earned him a measure of respect from other inmates and also from the boys he resumed running with after release. Michael made an effort at legitimate employment, but his earnings were meager and the call of the streets was strong. His involvement in delinquency continued. Over a period of several months, he and his companions gradually began committing armed robberies. At age 17 he was rearrested, held in jail for nearly six months, and sentenced to 3–10 years at Lorton. Michael had a very difficult time reconciling to and serving his sentence:

Q: You say you were a "fuckup" in Lorton. In what sense?
A: I did a lot of things to stay in trouble. I was young, you know, when I caught the 10 years. . . . And I was one of those rebellious types, you know. I was buckin', you know, because I was just fucked up with the world, you know. I had the 10 years, man, you know, [but] I just, I just couldn't adjust, you know, to doing the time, especially at the place where I was at, you know. There was a lot of prejudice there, you know, hacks there, man. . . . The cats was prejudiced. It was very prejudiced. Everybody was somebody's uncle or cousin, you know, all the captains and shit. And they was, hey man, they did a thing to you. I had some hacks there that couldn't read my name, couldn't spell my name, you know. But I got to say "sir," you know, speak to them as "sir," and shit like that. And they called me "boy," and stuff like that, you know. And it just fucked me up, and I couldn't cope with it, you know. So I would buck, you understand. I was a 'buckin' dude,' you know. Call him 'sir'! I wouldn't call him shit, you know. And so I just got wrote up all the time, and I stayed in the hole.

Assuming he had little chance of being paroled after serving his minimum sentence, Michael declined even to appear before the parole board.

More important than the difficulty he had adjusting to imprisonment, Michael began using narcotics and learned to hustle while incarcerated. When he went to Lorton, Michael says that he

> was actually square, as far as narcotics was concerned, you know, really square 'til I was in the joint, you know. And I just got associated with the people that dealt with that type thing, you know, and that's when I started, you know. Right now, drugs is like, getting drugs in the joint now is like getting them in the street. But at the time I was there, it was hard. Then we used a lot of synthetic drugs, you know, a lot of stuff we was gettin' out of the hospital. We had drugs come in, but it was harder to get in. But now, you know, it's like dealin' on the streets.

After he was incarcerated a few years, Michael started "messin' with these slickers and things, you know, [and] I thought I was half slick, too. And that was it. My whole life changed."

After serving more than six years of his sentence, Michael was released via conditional release. He returned to D.C., began using heroin, and soon became addicted. For several months he worked at landscaping, a job his parole officer secured for him and insisted he try. But "even though I was doin' that landscaping, you know, I was messin' with those narcotics. And the salary itself couldn't support my habit, you know, and leave anything. And so, during the time I was working, I was still stealing, you know. It was an everyday thing." He also began selling drugs. After one year on the streets, because he did not maintain regular employment, associated primarily with other thieves and hustlers, and generally refused to cooperate with his parole officer, Michael was returned to prison as a conditional release violator.

Released at the expiration of his sentence more than two years later, Michael resumed his former pattern of hustling and selling drugs: "I was strictly hustling, you know, full time. It was a job. That was my work, full-time job. . . . I got to the point, you know—hustling—I could do any kind of hustle, you know. You better believe it. I've done it all." Interpreting this period of his life, Michael says, "I had to be part of the scene" and that "after I got into it, I wanted to be the best, you know. I knew I was good because, for one thing, I kept money in my pocket, I kept my habit going, and I kept my clothes, you know, pretty." He was arrested for housebreaking and later for carrying a pistol, but he managed to "wiggle out" of both charges. Two years later, however, he was arrested for selling drugs and spent eleven months in jail while facing a possible sentence of 20 years:

> I refused to go, you know, at the time, to go into court because, like I told my lawyer, I needed some help. I didn't need the 20 years, you know, I needed

help. I was an addict, you know, not a profiteer. I was sellin' but I wasn't a profiteer. More like I was sellin' them, more like, to support my own habit. I wasn't actually getting no, you know, making no money.

Although Michael received a 10-year sentence, under the terms of then new federal legislation he was committed to the U.S. Public Health Service Hospital at Lexington, Kentucky. Six months after his release and return to D.C., he "started messin' around, you know, with narcotics, again . . . hustling, stealing, forging checks and shit." Still facing the prospect of a lengthy prison sentence, Michael instead was returned to Lexington for another seven months. Following his second release, Michael again resumed using heroin and hustling. He was arrested for shoplifting and spent 30 days in jail. After release he resumed using heroin, his fortunes steadily deteriorated, and soon he was "sleepin' in empties [abandoned houses]."

Matters improved substantially when Michael met a woman, moved into her home, and resumed working. Although the work was seasonal, the fact that his partner was receiving welfare assistance relieved the financial problems he normally would have during the winter months. His partner already had two children, and Michael happily put himself "into a family situation. I was playing, like, a father role, you know, and I enjoyed it." He avoided serious crime for the six years they were together:

> Hey, man, I was square as square can be, you know. Because I really cared for the woman. I was in love with the woman. I cared for her, you know. . . . And that was it, you know. It was her. I had straightened up, I was really straight. I wasn't doing no stealing, you know, not in the hustling sense, you know. Little petty shit, you know. I'd be shopping, I might be in the Safeway. I might see something, deodorant or something, you know. Instead of paying the money for that, something small like that, I might stick it in my pocket, or something of that nature, you know. I might put it in my pocket, you know, just to be doin' something. [And] I'd smoke a little reefer.

Michael's relationship with his partner ended, according to him, because of a "misunderstanding" exacerbated by interference from members of her family. Michael's niece related that Michael's partner "got saved" and urged Michael to begin attending church with her. When he balked, she threw him out of her house.

In 1981, when I first met and interviewed Michael Preston, he was unemployed and living with another woman in public housing. He had worked for several months as a concessionaire at a local sports arena, a position that enabled him to make extra money by exploiting the hustling opportunities it offered, but he had been without steady employment for several years. He was unhappy over his inability to secure gainful em-

ployment of the kind he wanted and uncertain of his ability to avoid returning to full-time hustling:

> I know I spend more time in the street now, you know. I'm back in the
> streets. . . . And like, you move around, you know, [and] you see fellas doing
> things. . . . I have offers, dudes come to me, man, want me to sell narcotics
> and things. But, like I say, man, I turned them down, you understand. But I
> wouldn't say I'm in any danger of doing anything.

When I asked him if he was "messing with narcotics," he responded,
"Yeah, I chips every now and then. Sometimes I get depressed, you know,
and I go on and chip. But I haven't got to the point where I done got
strung out, where I need narcotics." He attributed to "experience" his
ability to use heroin occasionally while avoiding addiction.

Looking back on the fourteen years he spent in confinement, Michael
sees fundamental changes in himself:

> I done got to the point, man, where at one time, a lotta things that people say
> to me now, I wouldn't take, you know. Because I done got to the point, you
> know, I'm gettin' old. And my life, man, seem like it's been, it's somewhat
> changed me, man. I done got, you know, I wants to do right. I wants to con-
> tribute to society. I wants to do this, I mean, seriously speaking. I really do.
> But I just can't seem to find a job that will allow me to work year 'round, dis-
> play my abilities.

Although Michael was doing some hustling, he could see no circumstances under which he ever would commit robbery or a similar crime: "I
can't imagine me putting no gun in my hand now and sticking nobody
up, you know. I'd be shaking, trembling, you know. I'd be scared." He believes that he "threw away" some of the best years of his life: "I didn't see
none of my teens, you know. All my teen years was in the joint."

After I met Michael Preston, several years passed without any further
contact between us, but we now have maintained contact over more than
a decade. Michael Preston today is 61 years old and for the past 10 years
has lived with a woman who manages a branch department store. Always
proud of his prowess with women, Michael said that when the two of
them met, his "charm swept her off her feet." Michael's niece related to me
that Michael moved in with her only days after his former partner threw
him out of her home. Michael says simply that "I can't get along without
a woman." Michael has changed little in the past 15 years. His health is
good. Although he has had no stable employment, Michael did work occasionally doing drywall installation and other construction work. He continues to use heroin occasionally but has not been readdicted.

"Red" Jackson

Red Jackson was in his early 40s when I first met him. He had been convicted of felonies on four different occasions and had spent approximately 17 years in prison. Another persistent thief and ex-convict referred Red to me, and I interviewed him at the motel where I was staying while visiting his home city. Red was on parole at the time, having been released from the penitentiary several months earlier.

Red Jackson was born in Baltimore and reared in a small, intact family. His first arrest, at age 11, was for burglary, which resulted in probation. Three years later he was arrested for auto theft and sentenced to the state training school, where he remained for nine months. After nearly one year on parole, Red was recommitted to the training school. He ran away less than two weeks later. Arrested in another state, Red was convicted of violating the Dyer Act (i.e., transporting a stolen motor vehicle interstate) and sentenced to federal confinement. He was three months shy of his eighteenth birthday when he began his sentence in a youth correctional institution. He served the entire 3-year sentence.

Correctional records indicate that Red experienced many problems. In the youth institution, he was involved in several fights with other inmates, was implicated or suspected of stealing from them, and generally displayed "aggressive tactics." Correctional officials charged that he had a "hostile and resentful attitude" and "constantly displayed contempt for the regulations and routine." After a few months of confinement, 18-year-old Red was transferred to a penitentiary. His behavior showed little change in the penitentiary setting, and he was tagged as a "paranoid schizophrenic." After a few months he was transferred to the Medical Center for Federal Prisoners, at Springfield, Missouri.

Red says today that because of his age and youthful appearance, he was subjected to sexual pressures from other inmates in the youth institution. Predictably, these problems persisted, if indeed they did not intensify, in the penitentiary setting.

I was way too young for that institution. And, yeah, there was so much pressure on me there. I think I just, well, I *did* lose it; there was no doubt about it. Then I went to [Springfield], I spent, all the time I was there I spent locked up.

Nevertheless, records from his stay at Springfield indicate that he was involved in an incident described as a "mutiny" and "riot," during which he was in "possession of dangerous instrumentalities." He is described as a "very dangerous, assaultive, and paranoid schizophrenic" who "has been involved in assaultive behavior and has shown a persistent pattern of hostility."

Looking back on his first term of felony confinement, Red says that it "was a hell of an experience for me" and "they really put it on me." He became extremely bitter about the treatment he received from justice and correctional officials. He harbors little bitterness toward fellow prisoners who preyed upon him during this time: "I was more pissed at authorities for putting me in a position where I would go through all that shit. . . . That's not only doing three years, that's putting me through a lot of torment besides."

Released at age 20, Red returned to his mother's home. Today, however, he says that when he "got out of that [institution] I wasn't really prepared to live anywhere else, other than a penitentiary. They really put a trip on me."

After a few months in the free world, Red was arrested on a charge of assault and battery. Convicted, he served six months in the county jail. A few days after his release, he was arrested for burglary and unarmed robbery. He was convicted of both charges—and also of a charge of attempted jail breaking—and sentenced to the Maryland state penitentiary. He served nearly six years before his parole. After less than two weeks in the free world, he was arrested on a charge of armed robbery and returned to the penitentiary, remaining there for an additional six years. Paroled again, Red remained in the free world for nearly five years before he was arrested for burglary and safe cracking. Sentenced to 2–10 years, he was paroled after a year and a half, several months before I interviewed him.

Red says that he did not get along well during his early prison terms and spent much of his time in "the hole." Later, this changed:

> I was in there so many years I finally began to, I learned how to manipulate the system, you know. And like, when I went back this last time, you know, when I went in I got the right cell block, the right job, you know. I manipulated the system to work for me. But most guys don't know how to do that. But it took me years to learn that, too. . . . Like this last ten years or so I done, it was real easy time. . . . I didn't do that much of it in the hole or anything. I didn't have that hard of a time.

Red completed many educational programs while in state prisons and also was an instructor in a prison vocational program.

During the early years of his second lengthy prison sentence—six years—Red resolved to turn away from crime and try to make it by working. He remained in the penitentiary for several more years and became increasingly pessimistic about his chances of succeeding at legitimate work. Nevertheless, when released on parole he felt that he "wanted to get a job and work for a living." Once again, however, he says he was not prepared for life in the free world:

I got released from a maximum security institution. And the whole line of thinking in one of them institutions . . . is altogether different than what it would be in the world, the free world. And my thinking was geared to that penitentiary. And . . . it took me a long time to sort of get my feet on the ground. . . . I was far too violent, for one thing. And people were uneasy around me, and it showed, you know. I was just too violent, and I probably brought a lot of that penitentiary paranoia out with me. So it seemed like the only people I could relate to . . . were other ex-convicts who'd done a lot of time, like I had. . . . At that time I didn't really feel like I had a whole lot to talk to [free-world people about]. I personally had never been out of the penitentiary enough.

Red made some effort to work but supported himself primarily by "petty hustles" he learned in the penitentiary. After one year on the streets, he decided to devote his time and energies to becoming a thief.

Red had a "good name" from his years in prison and also had established contacts with some men who were competent thieves, primarily burglars. He began stealing with them. He claims that the financial returns from their burglaries were high, and he lived well during more than five years of freedom, his longest period of uninterrupted freedom since age 15. His good fortune ended with arrest and a sentence of 2–10 years.

Red views his earliest criminality as nothing more than "getting into *trouble*," and he contrasts this with the crimes he committed in later years:

I started stealing when I was a kid. . . . [but] the trouble I got into, I was really never after no financial gain. I was just, it was more of a delinquent problem than I was trying to achieve anything. I never really decided that I wanted to steal anything for profit until I was about 35. . . . All the time I did prior to this last sentence, you know, I never made no money at all. . . . If I'd have got away with the things I *did*, I wouldn't have made no money. . . . Now I know that's [stealing] what I want to do. . . . I just don't want to hurt no one. I don't want to do anything violent to hurt anyone. . . . But I'm going to steal.

When I first interviewed him in 1981, Red already had resumed his criminal pursuits. He said that he had weighed the potential gains and losses carefully and concluded that he had little to lose by returning to theft. He wanted to be a "good thief." Asked why, he replied:

Well, at this stage of my life I think that's the only thing left open to me, that I can really profit from. I'm not going to be successful working. I don't want to work that day-to-day grind, and I don't want that regimentation that goes along with working a job.

So long as his crimes were nonviolent, Red believed he risked prison sentences of not more than 18 months. He was optimistic and confident. He did not "want to take unnecessary chances" but said he was "going to try to make some money":

All the experiences, all the things I've learned over the years, the people I've met—mainly the people I've met—just sort of finally gelled for me, you know. We're not talking about stealing no $300 or $400 or something. We're talking about, we're talking about pretty big money, you know. . . . I'm interested in stealing as long as the money's right. I'm not interested in stealing just to be stealing, I'm just strictly interested in the money. If it's profitable, I'll do it. And I think what I know, and the people I know, can be profitable now. . . . I *can* make money from stealing. The chances of me getting busted are pretty slim, you know. . . . I know the odds are on my side, as far as getting away with a crime.

Red indicated, however, that he would have only a few more years to devote to stealing—"another six or eight years, or something like that"—before he would be too old to continue. He intended to steal until age caught up with him, his skills became obsolete, or the threatened penalties were raised to a point at which he was unwilling to gamble his future.

For eleven years after I interviewed Red Jackson, I had no further contact with him. When I did talk with him again, I was not surprised to learn that he had been arrested in the mid-1980s and had spent additional time in prison. I was surprised to learn it was only six months. Apparently, Red was heavily involved in boosting (shoplifting) for several years after our interview. He has served no prison or jail time for the past 10 years. Today he explains that "when I got out that last time, I had a strong feeling I didn't fit in there [prison] no more." He expresses few regrets about the many years he spent in prison, largely because he is happy with himself now and believes that his prison years and the lessons he learned there were responsible in part for making him the person he is today. He says he eventually realized that "I ain't got too many years left, and I don't want to flush them away in there [prison]." Now 58 years old, Red has been unemployed for several years and receives a monthly social security benefit. Many of his friends are former thieves and ex-convicts. I told Red that when I initially interviewed him, he impressed me as either "terribly nervous or one of the most high-strung people I ever met." He responded simply that "I probably was high at the time." He also confirmed that he was supporting himself by stealing at that time. Of himself today, Red remarked, "I ain't gonna say that I don't ever break the law, but I don't steal anymore." Age has improved his ability both to see signs of potential trouble and to avoid it when he does. Red volunteered an example: "Two or three weeks ago, I was visiting a friend, and we were sittin' around smokin' dope. And someone came by to *buy* dope! I thought to myself, 'you really don't need to be here.'" Red does not reflect often about the past but does say he occasionally regrets that he never had children. "If I hadn't spent all my life the way I did, perhaps I would have had a family. But then I probably would not have been a good parent, so maybe everything's worked out for the best."

A Look Ahead

The interpretation of crime as choice will be the touchstone in the chapters that follow. The preponderance of interest sparked by the notion of crime as choice has been focused on the decision to commit discrete criminal acts. Generally there has been little interest in how the decisionmaker arrived at the point where he may be contemplating crime or assessing potential victims. Although its importance is undisputed, the decision to commit a crime is only the most immediate and visible one in a series of choices that eventuates in persistent theft. An adequate understanding of the behavior of persistent thieves requires examination of the consequences of some of their earlier choices, including both the choice of identity and the choice of lifestyle. In Chapter 2 I shall explore how the class background of persistent thieves limits their occupational options and their choices. Disproportionately products of the lower class, few of these men develop or sustain high aspirations whether in or out of crime. In Chapter 3 I examine how in a world of rapidly changing criminal opportunities their criminal options also are limited by their background. I also take up the question of crime specialization by persistent thieves and suggest an interpretation for why there is so little of it. In Chapter 4 I turn from discussion of how some persistent thieves embrace a criminal identity and some implications of this. Identity and character concerns, for example, can play an important part in decisions whether or not to get involved in crime. Much of Chapter 4 is devoted to a description of *life as party*, the immediate context for some of the most important decisions made by persistent thieves. Its constraining and distorting effect on their calculations and their approach to potential arrest will be highlighted. In Chapter 5 I employ a life-course perspective to describe and analyze the criminal careers of persistent thieves. I shall pay attention particularly to changes in offending that accompany aging and how these are explained by the changing calculus of decisionmaking. As it turns out, they are remarkably similar to age-related changes in noncriminal males. In Chapter 6 we explore both offenders' knowledge of legal penalties and changes in their perspectives and decisionmaking produced by experience with sanctions, particularly imprisonment. Often the effect is confidence and cockiness that "things will be different next time." In Chapter 7 I conclude with a discussion of how this analysis of thieves, their calculus, and their choices gives reason for substantially increased modesty on the part of those who employ the notion of crime as choice to justify increased use of punishment to control street crime.

Notes

1. Examples of this approach can be found in Gary Becker, "Crime and punishment: An economic approach," *Journal of Political Economy* 76(1968), pp. 169–217; John S. Carroll, "A psychological approach to deterrence: The evaluation of crime opportunities," *Journal of Personality and Social Psychology* 36(1978), pp. 1512–1520; John M. Heineke, editor, *Economic Models of Criminal Behavior* (Amsterdam, N.Y.: North-Holland, 1978); and Morgan O. Reynolds, *Crime by Choice: An Economic Analysis* (Dallas: Fisher Institute, 1985). For a review of the reemergence of the crime-as-choice interpretation of offending, see Bob Roshier, *Controlling Crime* (Chicago: Lyceum, 1989).

2. Daniel Glaser, *The Effectiveness of a Prison and Parole System* (Indianapolis: Bobbs-Merrill, 1964), p. 85.

3. All names have been changed to protect guilty and innocent alike.

4. Although it was impossible to determine with precision from examining his rap sheet, this sum seems too high.

2

Origins, Options, and Preparation

Over the past 40 years, U.S. social scientists carried out hundreds of self-report studies of juvenile delinquency, using as subjects primarily high school and college students. In a typical study, members of a sample complete a confidential questionnaire in which they are asked to report the number of times in the preceding, say, six months they committed each of a list of crimes. Taken together, the results of these studies show that participation in direct-contact theft is not limited to the disadvantaged to nearly the extent suggested by arrest statistics. Although important class differentials in delinquency are apparent even in the findings from self-report research, theft, it turns out, is a surprisingly democratic enterprise. The same, however, cannot be said about men who commit the most serious and largest number of direct-contact thefts and who often persist at doing so despite formal sanctioning by the adult criminal justice apparatus. Their backgrounds are noticeably tilted toward the lower reaches of the working class.

The reasons for this imbalance are numerous, but one of the most important is the distinctive qualities of their *cultural capital,* defined here as the "general cultural background, knowledge, disposition, and skills that are passed from one generation to the next."[1] Children of working-class origin inherit substantially different cultural capital than do middle-class children. The cultural capital of working-class males limits their access to the resources needed to entertain and to strive for options readily accessible to the more advantaged. When they make important and consequential life decisions, their attractive legitimate options are few, and their preparation to take advantage of them is weak or nonexistent. Their cultural capital leaves them no better prepared to take advantage of the safest and financially most promising contemporary criminal opportunities. For one thing, they lack both the normative commitment to inequality and the experience required to build and operate effectively hierarchical organizations. In this chapter I suggest some of the ways that the range of options available to the working class, particularly the most disadvantaged and disreputable fraction of it, is constricted. Except in passing, the interpretive focus is not the hard objective facts of class disadvantage; I present no data on education or income. The concern here instead is the cultural and social-psychological consequences of limited wealth and prestige and how these constrain the number and variety of options accessible to working-class men and women.

I will have little to say about the worsening condition of the working class generally in the past two decades. As entire industries have declined or disappeared, the high-paying manufacturing jobs that once were plentiful have been exported to countries where wage levels are far below what U.S. workers traditionally earned. This and other developments related to the growth of a global economy have increased the size, the misery, and the despair of the underclass, the poorest segment of the working class.[2] To many, for example, it has brought for the first time in their lives the fear of homelessness.[3]

Wealth, Subordination, and Repute

Firmly rooted in the working class, persistent thieves are distinguished principally by their limited wealth and income. All their lives most have been poor or just a financial crisis and a few paychecks away from it. No other aspect of their circumstances is so profoundly important for virtually every aspect of their lives, certainly not their often weak or chaotic family ties or their taste for illicit drugs and their effects. The observation that many working-class men and women traditionally have been able to purchase stereo equipment, automobiles, and other expensive consumer goods does not alter this fact. For every debt-free and satisfied owner of one or more of these marvels, there is at least one financially strapped other whose stereo system has been broken for months and whose 10-year-old automobile fails to start or run reliably. Describing the working-class families she studied, Lillian Rubin noted: "For them, . . . deprivation was real—real when they knew parents had trouble paying the rent, when they didn't have shoes that fit, when the telephone was shut off, when the men came to take the refrigerator away."[4] Consider, for example, the amount of space available to family members: "It is one of the distinguishing marks of . . . working-class family life that there's not enough room in the house either for the people who live in it or the things they collect as they pursue their lives."[5] Nor, for that matter, is there enough personal space, or even sleeping space, to permit privacy. Contrasting sharply with middle-class sensibilities and practices, in the poorest and the most crowded working-class households, bedrooms and even beds are shared with others.

Working-class men and women labor in hierarchically low-level, low-paying jobs, increasingly in service industries. When they have employment, they clean office buildings, load and unload machines that extrude endless streams of plastic products and parts, guard prisoners, hang drywall, and maintain the dossiers and files crucial to the smooth operation of countless bureaucracies. Much of their work is physically hazardous or harmful. To spend any time at all in their company is to be struck by the high proportion who suffer from work-related ailments and injuries. Infirmities ranging from painful joints to missing fingers and ruined lungs are commonplace. Normally they work under the direct supervision of and on schedules constructed by others. For most, their work neither requires nor permits them to set production goals or to plan and complete tasks as they see fit. This is done by superiors or by other subalterns and in any case is thought to be none of their business. Subordination is one of the most important distinguishing characteristics of working-class employment. Always it features bosses, schedules, and time clocks.

None of this is meant to ignore or obscure substantial variation in the conditions and rewards of working-class employment and lives. At one end of this range are men and women who earn high wages, who have adequate health insurance, and who may own a home. Their work, perhaps in the highly skilled and unionized construction trades, is challenging, allows for exercise of some self-direction, and results in visible, tangible, and enduring products that they often point to with pride.[6] At the other end are persons employed, for example, at the lowest levels of the nursing home industry; their work often requires cleaning the beds and bodies of incontinent residents. The nature of this work ensures that only those with few options choose to do it, particularly at the minimum wage it pays.

Notwithstanding important variation in the nature and conditions of their employment, few working-class citizens do work that is interesting, exciting, or newsworthy. Much of it is aptly described as "dirty work."[7] Dirty work is jobs or tasks that most people want carried out albeit the work is undesirable and morally "dirty." Collecting and processing household garbage and trash is an obvious example, but much of the work of criminal justice fits also. "Good people" do not do dirty work, and they prefer not to know very much about it or those who do it. They do not want to talk or know about how "things are going," just so long as they *are* going.

The conditions under which men and women earn their living are one of the most important sources of how they are regarded by others and how they regard themselves. Largely because they do work that few people aspire to and most try to avoid, working-class citizens are seen by many as less honorable or respectable than "better" citizens and treated accordingly. Physicians, supreme court justices, and CEOs of Fortune 500 corporations enjoy higher status and repute than men and women who work with their hands. Apart from their location in a wealth-and-property hierarchy, the working class also are located disadvantageously on this moral hierarchy. Those near its top are touted as exemplars of what is admirable and important; the strengths and virtues of working-class women and men generally are unacknowledged and unchronicled. Respectable people characteristically imagine the most disadvantaged and socially detached among them as shiftless and irresponsible. John Irwin suggested they are seen as "irksome, offensive, threatening, capable of arousal, even protorevolutionary."[8] Objects of scornful, if colorful, labels, such as "greasers" or "rowdies," in an age of television and the videocassette recorder, these morally dismissive labels are understood and used widely.[9] Throughout much of America, and particularly in the South, the disreputable white working class are dismissed as "rednecks." In an unusually candid characterization, rednecks are described as "trash," men with "rotten teeth" who "kill deer out of season" and perhaps "belong to the Klan."[10]

Working-class men and women are not unaware of the existence and the dynamics of moral hierarchies. They understand that persons above them in the wealth and status hierarchies are "in a position to judge them, and that the judgment rendered . . . [is] that working-class people . . . [can]not be respected as equals."[11] This can exact a heavy toll in self-esteem. About the families he knew while living on "Clay Street," Joseph Howell said they "felt scorned and looked down on by [those] more affluent than themselves."[12] Referring to a typical male informant, investigators who interviewed 150 Boston-area working-class men and women said that "he sees himself as receiving the ultimate form of contempt from those who stand above him in society: he is a function, 'Ricca the janitor,' he is part of the woodwork."[13] Reflecting on her own working-class background, Lillian Rubin noted that she was unable to examine it analytically for many years because "I was . . . eager to forget the pain and the shame of feeling deficient."[14] Even scholars and intellectuals are not immune from the tendency to see working-class women and men as unworthy. Part of the intelligentsia, the former characteristically see themselves as "people who hold the 'right' values [and] stand out from a mass whose understanding and sensitivity they believe inferior to their own."[15] For minority citizens, the result can be "wounding undercurrents of self-doubt, [grounded in the] suspicion that if whites [own] the world, there must be a reason."[16] For others, the result can be resentment and anger both over the nature and dynamics of moral hierarchy and the disrepute that looms as their destiny.

An important component of the individual-level impact and meaning of low status is a sense of personal *insignificance* that is only strengthened by working-class awareness that their views are not solicited and usually are not taken into account by economic and political leaders. Neither they nor their opinions matter much; they are taken for granted as a matter of course. Rarely are we surprised, therefore, when noxious industries, landfills, and freeways are sited in or traverse working-class neighborhoods. The great decisions that shape the lives of millions instead are made by remote others who pursue their objectives with little concern for working-class opinion. Thus the working-class patrons of a restaurant frequented by African American men

tend to be very cynical about the motives of the powerful institutions of their society. . . . [O]ne of the beliefs they hold is that the world they live in is controlled and manipulated by powers at the top. . . . When a man suggests that nothing is an accident, he is making reference to the "fact" that important events are brought about by those who hold the reins of power. . . . It is taken for granted that society is run by a set of elites and institutions that arrange the most important events.[17]

Although race undoubtedly is one source of this perspective expressed by working-class men, cynicism is not restricted to members of minority racial groups. Reporting on the white patrons of the working-class tavern where he was a participant observer, E. E. LeMasters noted:

It is quite evident that these men don't trust politicians—whether they voted for them or not. This attitude of cynicism is generalized to include business leaders and trade union officials. As a matter of fact, it is hard to think of any "big wheels" in our society that these men admire and trust.[18]

Nevertheless, the disadvantages of class and status are intensified enormously for residents of America's ghettos, barrios, and reservations. Their rates of unemployment are among the highest, and those who do have regular employment often are consigned to some of the dirtiest and least remunerative work. Nor can we ignore gender inequity. To the oppression of working-class women generally, the added burdens borne by those of minority status can be insurmountable. Despite racial, ethnic, and gender variation within the working class, however, "we cannot lose sight of the fact that we are always talking about one working class—divided as it may be." Thus, "the 'underclass' is not some peculiar distortion of Black culture or psyche; [they] . . . are members of the lowest sections of the working class."[19] This in no way denies that poverty, disrepute, and race all contribute something to the varied forms and meanings of lower-class street crime.

One of the most important consequences of life in the working class is that men and women generally do not aim high either educationally or vocationally. This is not hard to understand. It is difficult for the imagination to soar when life is consumed by the pressures of coping with routine exigencies and near-daily crises. Nor are working-class children exposed to the educational and cultural experiences that are fertile soil for imagining and comprehending alternatives. Commenting on his working-class childhood, Russell Baker noted that at age 14,

> [m]y ignorance of the world beyond schoolroom, baseball diamond, and family circle was remarkable. . . . I had spent my childhood in the blue-collar world where there was neither money, leisure, nor stimulus to cultivate an intelligent world view. I had never been exposed to art, nor attended a concert, nor listened to a symphony even on records. . . . The fierce political passions of the 1930s, the clash of ideas about communism, fascism, socialism were very remote from the gray depths we inhabited.[20]

Children reared in working-class worlds frequently do not aspire beyond a good-paying blue-collar job, perhaps in the construction industry, or service in the military. Of all the consequences of poverty and disrepute, perhaps none is as consequential as this stunting effect on their dreams and imagination.

The limited aspirations of these children generally are buttressed by their school experiences. Because of their speech, their behavior, and other aspects of their cultural capital, they are tagged as students unlikely to succeed:

> By embodying class interests and ideologies, schools reward the cultural capital of the dominant classes and systematically devalue that of the lower classes. Upper-class students, by virtue of a certain linguistic and cultural competence acquired through family upbringing, are provided with means of appropriation for success in school.[21]

It does not take long for many working-class children to tune out of the school scene, not because they believe "success in school is irrelevant but rather that the odds of 'making it' are simply too slim to bet on. . . . [They] conclude that the possibility of upward social mobility is not worth the price of obedience, conformity, and investment of substantial amounts of time, energy, and work in the school."[22] It is not difficult to see why working-class children, even if they do not expect it, at least are prepared to accept limited aspirations and accomplishments. This objectively based but self-reinforced damper on dreams and achievement limits their legitimate and illicit pursuits alike. Even their criminal dreams and accomplishments are drawn to modest scale.

Family and Peer Group

The degree to which families remain stable and intact despite the problems of working-class life ranges on a continuum from hard living to settled living.[23] The settled working class are those with an adequate and stable income, many of whom own their homes. They are

> the single largest group of families in the country. These are the men and women, by far the largest part of the American work force, who work at the lower levels of the manufacturing and service sectors of the economy; workers whose education is limited, whose mobility options are severely restricted, and who usually work for an hourly rather than a weekly wage. They don't tap public resources; they reap no benefit from either the pitiful handouts to the poor or from huge subsidies to the rich. Instead, they go to work every day to provide for their families, often at jobs they hate.[24]

Another observer has called them "maintainers," adults who "reproduce society through the enactment of recurrent processes in the framework of established institutions" and, therefore, play an extremely important part in the life of working-class communities.[25] These men and women often are active in community activities. Whatever the reasons they are able to rationalize their lives and activities, the availability of an adequate income surely is one of the most important.

In contrast to the settled-living, the hard-living generally seem to live from crisis to crisis. Their lives have a chaotic quality. Alcoholism, unstable work histories, and unstable marital and live-in relationships are commonplace. It is this fraction of the working class that commonly is designated *lower class*. Most of the analysis in this chapter applies particularly to them. Whether they are unable or simply unwilling to rationalize their lives and pursuits is unimportant when weighed against the consequences of the fact that they do not:

> They are the men and women who rebel against the grinding routine of life; the dulling, numbing experience of going to the same mindless job every day; of struggling with the same problems of how to feed, clothe, and tend the children without adequate resources; of fighting an endless and losing battle with roaches, rats, sore throats, and infected ears.[26]

It is characteristic of working-class life and neighborhoods that settled families and hard-living families often live in close geographic proximity.

The importance of the family in mediating the effects of overarching economic and status hierarchies is affirmed clearly in Jay MacLeod's study of the "Hallway Hangers" and the "Brothers," two groups of young men residing in a public housing project in a northeastern U.S. city. The former, all of whom were white, had turned off to school and had leveled aspirations; they aspired to nothing beyond

> the only jobs that they perceive to be available—unskilled manual work. Many expect to enter military service, not because they find it particularly appealing but because of the paucity of other opportunities. The concept of an aspiration is essentially alien to the Hallway Hanger. Most simply expect to take whatever they can get.[27]

The Brothers, who were African American, offered a contrast. The parents of these boys had seen improvement in their own lives and had conveyed to their children a sense of optimism and hope.[28] As a result, the Brothers had not lowered their educational and occupational aspirations. The family clearly can reinforce, blunt, or defeat the threat of leveled aspirations.

And there is no doubt some families, particularly the ones that are better off financially than others, make at least a modest effort to inspire their youngsters. Typically, this takes the form of urging them to get an education or to acquire occupational skills—electrical wiring, perhaps—that will pay off later. Beyond these ambiguous admonitions, however, most working-class parents may have little to offer, and even a directional heading is more than some can provide.

The circumstances and motivations of parents who do not encourage their children to set lofty goals for themselves can be varied and complex. For many it simply is lack of knowledge; they may not know how to identify key reference points or to provide adequate guidance to those with ambition. Buffeted by the consequences of alcoholism and unstable employment, other parents are so overwhelmed by living day to day that they cannot imagine a future different from what they know. Coping with daily crises simply leaves no time or energy for it. Some parents may not inspire their children intellectually or vocationally for fear that the cost to the latter in frustration and devastated self-esteem if they do not "make it" is too much to risk. Perhaps, as these parents see things, it is best not to "put ideas in their heads."

Parents and other adults are the most important transmitters of cultural capital, but the peer group is important also. It can reinforce or turn on its head perspectives formed in the world of adults and in relations with authority figures. The results of interviewing and participant observation in a British working-class neighborhood and school demonstrate this point. The investigator found and described two groups of boys, the "lads" and the "ear'oles."[29] The former were distinguished by their opposition to the culture of the school and the objectives of teachers; the latter were conformist in orientation and behavior. Boys who gravitated toward the lads in the process became less conformist in their stance toward school. The fact that working-class male children are granted autonomy at an early age simultaneously diminishes the influence of parents and increases the potential impact of the peer group, whether it is conformist or oppositional. It is here, for example, that lower-class aversion to many types of white-collar work as unmanly often finds reinforcement. Substituting a white collar for a blue one, as they see it, does not guarantee upward mobility or success. Income and working conditions are critical also. Generally, white-collar employment that subjugates one to a rigid schedule and close supervision is devalued. Tenured full professors at major universities are viewed as successful, accountants are not.

Cultural Constraints

Beyond economic precariousness, an air of inferiority and insignificance, and the leveled aspirations that are staples of lower-class worlds and lives, experiences of the kind I have sketched give to their cultural capital distinctive qualities. The economic and status realities of "working-class life," Lillian Rubin noted, "and the constraints they impose upon living are the common ingredients from which a world of shared understandings arises, from which a consciousness and a culture grows that is distinctly working class."[30] Noteworthy are two normative commitments and personal styles that are valued positively, particularly by males with origins in the lowest fraction of the working class.

Independence and Autonomy

Those who have spent time in working-class worlds invariably point to the importance males place on personal independence and autonomy. The independent and unencumbered male ideal is valued highly. As they understand it,

> [i]ndependence . . . means "minding one's own business" or not meddling in other people's business and, at the same time, expecting to be left alone in managing one's own affairs. This concept is expressed most frequently in the simple phrase, "Ain't nobody gonna tell me what to do."[31]

Doubtless one reason working-class males value highly independence and autonomy is because, as the children of families with limited financial resources, they achieve financial independence at an early age. When parents simply lack resources to provide beyond the necessities, their children are aware of it and have little choice but to adapt accordingly. Working-class males understand without being told that whatever they acquire in life will be by their efforts alone. There will be no inheritance or trust fund, no parental indulgence while they take time off to "find themselves," and no high-powered connections to draw on. In marked contrast to children of the professional middle class who enjoy "an extended adolescence—often until the mid-twenties and later," these working-class children "grow up so fast" because the "moratorium on assuming adult responsibilities is a luxury that only the affluent sector of the society can afford."[32] Jay MacLeod described the Hallway Hangers: "At sixteen, seventeen, and eighteen years of age, [they] have gained a maturity . . . that is incommensurate with their chronological age."[33]

One of the taken-for-granted defining characteristics of the status of adult is the demonstrated ability to provide for oneself all or a substantial proportion of the wherewithal needed for food, clothing, and shelter. As young males achieve financial independence and adult status in the realm of occupational performance, others begin treating them as equals in other spheres as well. And what begins as economic necessity and cultural norm is converted gradually into personal and social right. Bear in mind that young working-class males usually hold a variety of jobs, many for no more than a few days. Often they are paid cash, in transactions that are unreported. Stable, skilled, and well-paying employment at work with a future remains their ideal, however.

In addition to employment stability and a good income, work that permits one to operate independently is preferred. This helps explain why many of them hope to acquire specific work skills while young:

> Having a job skill was important because the work itself was more rewarding than unskilled work, because the jobs paid more, and because a skill gave a person more independence. . . . [S]ubcontracting was popular. . . . The least desirable jobs were factory jobs or jobs where you had to take orders all day and had no freedom.[34]

Many of these men gain a familiarity with the requisite tools, skills, and organization of construction while young, which facilitates later employment in this industry. The absence of formalized credentialing processes and career lines also makes it attractive.[35] An informant once told me that those who do the hiring on construction sites "don't care whether you come from Yale or from jail. All they care about is whether they can make any money with you." Describing how he began working as a bricklayer, the same informant went on to say:

> When I got out of prison [the second time] . . . I sold a suit for $10 and I bought [some tools], just the bare necessities of what I needed, and I met a

guy who carried me on the job.... So at that time I could make $160 a
week.... And with this earning power, I didn't have ... I didn't have to
steal.... This was right down my alley.

Subcontracting, which is commonplace in the social and economic organization of construction work, only increases its appeal for the indepen-
dent-minded.

Most working-class males, however, have misinformed or severely distorted notions about the realities and risks of self-employment. Given
their subordinate origins, few of them fully comprehend the discipline
and long hours often required to make a go of things as a budding entre-
preneur and business owner. In the words and the fantasies of a hustler,
"When you work for somebody, he tells you this or that and if you don't
do it he beefs with you. I don't want to work for *nobody*. That way, I got
no beefs, and I can keep my own hours."[36] Reality does not concern them;
experience with subordinated and unremunerative jobs has convinced
them self-employment is better. Those who venture into entrepreneurship
generally find that it requires a degree of rationality and discipline they
cannot or will not devote to it. During the one year he lived in south
Philadelphia, Dan Rose was employed by a man who owned and operated an automotive transmission repair shop. The business did not run
smoothly, and there were endless problems. According to Rose, it was as
if the owner-proprieter "wanted to turn the street hustle ... into a capi-
talist enterprise but with none of the market rationalities of ownership,
legitimacy, licensing, or access to wholesale parts and supplies."[37] Entrepreneurship and a rationalized life hold little appeal for men like him
who want nothing so much as to be free of external constraint. For those
accustomed to the freedoms and the rhythms of the street, operating a
business prudently and closely is too much like confinement.

Egalitarianism

Although I have elected not to dwell on the pathologies and shortcomings
of working-class males, they should not and cannot be ignored entirely. It
is useful to bear in mind that the values and personal styles of working-
class males are celebrated and pursued in a patriarchal world:

In much the same way that it takes a number of support troops to maintain
one soldier on the front line, it takes a number of seemingly compliant people to supply the make room for one individualist at home—to honor his
whims, provide an audience for his acts of self-expression, and populate the
world over which he has dominion. In this, as in so many other respects, one
person's freedom of action can easily become another's bondage.[38]

Nor can the racism and high levels of interpersonal violence that flourish among lower-class males be overlooked.

In the corners of their patriarchal, racist, and classist worlds, however, working-class males endorse and expect egalitarian relations with one another. Remarking on the black males he knew in south Philadelphia, Dan Rose noted that "the autonomy of the self led to a society of autonomous selves that were radically democratic."[39] They are more democratic in some respects than in others. Working-class males do not treat one another without regard for rank of some kind, even if it is informal and reputational. Rank is important. The fact is that some men are looked to with respect, others with fear, and still others with contempt. They are not democratic if by this is meant that all are treated alike.

But they are democratic in believing that interactionally ostentatious displays of the right to give orders generally is unacceptable behavior. None should behave as though deference and command are personal entitlements. Egalitarianism and authority generally are seen as incompatible. This is one of the reasons working-class males may be reluctant to assume an interactional posture with their peers that could be interpreted as "trying to give orders."

The high value placed on egalitarianism and opposition to those who behave as though they are superior finds expression in respect for the unabashedly common. To embrace egalitarianism completely is to revel in being and being seen as one of the "common folk,"[40] someone who is "never too good to speak to you." On Clay Street, "a given personality or individual could be admired and accepted regardless of his social position, just so long as he seemed to be an 'okay guy.' Being an 'okay guy' meant among other things . . . being . . . unpretentious. The worst kind of person was a snob."[41]

When egalitarianism is coupled with strong support for class or peer-group solidarity, it can make for reluctance to move out of the familiar world and to regard those who do as traitors. Peer-group influences that cause members to limit their individual aspirations in favor of loyalty to the group have been noted in research from New York ethnic neighborhoods to rural West Virginia.[42] One of the characteristics that distinguished the "lads" and the "ear'oles" was the lads' desire to maintain the identity of the group. In his account of the Brothers and the Hallway Hangers, Jay MacLeod noted that members of the latter placed great emphasis on group identity.[43]

The working-class male cultural emphasis on democratic relations is a mixed blessing, however. It makes these men less likely than contemporaries reared at other levels of the class hierarchy to strive for and to seek out positions of leadership. They do not relish acquisition or effective use of the skills or the trappings of superordination. Left to themselves, few would choose to become "boss." Lacking experience as organizers and leaders, it is hardly surprising they also lack confidence in their ability to do these things. Thus, the emphasis on egalitarianism augments the leveling of aspirations produced by class and school experiences.[44]

For individuals, as for families, the consequences of disadvantage and disrepute and subordination are not invariant. Limited resources and a bleak assessment of prospects for becoming successful through honest endeavor can lead alternately to a profound sense of futility or to rage.[45] Spurred by identical structural and cultural constraints, some individuals respond with willingness to drive themselves unsparingly on the assumption that anything less only guarantees the quiet fate that awaits most. Regardless of whether they are determined to succeed or simply determined not to fail, these men will not be snared or defeated without struggle. Class and racial memberships that destine one for a life of disrepute and insignificance cause them to elevate near the top of their motives a drive to be noticed and respected. They are less willing than their siblings and peers to rule out criminal options if need be. Even if it must be secured with a pistol, these men will have the wealth and leisure denied to their parents and older neighbors. Asked what made him a criminal, an aging English thief replied, "Seeing my father, a straight man, getting only poverty all through his life for being straight."[46] Another man is more expansive:

> You know, [there's] a thing the smart-boy preachers and professors and all ought to remember: all the crap they hand you in Sunday school and over the television and the radio and through newspapers and books about how you got to be good and work hard and go to church and mind your manners and wash your face and comb your hair and clean your fingernails and spray under your arms and say sir to the boss and punch the time clock and tip your hat to the cop and respect the mayor or governor or president, all those things if you want to live a happy life, that's a lot of goddamn lies, and if *they* know it, what makes them think someone else can't figure it out, too?[47]

To be successful, these men must construct a life experienced as satisfactory on dimensions such as "dignity, fulfillment, achievement of life goals, or level of gratification."[48] They are capable of enormous self-discipline and rationality in pursuit of a life better than the one their parents attained. Although their numbers proportionately are not large, the toll they exact is substantial, for they are among the most rational and successful of all whose criminal beginnings stem from the inequity of class.

Responses to class and status inequality can take meaner forms as well. Nursing anger and resentment, other men situated near the bottom of class and moral hierarchies are prepared to use threat or force to acquire what is denied them by inequality. Wealth and leisure are important components of their motivational quest, but self-validation or recognition is added to the mix. In this way, crime can be a mechanism and an interactional forum for extracting from an indifferent or hostile world the attention and respect men would not know otherwise.

Class, Constraints, and Decisions

The theory of crime as choice predicts that persons who have few legitimate options, attractive illicit ones, and little fear of the risk of being caught if they choose the latter are more likely to engage in criminal activity than are those who have attractive, attainable legitimate options, few if any illicit ones they are aware of, and fear of the consequences if they are arrested. The reasons working-class men are more likely than middle-class thieves to persist at street crime are easy to understand and entirely consistent with this theory. Working-class men are unlikely to have access to attractive legitimate opportunities or to be sufficiently confident of themselves and their skills to pursue the ones that are available. In a word, they are among the least likely to find close at hand the resources needed to construct and maintain successful lives legitimately. Some of their own decisions limit them even further; they drop out of school and in other ways make decisions that limit what they will be able to accomplish.

If it is understood properly, the decision to commit a crime must be seen in this larger context of prior decisions and constraints. We never have unlimited options in the choices of everyday life. Always our options are constrained by considerations that cause us to ignore or to rule out some. Lower-class children generally do not entertain as a career option becoming a physician, although this is not because they lack potential. Instead, it is because this is not held out to them as a "realistic" or attainable goal by their parents or by school officials, and consequently most do not aspire to become physicians. At some point we must acknowledge and examine how the class and status origins of many men who persist at direct-contact theft and the characteristics of their cultural capital constrain their legitimate options. These factors have the same effect on their criminal options.

Class and Compliance

Several years ago, a team of researchers at Stanford University conducted a study of psychological reactions to the experience of imprisonment.[49] The key component of the research was a simulated prison operated by the investigators. They first advertised for volunteers, who would receive $15 per day for participating in the study. Seventy males, predominantly young, middle-class college students, applied, and two dozen eventually were selected to participate in the study. Half the volunteer participants were arbitrarily designated as guards and the others as prisoners. As one of the investigators later explained:

> These were the roles they were to play in our simulated prison. The guards were made aware of the potential seriousness and danger of the situation and their own vulnerability. They made up their own formal rules for maintaining law, order and respect, and were generally free to improvise new ones during their eight-hour, three-man shifts. The prisoners were unexpectedly picked up at their homes by a city policeman in a squad car, searched, handcuffed, fingerprinted, booked at the Palo Alto station house, and taken blindfolded to our jail. There they were stripped, deloused, put into a uniform, given a number and put into a cell . . . where they expected to live for the next two weeks.[50]

All activities taking place in the mock prison were observed and video-taped. Participants also were tested and interviewed at various points during the study.

"Guards" quickly developed exaggerated roles of the kind found in real prisons, becoming high-handed and tyrannical in the process. "Inmates" became docile and showed signs of extreme emotional stress. Three prisoners had to be released in the first four days because of "acute situational traumatic reactions," such as hysterical crying, confusion in thinking, and severe depression. Others begged to end their participation early. These and other reactions by guards and prisoners caused the investigators to terminate the study after only six days.

The participants in the Stanford research primarily were middle-class university students.[51] Just as they found confinement to be extremely unpleasant, men from white-collar backgrounds who chance to spend any appreciable time in real confinement often find it unusually demeaning and difficult. An ex-convict and former thief made this accurate observation:

> Straights doing time can't relate to the lifestyle inside, can't make peace with being caged, and can't accept the con code. They don't know how to keep to themselves, to see nothing, hear nothing, talk about nothing. They don't know how to protect themselves from the dangers, like wolves that prey on weak, scared cons. They don't understand that you mustn't trust no one, mustn't injure anyone's feelings, and mustn't lose at gambling any debts you can't pay. Squares don't know how to wheel and deal to stay alive.[52]

When they do become ensnared by the criminal justice apparatus, respectable white-collar citizens characteristically apply to their criminal acts linguistic techniques that enable them to deny or to minimize the fact they are *criminals*. They may interpret their arrest and conviction, for example, as evidence of political pressures exerted on or personal bias on the part of prosecutors. Once in custody, they complain, make claims for special treatment, and burden others with accounts of the mistreatment and injustice they have suffered.[53]

How different they are from working-class males who, once they are arrested and sentenced, typically refer to their activities as "stealing" or "doing wrong" and who rarely dispute the state's formal right to punish them. It is a fundamental and inescapable fact, moreover, that the penalty of imprisonment is limited principally to blue-collar men and that one of the more noteworthy aspects of their adaptation to it is a high level of taken-for-granted compliance. Reflecting on many years spent in juvenile and adult institutions, an alcoholic former thief and heroin addict could be speaking for many working-class males who, like him, chance to end up in prison:

> [N]obody's done anything to me that I haven't gone clean out of my way to ask for. And I've never complained about being picked on, really. I've never had complaints about parole officers or police. I never have felt that, because I've always known that each time that I got here I worked hard to get here. I truly worked harder than other people to get myself put in this goddam place, you see, and I think the way that I did my time also indicated my willingness to accept the punishment as my lot.[54]

Save for the day-to-day violence inmates inflict upon one another, occasional inmate assaults on staff, and the waves of riot that periodically course through them, U.S. prisons are calm places. Active, open resistance to institutional personnel and regimens is as rare as emotional responses were commonplace in the "Stanford County Jail." The same handicaps and cultural biases that prepare working-class men for street crime also prepares them for punishment when they are caught.

Those charged with running places of involuntary segregative confinement face the challenge of inducing inmates to contribute to the smooth operation of their facilities or at least not to disrupt daily operations. The challenge of maintaining order and routine in jails and prisons is reduced when prisoners can be made to discount or ignore entirely the possibility of joining with their peers to challenge staff actions or to insist upon improvements in their common conditions of confinement. Their acquiescence is facilitated not only by administrators' calculated actions to divide inmates but also by the fact that working-class men respond to incarceration in ways that reflect aspects of their cultural background and common values. Their experience leads them to see as legitimate and to accept as proper an unambiguous link between crime and punishment. Working-class men are *prepared* to submit to criminal justice authority. Two aphorisms often heard in the prison world are "If you can't do the time, don't do the crime" and "If you wanna play, you gotta pay." They attest to the clear relationship between crime and punishment that is taken as a given by prisoners from poor and minority backgrounds.

The value they assign to independence and autonomy is particularly important in this regard. Prison officials promote a "do-your-own-time" interpretation of prisoners' plight, one that resonates comfortably with the self-defined independent working-class male. Describing how he settled into doing his second prison sentence, Roger Morton said:

> I just laid back and let people do what they wanted to do, just as long as it didn't involve me. Just laid back and done my time. I was the only one there to do it. I just let most folks alone, I tried not to get involved in loanin' money or borrowin' money, or get into the drug thing. Every now and then we might throw us up a little julep or something, to celebrate.

This normative ideal and strategy of "live-and-let-live" atomizes the prisoner group and complicates enormously the task of anyone who would call for more interaction and trust among prisoners. It is not because of the actions of guards alone that U.S. prisons "are among our last bastions of the idea of the insurmountable, free individual."[55]

The brand of egalitarianism valued so highly by working-class males also finds expression in their compliant behavior when they are in custody. The notion of differential authority and leadership is for them of such uncertain legitimacy and distasteful as well that they are reluctant to involve and submerge themselves in organization. They are not the kind of men who align themselves with or subordinate quickly to self-proclaimed leaders. This wariness decreases further any prospect for a collective, perhaps oppositional, response to their treatment.

The emphasis working-class men place on egalitarianism also makes the task of controlling them easier when they are in the clutches of criminal justice functionaries and bureaucracies. They are slow to step forward from the ranks, but they are quick to mistrust those who do. This effectively denies to them all hope of acting purposefully and collectively. They are leaderless because it satisfies their egalitarian impulses, because they are slow to subordinate themselves voluntarily, and because they lack experience organizing and leading. In Chapter 3, we shall see how these same cultural biases limit their ability to exploit crimes that pay well with little risk of arrest or severe penalty.

Notes

1. Jay MacLeod, *Ain't No Makin' It* (Boulder, Colo.: Westview, 1987), p. 12. For an extended development of the concept of cultural capital, see Pierre Bordieu, *Outline of a Theory of Practice* (Cambridge: Cambridge University Press, 1977); and Pierre Bordieu and Jean-Claude Passeron, *Reproduction in Education, Society, and Culture* (Newbury Park, Calif.: Sage, 1977).

2. William Julius Wilson, *The Truly Disadvantaged* (Chicago: University of Chicago Press, 1987). The underclass thesis has been the focus of considerable if often arcane scholarly debate in which the lived experience of underclass women and men is all but ignored. For an exception, see Ken Auletta, *The Underclass* (New York: Random House, 1982). The utility of the underclass concept certainly is not limited to urban minority populations. Its application to Appalachia is argued in Lynda Ann Ewen, "All God's children ain't got shoes: A comparison of West Virginia and the urban 'underclass,'" *Humanity and Society* 13(1989), pp. 145–164. A discussion of the underclass concept and the controversy generated by it is Carole Marks, "The urban underclass," *Annual Review of Sociology* 17(1991), pp. 445–466.

3. Sympathetic and insightful accounts of some of these changes include Terry M. Williams and William Kornblum, *Growing Up Poor* (Lexington, Mass.: D. C. Heath, 1985); and Gregory Pappas, *The Magic City* (Ithaca, N.Y.: Cornell University Press, 1989). On the fear of homelessness, see Lillian B. Rubin, *Families on the Fault Line* (New York: HarperCollins, 1994), especially pp. 113–116.

4. Lillian Breslow Rubin, *Worlds of Pain* (New York: Basic Books, 1976), p. 30.

5. Lillian B. Rubin, *Families on the Fault Line* (New York: HarperCollins, 1994), p. 17.

6. E. E. LeMasters, *Blue-Collar Aristocrats* (Madison: University of Wisconsin Press, 1975); and Studs Terkel, *Working* (New York: Pantheon, 1974).

7. Everett C. Hughes, "Good people and dirty work," In *The Sociological Eye*, vol. 1, edited by Everett C. Hughes (Chicago: Aldine Atherton, 1971).

8. John Irwin, *The Jail* (Berkeley: University of California Press, 1985), p. 2.

9. Herman Schwendinger and Julia R. Siegel Schwendinger, *Adolescent Subcultures and Delinquency*, research edition (New York: Praeger, 1985).

10. This characterization of Bernard Welch, the man who murdered her spouse, was given by Dr. Halberstam's widow on the day Welch was sentenced to imprisonment. Mrs. Halberstam, who grew up in the Deep South, said she had known men like Welch "all my life." See *Washington Post*, "Welch convicted of murder, robbery, nine other counts," April 11, 1981, p. A1.

11. Richard Sennett and Jonathan Cobb, *The Hidden Injuries of Class* (New York: Alfred A. Knopf, 1972), p. 38.

12. Joseph T. Howell, *Hard Living on Clay Street* (New York: Anchor Books, 1973), p. 327.

13. Richard Sennett and Jonathan Cobb, *The Hidden Injuries of Class* (New York: Alfred A. Knopf, 1972), p. 50.

14. Lillian Breslow Rubin, *Worlds of Pain* (New York: Basic Books, 1976), p. 13. Of her childhood spent in rural poverty, songwriter and singer Dolly Parton noted simply that "The worst thing about poverty is not the actual living of it, but the shame of it." See Dolly Parton, *Dolly* (New York: HarperCollins, 1994), p. 51.

15. Richard Sennett and Jonathan Cobb, *The Hidden Injuries of Class* (New York: Alfred A. Knopf, 1972), p. 69. Although many middle-class academics and activists claim to understand and to act in the interests of working people, in truth most do not bother to acquaint themselves firsthand with working-class lives and perspectives. The fact that affirmative action programs were designed and operate with apparent indifference to the handicaps of class is particularly revealing. The gulf between middle-class and working-class perspectives and its consequences are explored in David Croteau, *Politics and the Class Divide* (Philadelphia: Temple University Press, 1995). A popular treatment of some of these issues is E. J. Dionne, Jr., *Why Americans Hate Politics* (New York: Simon & Schuster, 1991).

16. Sylvester Monroe and Peter Goldman, *Brothers* (New York: William Morrow, 1988), p. 161.

17. Mitchell Duneier, *Slim's Table* (Chicago: University of Chicago Press, 1992), p. 74.

18. E. E. LeMasters, *Blue-Collar Aristocrats* (Madison: University of Wisconsin Press, 1975), p. 184.

19. Lynda Ann Ewen, "All God's children ain't got shoes: A comparison of West Virginia and the urban 'underclass,'" *Humanity and Society* 13(1989), p. 154.

20. Russell Baker, *Growing Up* (New York: Congdon and Weed, 1982), pp. 198–199.

21. Jay MacLeod, *Ain't No Makin' It* (Boulder, Colo.: Westview, 1987), p. 12.

22. Jay MacLeod, *Ain't No Makin' It* (Boulder, Colo.: Westview, 1987), p. 104.

23. The distinction between settled living and hard living is made and discussed in Joseph T. Howell, *Hard Living on Clay Street* (Garden City, N.Y.: Anchor, 1973).

24. Lillian B. Rubin, *Families on the Fault Line* (New York: HarperCollins, 1994), pp. 30–31.

25. Mitchell Duneier, *Slim's Table* (Chicago: University of Chicago Press, 1992), p. 131.

26. Lillian Breslow Rubin, *Worlds of Pain* (New York: Basic Books, 1976), p. 34.

27. Jay MacLeod, *Ain't No Makin' It* (Boulder, Colo.: Westview, 1987), pp. 67–68.

28. Jay MacLeod, *Ain't No Makin' It* (Boulder, Colo.: Westview, 1987), especially pp. 137–162. The same racial difference is reported in Mercer L. Sullivan, *"Getting Paid"* (Ithaca, N.Y.: Cornell University Press, 1989).

29. Paul E. Willis, *Learning to Labour* (Farnborough, U.K.: Saxon House, 1977).

30. Lillian Breslow Rubin, *Worlds of Pain* (New York: Basic Books, 1976), p. 210.

31. Patricia Duane Beaver, *Rural Community in the Appalachian South* (Lexington: University of Kentucky Press, 1986), p. 153.

32. Lillian Breslow Rubin, *Worlds of Pain* (New York: Basic Books, 1976), p. 30.

33. Jay MacLeod, *Ain't No Makin' It* (Boulder, Colo.: Westview, 1987), p. 55.

34. Joseph T. Howell, *Hard Living on Clay Street* (Garden City, N.Y.: Anchor, 1973), p. 343.

35. For example, Dermot Walsh, *Heavy Business* (London: Routledge & Kegan Paul, 1986), p. 59.

36. James Willwerth, *Jones* (New York: M. Evans, 1974), p. 186.

37. Dan Rose, *Black American Street Life* (Philadelphia: University of Pennsylvania Press, 1987), p. 120.

38. Kai T. Erikson, *Everything in Its Path* (New York: Simon and Schuster, 1976), p. 91.

39. Dan Rose, *Black American Street Life* (Philadelphia: University of Pennsylvania Press, 1987), p. 175.

40. Patricia Duane Beaver, *Rural Community in the Appalachian South* (Lexington: University of Kentucky Press, 1986), p. 165.

41. Joseph T. Howell, *Hard Living on Clay Street* (Garden City, N.Y.: Anchor, 1973), p. 348.

42. Compare, for example, Herbert J. Gans, *Urban Villagers* (New York: Free Press, 1962) and Jack E. Weller, *Yesterday's People* (Lexington: University of Kentucky Press, 1965).

43. Jay MacLeod, *Ain't No Makin' It* (Boulder, Colo.: Westview, 1987).

44. Paul Willis, *Learning to Labour* (Farnborough, U.K.: Saxon House, 1977); and Jay MacLeod, *Ain't No Makin' It* (Boulder, Colo.: Westview, 1987).

45. Jay MacLeod, *Ain't No Makin' It* (Boulder, Colo.: Westview, 1987).

46. Tony Parker and Robert Allerton, *The Courage of His Convictions* (London: Hutchinson, 1962), p. 106. "Robert Allerton," the thief and ex-convict whose life history is the subject of this book, would go on to serve at least one additional prison sentence after it was published.

47. Ted Thackery, Jr., *The Thief* (Los Angeles: Nash, 1971), p. 72.

48. John Irwin, *The Felon* (Englewood Cliffs, N.J.: Prentice-Hall, 1970), p. 177.

49. Philip G. Zimbardo, "Pathology of imprisonment," *Society* 9(1972), pp. 6–8.

50. Philip G. Zimbardo, "Pathology of imprisonment," *Society* 9(1972), p. 6.

51. Philip G. Zimbardo, "Pathology of imprisonment," *Society* 9(1972), p. 6.

52. Marlene Webber and Tony McGilvary, *Square John* (Toronto: University of Toronto Press, 1988), p. 74. For examples of how incarcerated squares are exploited, see Pete Earley, *The Hot House* (New York: Bantam Books, 1992), pp. 156–158; and Nathan McCall, *Makes Me Wanna Holler* (New York: Random House, 1994), pp. 154–156. In recompense for incarceration with those they typically regard as social inferiors, some respectable ex-prisoners write scornful, classist accounts of their peers. For an example of this, see Jean Harris, *Stranger in Two Worlds* (New York: Macmillan, 1986).

53. See, for example, Michael L. Benson, "Denying the guilty mind: Accounting for involvement in a white-collar crime," *Criminology* 23(1985), pp. 583–607.

54. Eugene Delorme, *Chief,* edited by Inez Cardozo-Freeman (Lincoln: University of Nebraska Press, 1994), p. 153.

55. Joan Smith and William Fried, *Uses of the American Prison* (Lexington, Mass.: Lexington Books, 1974), p. 58.

3

Changing Criminal Opportunities and the Unskilled

When Karl Marx observed that humans "make their own history, but they do not make it just as they please," he was calling attention to the fact that in addition to the constraints of class and status, our options are constrained also by historical conditions. No one entertained the option of automobile theft in nineteenth-century Boston—or anywhere else, for that matter—for the obvious reason there were no automobiles to steal. Criminal options are not historical constants. Whether viewed over the span of a few decades or the sweep of centuries, historical change modifies both the nature and the number of criminal opportunities available to motivated thieves.

The same handicaps that limit access by persistent thieves to well-paying, respectable, and legitimate means of livelihood also reduce their ability to take advantage of some of today's most attractive criminal opportunities. Most contemporary persistent thieves either are unable or else they refuse to exploit these opportunities, and they continue instead to mine the low-grade but readily accessible ore of unremunerative crime. In this chapter we examine both historical and contemporary changes in criminal opportunities, the skills needed to exploit them, and the consequences for men who lack these skills.

Historical Change and Criminal Opportunities

The attractive or bountiful criminal opportunities of one place or time can be transformed or even disappear in a few short years. Commenting, for example, on changes in theft in post–World War II England, a persistent but unsuccessful British thief noted:

> In the late 1940's smash-and-grab raids were all the fashion in the criminal fraternity. Crime moves in cycles, of course, following things like supply and

demand or just exploiting weaknesses in security. At this time jewelers' windows were an easy thing. . . . But the whole smash-and-grab thing went out of fashion because the jewelers got wise. They put in grilles and other devices to make life difficult for us.[1]

Train robbery, which emerged and flourished in the United States in the late decades of the nineteenth century, is instructive also. The historical appearance of train robbery was stimulated by a host of circumstances peculiar to the frontier West, including disorganized law enforcement and the fact that the skills required to commit it were simple and straightforward. Security arrangements on trains that carried cash shipments initially were weak, and law enforcement responsibilities were lodged in local and state authorities. Robbers not only could stop, board, and rob trains with little fear of personal harm but the absence of federal enforcement meant that they also could escape into bordering states where they were virtually free from apprehension. As these conditions gradually changed, train robbery became less attractive. As one commentator noted:

Baggage cars were equipped with ramps and stalls containing fast horses for the immediate pursuit of bandits; detectives and guards rode unobtrusively in coaches; single locomotives were kept ready on sidings to speed alarms and transport posses; express cars were made with finer precision and strength; substantial rewards were offered; and federal involvement extended investigations beyond county and state boundaries. Technology . . . [provided] more efficient communication and transportation, and forensic science made identification and apprehension less difficult.[2]

As a result, train robberies, which numbered 29 in 1900, declined to 7 in 1905 and never increased significantly thereafter.[3] By the 1920s, train robbery and train robbers had disappeared from the American scene.

The historical transformation and eventual decline of safecracking in the United States offers a more contemporary example and one with more relevance for the activities of contemporary persistent thieves. In the early 1900s, manganese steel was used widely in the construction of American money safes. Because it was resistant to attack by drilling and also offered resistance to fire, manganese in many respects was ideal for the purpose. Widespread adoption of the oxygen-acetylene torch soon after World War I, however, left manganese safes vulnerable to a new form of attack.[4] To counteract this threat and to reduce production costs, manufacturers responded by developing laminated money safes constructed of alternating sheets of copper and steel. Its heat-diffusing properties make copper extremely difficult to burn, and use of it in combination with manganese or case-hardened steel provided resistance to attack by torch and by most burglary tools.

Confronted with the new technical challenges, many safe burglars shifted their point of attack on money safes in use in the 1925–1950 era to features that remained vulnerable, particularly their locks and locking mechanisms. A variety of techniques were developed and used to defeat these. After removing the lock's knob, burglars often used a hammer and punch to drive the stem through the lock's rear plate, rendering the lock inoperative. Instead of punching the lock stem, other burglars devised or adapted techniques for pulling it from the lock. A career thief recalled an occasion, for example, when

> we tried something . . . called a come-along. . . . The come-along is a malleable steel collar with bolt holes coming through the edge of it to fasten on right behind the knob of the combination. It is about six inches round and it looks like a doughnut with a two-and-a-half-inch hole in the center. It slips over the knob then you tighten up against the front of the safe door, so that the plate exerts outward pressure on the knob, pulling the stem loose from the tumblers.[5]

Still other burglars successively peeled the metal sheets of the laminated walls. Although techniques such as punching and peeling were employed by only a small proportion of burglars, a much larger number were aware of these techniques even if they never used them successfully. Certainly, money safes with commonly known and exploitable design and construction features were enticing criminal opportunities to burglars in the early decades of the twentieth century.[6]

Carbide drill bits, which came into general use after World War II, presented a new challenge to safe manufacturers. Because not even casehardened steel is a match for them, money safes that formerly were tool resistant were no longer so. To counteract both this innovation and the diamond-tipped core drill that followed soon after, manufacturers developed new metals to use in combination with multiple sheets of copper in money safe construction. Copper resists torch attacks, and the new metals twist, chip, or break most drill bits. These cumulative developments have made today's money safes an insurmountable challenge for the vast majority of contemporary thieves, and safecracking, as an attractive and potentially lucrative career option for thieves, has declined.[7] As a persistent thief remarked, "Safes today are a dead issue really."[8]

As was true of both the smash-and-grab in post–World War II England and train robbery a half century earlier, developments in security arrangements and technology also contributed to the decline of safecracking in the United States, particularly the increasing sophistication of burglar alarms and security technology. Electric "eyes" (i.e., beams of light) were widely used in burglar alarms in the middle decades of the twentieth century. Located at door openings, for example, anytime the light beam was interrupted between its source and receiving eye, an alarm was triggered. Burglars quickly learned how to defeat these rather primitive alarms, for example, by taping a flashlight over the latter. The years after the Korean War, however, brought the development of alarms more difficult to bypass. Sonar and motion detection technology were copied by the security industry and incorporated in alarm systems. Ultrasonic alarm systems, which fill a protected space with sound waves, are triggered whenever objects move in this space. In recent years the price of these devices has fallen substantially, making them available even to many middle-income homeowners.[9] It is possible today to purchase an ultrasonic alarm system for less than $500. Development and diffusion of these electronically sophisticated alarms necessitate that thieves bent on neutralizing them acquire expensive electronic equipment and specialized expertise. Most thieves are unable to do so and therefore must bypass safecracking and other lucrative burglary opportunities.

The Growth of Fraud

A more important reason for the decline or transformation of safecracking and other forms of crime that once offered attractive opportunities to thieves is fundamental and dramatic changes in the public welfare functions of the state, in communications technology, and in the post–World War II U.S. economy. Widespread availability and use of consumer credit, telecommunications, and electronic financial transactions have hastened the approach of a cashless economy and a veritable explosion of new, lucrative, low-risk criminal opportunities.[10]

Through the early decades of the twentieth century, goods were purchased from vendors and bills were paid in cash, and thus commercial establishments kept substantial sums of cash on premises in money safes. But the use of cash in financial transactions has declined, and money safes rarely contain large sums of it today. Financial transactions increasingly are conducted electronically; bills are paid and funds are moved without the need to do so physically. They can be transferred from one account or company to another by use of computers, telephone lines, and satellite networks. Automatic teller machines (ATMs), home banking, and electronic financial transfers (EFTs) among banks and businesses now are used routinely throughout much of the world. As a result, even when the ordinary burglar, through ingenuity or good fortune, manages to open a money safe, it is unlikely to be as rewarding as in earlier eras.[11] In a self-parody, the ex-convict Malcolm Braly described one experience:

> One night I broke a safe in a drugstore, using the small pry bar they kept in the storeroom to open crates, and once I had a peel started, I continued the

opening by driving in a number of softball bats I found on display. Here was the expert safecracker at work . . . pounding in ballbat after ballbat like an insane beaver, until, finally I broke the lockbox and opened the safe. I took three hundred dollars in bills and change.[12]

The effort is hardly worth the candle, particularly in a world where far more lucrative opportunities can be found elsewhere.

The massive growth of consumer credit and computer-based electronic transactions, coupled with an enormous expansion of government largesse for wealthy and poor alike and mass marketing of insurance, have generated a host of criminal opportunities, primarily for fraud. The defining characteristic of fraud is use of deception to secure unfair or unlawful gain.[13] Whereas robbers, burglars, and automobile thieves make no pretext of their intentions when confronting their victims or stealing their property, perpetrators of fraud use guile and deceit to create for illicit advantage the appearance of a legitimate and routine transaction. The increasing use of ATMs is an example. Developing with this change have been the emergence and growth of ATM fraud. In 1983 there were 2.7 billion transactions involving $262 billion processed through ATMs. Data from a 1983 survey of 16 U.S. banks, all but one with deposits in excess of $1 billion, revealed that 45 percent of ATM incidents resulting in account-holder complaints were found to be potentially fraudulent, involving, for example, unauthorized use of lost or stolen cards, over-drafts, and "bad" deposits. Rapidly increasing opportunities for fraud have been met with an array of criminal responses. Nationwide, bank losses from ATM fraud during 1983 were estimated in the range between $70 and $100 million.[14] These losses dwarf monetary losses from street crimes; in 1983 the estimated financial value of all property stolen in crimes reported to police departments throughout the United States was $8 million.[15] An example of unusually imaginative ATM fraud was reported in 1993 in the northeastern United States:

For two weeks, an ATM machine—ordinary-looking in just about every way, but completely bogus—operated in a shopping mall near [Hartford, Connecticut], giving nothing but apologetic receipts that said no transactions were possible. Meanwhile, police . . . and bank officials say, the machine was recording the card numbers and the personal identification numbers that hundreds of customers entered in their vain attempts to make the machine dispense cash. [A few days later], while the machine was still running . . . , the first withdrawals began. Using counterfeit bank cards encoded with the numbers stolen from Connecticut customers, the thieves strolled through midtown Manhattan, tapping into the 24-hour automated teller network, and netting . . . at least $50,000.[16]

Opportunities for fraud have expanded also because of governmental programs that make available to citizens and businesses an array of subsidies, tax breaks, welfare, and other forms of largesse. Defense procurement fraud, financial institution fraud, and securities and commodities fraud are some examples of criminal responses, primarily by white-collar, professionally employed citizens and corporations.[17] Losses from health care fraud and insurance fraud, in which, for example, fake automobile accidents result in bogus insurance claims, are estimated to exceed $500 million a year.[18] Health care has become increasingly attractive to fraudulent exploitation of insurance programs. In one type of scam, so-called rolling labs are used to conduct unnecessary and sometimes fake tests on unsuspecting patients, and the cost is billed to insurance companies or the government. One case, which resulted in $50 million in losses to government and private insurers, began with telephone sales representatives offering free physical exams to patients. Those who took advantage of the offer completed medical history forms that later were used to justify both the "medical necessity" of the tests and payments by government or private insurers.[19] Other scams focus on and take advantage of the movement toward increased use of home health care, often billing for substandard or undelivered services. A third type of scam is practiced by crooked suppliers of health care equipment who provide unnecessary or inferior products and bill the government at massively inflated prices. Exploiting some of the new opportunities for fraud requires "not much more than the ability to read, write, and fill out forms, along with some minimum level of presentation of a respectable self."[20]

Many new opportunities for fraud are provided by the emergence and growth of the credit-based economy. It is not an exaggeration to say that "credit cards produce credit fraud."[21] In the late 1960s, as consumer use of credit cards became increasingly commonplace, criminal activity centered on lost and stolen cards. Soon, however, it moved to manual alteration involving counterfeiting and white plastic. "White plastic" refers to regular size, plain, blank plastic cards that are embossed with an account number, cardholder name, and expiration date. Collusive merchants accept the cards and make money by submitting phony sales records to banks. Fraudulent cards can generate hundreds of dollars of purchases and cash advances before they are blocked by the issuer. Subsequently, a new fraud surfaced: fraud utilizing not the card itself but the account number. Offenders have devised several different ways to obtain valid account numbers without the cardholder knowing that it will be used by another person. Account data can be extracted from carbon slips used in valid card transactions and either discarded by the merchant or memorized by the perpetrator while the cardholder is making a legitimate purchase. Alternatively, account data can be conned from the cardholder directly, generally over the telephone, by representations that the perpetrator is the bank confirming the account information. Genuine account numbers can be used on unauthorized sales slips by dishonest merchants, or they can be used to purchase goods from telephone mail order houses. Goods can be shipped to a temporary address given by the perpetrator, who can change locations before the cardholder can report the unauthorized transaction from his or her billing statement. Financial data provided by VISA and MasterCard show that losses from fraudulent credit card transactions increased from $10 million in 1973 to nearly $130 million in 1982.[22]

Perhaps the most lucrative and least risky opportunities for fraud are in the area of telemarketing. Typically, a consumer receives a phone call, often from a so-called boiler room, rented offices with banks of telephones operated by high-pressure operators or salespersons. The telephone callers solicit funds or sell products based on untrue assertions or outrageous claims. They often use names that sound similar to bona fide charities or known legitimate organizations. Alternatively, consumers receive in the mail a postcard asking them to call a telephone number. When they do so, they are told or promised virtually anything it takes to get their credit card or checking account number. Telemarketing scams offer an enormous variety of products or services including travel clubs, skin care products, calendars, coins, jewelry, water filters, government lists, scholarships, vitamins, investment opportunities, pen sets, and employment opportunities.[23] Business opportunity and franchise frauds often victimize persons who dream of being self-employed entrepreneurs. Certain vitamin scams and other health product scams appear to be designed specifically to appeal to older citizens. Goods or services either are never delivered or are substantially inferior to those that were promised. The typical owner of a telemarketing firm uses multiple aliases, telephones, mail drops, and business locations. These operators can change their method of solicitation, product line, and other recognizable traits overnight. Their operations are mobile.

The operations of an Atlanta, Georgia, entrepreneurial criminal organization illustrate how telemarketing was used in a larger pattern of fraud:

> Federal authorities announced [yesterday] that they have smashed a ... fraud ring that from its base in Atlanta stole more than $10 million in dozens of states, at least partly by recovering discarded checks, deposit slips and credit-card receipts from trash containers.
>
> Using information gleaned from the garbage, members of the loose-knit group used high-quality computer graphics to create fake driver's licenses, Social Security cards and other forms of identification that were then used to create bogus checking accounts, cash counterfeit checks, make unauthorized credit-card purchases, and file false tax refunds.

They also staged automobile accidents to collect fraudulent insurance payments, set up dummy corporations that purchased clothing and other goods without paying vendors, and established several telemarketing boiler rooms that were used to collect credit information from victims, many of them elderly.[24]

Refinements in telemarketing schemes have become significantly more sophisticated. Many now are structured to involve lengthy delays between the time charges are incurred on the credit card and the delivery of the promised goods or services. Consequently, many consumers fail to realize they have been victimized until a substantial period of time has elapsed and the fraud is uncovered. Under travel scam programs, for example, victims generally are charged for a "bargain" travel package shortly after providing their credit card number to the fraudulent telemarketer although they typically plan not to take the purchased trip until several months later. Selling bogus products and services via 900 telephone numbers is a growing enterprise in the 1990s also. Estimates of annual financial losses resulting from telemarketing fraud range from $1 billion to $40 billion.[25]

Although surprisingly little is known about how many Americans are victimized by fraud, the numbers clearly are large. A 1991 survey of 1,246 households found that compared to crimes such as burglary, robbery, assault, and theft, "personal fraud . . . appears to be very common."[26] The Federal Bureau of Investigation does not publish annual data on the number of fraud crimes reported to the police in the United States, but it does report the number of arrests for fraud. Temporal changes in arrests are a less than perfect indicator of change in the rate of crime commission, but they do suggest both that fraud is gaining in popularity and that it is doing so faster than more traditional forms of property crime. Figure 3.1, which depicts changes in arrest rates over the period 1964–1992, shows that arrest rates for robbery, burglary, automobile theft, and larceny increased 143.7 percent, 19.4 percent, 9.3 percent, and 123.7 percent respectively. During the same period, the arrest rate for fraud increased 367.7 percent.[27] In Britain, losses from check and credit card fraud nearly doubled between 1988 and 1991 alone.[28]

The appeal of the new criminal opportunities is only enhanced by the fact that legislation and security countermeasures generally have lagged behind their emergence.[29] A statutory example:

A person who steals a credit card in Texas . . . and who uses it to charge $100,000 in goods but who always charges items that cost less than $750 is guilty of multiple misdemeanor offenses, not a felony. Thus, a person could have used a credit card illegally 1,000 times, charging $100 each time, and not be guilty of a felony.[30]

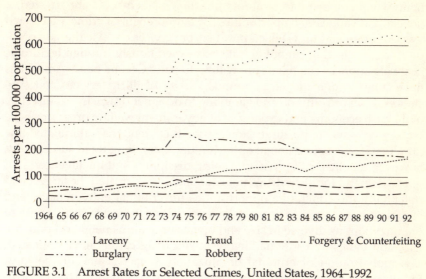

FIGURE 3.1   Arrest Rates for Selected Crimes, United States, 1964–1992

SOURCE: Federal Bureau of Investigation, *Crime in the United States: Uniform Crime Reports* for 1964 through 1992 (Washington, D.C.: U.S. Government Printing Office, annual).

Fraud is low-risk crime. First, when compared to those victimized by street crimes, victims of fraud are much less likely even to be aware they have been victimized. And they are less likely than victims of street crime to report it to authorities.[31] Believing they should have been more careful in the first place, many feel a sense of embarrassment and shame and certainly do not want others to know what has happened to them.[32] Local-level law enforcement and prosecution generally are no match for criminals whose operations span state borders via the telephone or the U.S. mail. Further, those who are prosecuted for fraud enjoy a considerable advantage at the hands of the criminal justice system when compared with those charged with robbery and burglary. Defendants convicted of fraud in federal and state courts generally are sentenced to incarceration less often than defendants convicted of committing direct-contact theft.[33]

Entrepreneurial Options

For ambitious, imaginative, and intelligent offenders unable or unwilling to exploit new criminal opportunities, there are other options, in particular *entrepreneurial crime.* Entrepreneurial crime is low-level organized crime. It requires differentiated roles, organization, and leadership. In contrast to *syndicated crime* of the kind represented by La Cosa Nostra, the organizations created by entrepreneurs generally are small and impermanent; when one or more of an organization's "members" are arrested, it generally disappears. Opportunities for entrepreneurial crime are created by public demand for (1) illicit products or services or (2) legitimate products or services that cannot be satisfied expeditiously through legitimate channels at prices customers are willing to pay.[34] On one hand, Americans have come to demand an enormous variety of illicit services and substances, from prostitution and gambling to designer drugs. Even as decline of the cash economy and expansion of government welfare programs have created massive opportunity for fraud, this trend has stimulated the growth of these new criminal opportunities. Exploiting them successfully, however, requires entrepreneurial spirit, discipline, and intelligence.

The demand for illicit drugs unquestionably has created the largest and potentially most lucrative opportunities for criminal entrepreneurs and organizations. To meet the inelastic demand for these products, criminal organizations as diverse in size and operating scale as neighborhood distribution gangs and internationally linked drug cartels have appeared. The globalization of criminal organization in fact is one of the most important changes occurring in contemporary criminality. The opportunities presented by the market in illicit drugs have been exploited by ghetto youth and thieves alike.[35] Street-level theft and drug use are inextricably linked, and many ordinary thieves and hustlers are familiar with low-level drug entrepreneurs. At some time or another, most of them attempt the same course, generally as a way of earning income while also ensuring a supply of drugs for their own needs.[36] The practical demands of the business can be extremely trying, and these efforts typically are at a low-level and, more often than not, end in voluntary termination, arrest, and penury. A former offender gave this assessment after trying unsuccessfully to make a go of drug dealing:

> I finally had to admit that I lacked the discipline to be a good dealer. Dealing drugs is harder than any job I've had, then or since. To this day, I laugh when I hear folks say drug dealers are lazy people who don't want to work. There's no job more demanding than dealing drugs. It's the only thing I've really tried hard to do, and failed at.[37]

Given most offenders' class and status origins, this admission should come as little surprise. It is primarily the young and the cocky who try drug dealing. Self-discipline is not their strong suit. And the rewards of drug dealing often prove to be illusory in any case. A study of street-level heroin dealers in Detroit found that runners earned an average of $160 per day, or $14 per hour.[38] Counted as the wage for a few hours of work, this is not a bad return. However, bad planning, bad execution, and bad luck all take their toll on overall earnings.

On the other hand, in the decades following World War II, U.S. industry began to mass produce commodities to meet new and rapidly growing legitimate consumer demand. Houses, refrigerators, automobiles, and electronic goods were marketed in enormous volume as Americans, to a historically unprecedented degree, accumulated a wide array of personal property.[39] Desire to own at least a portion of these consumer goods has become a powerful force, driving not only the legitimate economy but strengthening the underground economy as well.[40] The example of recorded music is instructive.[41] Until the 1960s, counterfeiting and piracy of audio recordings of popular musical artists were uncommon. So long as the vinyl phonograph record was the principal medium for marketed recordings, the technology required to copy recordings was expensive and generally not available to the public. By the early 1970s, however, the popularity of the vinyl record was rivaled if not surpassed by cassette tape recordings. Electronic equipment for playing and copying audiotapes became popular and available to the public at modest prices. The capital outlay required to purchase equipment for duplicating popular recordings decreased dramatically as the demand for tape recordings escalated. This combination of circumstances created lucrative criminal opportunities and stimulated creation of an illicit industry. Some indication of the size of the industry can be gained from statistics on seizures of counterfeit or pirated cassettes and actions taken against suppliers and distributors of them. In 1992, law enforcement officials throughout the United States seized more than 2.5 million cassettes and secured guilty pleas or verdicts against 128 persons.[42] It is unclear how the development of compact disc technology will affect this development. In 1993, however, counterfeit or pirated compact discs (CDs) numbered 17,845, a substantial increase from the 15 seized in 1988.[43]

The emergence and persistence of automobile theft rings and chop shops are another example of how demand for legitimate products at reasonable prices can produce criminal opportunities and entrepreneurial criminal organizations.[44] These enterprises proliferated during the 1970s in response to circumstances in the market for automobiles and automobile parts. Initially, the legitimate price of luxury American automobiles increased dramatically, as did the price of "crash parts," such as front fenders, grilles, and hoods, which often are damaged in collisions. This was compounded by a lengthy increase in the time required to fill orders for new crash parts. A widespread demand for cheaper luxury cars and readily available crash parts presented opportunities for criminal entrepreneurs. One result has been that the proportion of stolen automobiles that are recovered has declined considerably over the past two decades.[45]

Auto theft rings produce products for two markets: automobile body parts, which are sold primarily to auto salvage yards and body shops, and "retagged" or rebuilt automobiles with modified or fraudulent identification numbers and papers that are sold to individuals or dealers. Typically, the product process begins with one or more members of the organization taking orders from individuals or business firms. Many orders come from "long-lines," special telephone intercoms that may link as many as 200 automobile salvage yards in a multistate region. Whenever a salvage yard needs a particular part, it will make its requirement known on a long-line.

Entrepreneurial crime requires offenders to bring to bear resources and factors that are unnecessary so long as they limit their activities to predatory street crime. At the very least, it requires rationality and planning, neither of which is highly valued by many working-class males. The changes and adjustments required if one is to move into entrepreneurial crime are simply too high a price for some men:

> I could be moving into the higher echelons of things, but I'm staying away from it. When you get seriously involved in the drug business, there's thousands of dollars at stake. It's a lot more pressure, a lot more hassles. You have to worry about people making deals with the D.A. You could get bumped off. People think you're moving in on their territories. They rip off your workers, your spots. They be diming on you. I really don't have to worry about that at my level.[46]

The financial opportunities created by public demand for drugs and the goodies of a consumer economy have attracted the kinds of offenders who in earlier times would have resorted to more lucrative forms of burglary and robbery. Whether it results from lack of ambition, lack of imagination, absence of connections, or insufficient control of their emotions, most ordinary thieves continue to mine the low-grade ore represented by individual victims, who often are of modest means. Beyond a simple intention to make money quickly and easily, the crimes they commit require neither personal distinction nor highly developed technical skills. Unlikely candidates for fraudulent manipulation of ATMs, they are more likely to lie in wait and employ old-fashioned criminal skills to victimize legitimate users of the new technologies. Robbery of persons at ATM machines has increased in frequency. Today's persistent thieves continue to pursue the old forms of crime not only because they are incapable of exploiting or unwilling to exploit the new opportunities but also because there is a bountiful supply of the older ones providing returns that, seen through their eyes, are satisfactory albeit far from optimal.

Enticing Munificence

Even as opportunities for fraud and entrepreneurial crime have increased, the supply of opportunities for more traditional, if pedestrian, forms of theft paradoxically has never been greater. The credit economy, new developments in communications technology, electronic fund transfers, and welfare programs for rich and poor have opened up new criminal opportunities, but other changes in American life have functioned to ensure there will be no shortage of traditional ones. In 1960, 13.1 percent of American households were composed of single individuals; by 1990 this had increased to 24.6 percent.[47] In 1960, only 37.7 percent of American women were employed outside of the home; by 1990 this had increased to 57.5 percent.[48] The decline of the extended family, the growing proportion of the population who reside alone, and the rapidly increasing employment of women outside the home have combined to make household burglary increasingly attractive to many offenders. Growing numbers of two-income families and individuals who live alone have made apartments and houses unoccupied for much of the day available to a broad range of thieves.[49] The mobile lifestyles of contemporary Americans means that during evening hours also homes often are unoccupied while residents eat out or run errands they could not complete during the daytime hours. Construction materials and locks used in many contemporary apartments and homes, moreover, present less of a challenge to thieves. Together with reduced rates of daytime occupancy, these developments have made today's homes and apartments easy to plunder. And the home electronics revolution virtually ensures that every home will have portable, high-demand television sets, videocassette recorders, and stereo sound equipment that can be sold quickly and easily. In the past three decades, the rate of household burglary soared, far outstripping the increase in commercial burglary. In the period 1962–1992, the proportion of all burglaries reported to local police in which households were the target increased from 44.3 percent to 66.2 percent.[50] The fact that nearby apartments and homes are more likely today to be unoccupied has reduced the risk of these burglaries substantially. During the same 30-year period, the clearance rate (the proportion of reported crimes that result in arrest) for burglary fell from 26.9 percent to 13 percent.[51]

The decline of extended families, the growth of two-income families, and the increasing proportion of persons residing alone have coincided with the emergence of convenience lifestyles. Convenience stores and fast food restaurants, institutional mainstays of this lifestyle, typically open early and remain open until late at night.[52] From 1972 to 1992, the number of convenience stores in the United States increased from 19,000 to 64,482.[53] Many predators view them as "poor people's banks." After 1955, the number of branch banks in the United States proliferated, placing them in ready access to every citizen.[54] The declining importance of burglaries in which bank vaults are targets of attack has been matched by the increasing appeal of bank robbery.[55] The development of interstate highways and other high-volume transportation arteries has brought these convenience institutions into easy driving range of ever growing numbers of Americans, including predators.[56] Thieves now have the kind of rapid, easy access to targets that reduces the risk of robbing them. Between 1960 and 1993, the clearance rate for robbery declined from 38.6 percent to 24 percent.[57]

Crime Specialization

It is often supposed that the area of crime thieves specialize in distinguishes various categories of them and can be used for analytic and policy purposes. Although use of statistical techniques permits investigators to sort offenders into an array of types, their boundaries remain ambiguous and fluid and the policy payoff from these exercises is yet to be demonstrated.[58] The principal reason for this indefiniteness is that crime specialization is very limited. Self-report survey data from 88 incarcerated burglars not only showed this but also revealed that thieves who were most heavily involved in and identified with theft committed a greater variety of criminal acts than their noncriminal peers.[59] Self-report data collected from 49 convicted robbers in a California prison showed, in fact, that they had committed three times more burglaries than robberies during their criminal careers.[60] Ethnographic research on active burglars, contacted without assistance from criminal justice agencies or personnel, found that "while it may be convenient to think of these subjects as 'residential burglars' for the purposes of the present study, . . . many of them are more criminally versatile than such a label implies."[61] A British thief could have been speaking for the substantial majority of thieves and hustlers when he remarked:

> This has always been my theory, that I'll take whatever job comes along. If there's a vanload of stuff to be pulled, I'll pull it; a screwing job [burglary], I'll screw it; a safeblowing, I'll blow it—and so on. And if it's a coshing job [robbery facilitated by assault], well then, I'll use a cosh.[62]

These comments are echoed by an American thief: "During the course of my larcenous career, . . . I worked confidence rackets, I swindled gambling establishments and, with varying degrees of success, I also doubled as a burglar, safe cracker, car thief, armed robber, and you name it."[63] Data collected from prison interviews with 77 robbers and 45 burglars led the investigator to conclude that "[v]ery few men seemed to be specialists and most appeared to be generalists, 'jack of all trades, master of none' in the criminal world."[64] The image of thieves as crime specialists clearly does not apply to the great majority of contemporary persistent thieves.

The reasons for minimal specialization need not detain us long and should come as no surprise in any case. Large pools of cash or high-value commodities that can be stolen are difficult to identify at any time and, because of the economic and other changes described here, have become even more so in recent decades. Simply put, "it's a hard thing to steal for a living. . . . When you're stealing for a living that means you're out every day. And you're not going to run into any gravy every day of the week."[65] Today, more than ever before, sustained direct-contact theft is unlikely to produce the mythical "big score."[66]

But while labels such as "burglar" and "robber" have limited value as a means of distinguishing types of offenders, this is not to say that thieves and hustlers lack strong or specific crime *preferences*. The fact is that a fundamental decision awaits all who commit direct-contact theft: whether to avoid or to confront their victim(s). Brian Biluszek, who committed as many as 550 burglaries but no robberies, said:

> I think, if you're *robbin'* somebody, there's an interpersonal thing, I mean, you're doing something to somebody. And if I'm just stealing, you know, I can justify that I'm just, you know, there's no *personal* connection with another person, I'm just in his house, taking "stuff."

Robbery strikes many who commit it as extremely easy, particularly when it is compared with burglary and other crimes. Instead of going through all the hassles of burglary, why not, as they see it, simply steal *cash?* There is no need for it "to be cut, melted down, recast or sold. There are no treacherous middlemen, insurance adjustors, or wiseguy fences involved. A guy can spend it walking out the door."[67] Still, robbery requires different skills, develops at a different pace, has a drama all its own, and evokes it own emotional rewards. It also presents those who commit it with an opportunity to show courage, gameness, and forthrightness, personal qualities they regard highly.

Some armed robbers, moreover, revel in confronting their victims and using threat or terror to steal from them. Often described as *hardmen* or *badasses*, these offenders avoid burglary, seeing it as boring, too slow to develop, and too risky when one must dispose of stolen goods. Choosing instead to confront and compel compliance from their victims means, as one offender put it, that "nothing can beat a robbery for the sheer drama of personal confrontation."[68]

> Sticking up gave me a rush that I never got from B&Es. There was an almost magical transformation in my relationship with the rest of the world when I drew that gun on folks. I always marveled at how the toughest cats . . . whimpered and begged for their lives when I stuck the barrel of a sawed-off shotgun into their faces. Adults who ordinarily would have commanded my respect were forced to follow my orders like obedient kids.[69]

The sense of power and mastery they derive from their exploits can become a strong component of some robbers' motivation. Reflecting on a period of his life when he lived by committing robberies, an informant said simply, "I was addicted to the pistol."

The robber recognizes the element of unpredictability in the victim's response to robbery, and he plans accordingly. Boldly and openly, he commits to and embarks upon a project of uncertain exigencies and outcome, the very element of robbery that makes others fear and avoid it:

> I went through a couple of months playing with a gun. Did a little shooting for a while there, but I didn't like it. I didn't really like to threaten the people, taking that much of a chance on killing somebody. You're always on the verge, you know. It could happen by accident. And a lot of times it does happen by accident.[70]

There is the uncertainty of whether the victim may "try to be a hero" and the robber, in order to escape, would end up shooting him. It is not surprising that techniques for immediately sensing noncompliant victims and maintaining command of the situation figure prominently in the robber's criminal-skills repertoire.[71] Victims who resist are thought stupid and deserving of whatever countermeasures they necessitate:

> [I]f some [bank] teller tries to play hero when I'm pointing a shotgun in his face, sure I feel bad about that, but it really isn't my fault because I tried to be professional and plan the robbery and do a good job without anyone getting hurt. He's the one acting like a fool trying to stop me.[72]

Thus the robber converts resistance by victims into unjustified provocation,[73] as in the robbery of a McDonald's restaurant:

> Out of the corner of my eye, I noticed the store manager trying to ease his way into a side office. I pointed the .32 pistol at him and said, "Freeze!" Minutes later he tried it again. . . . . All I wanted to do was get the cash and dash. But I made up my mind that if he moved again, I *had* to smoke him. I hated him for putting that pressure on me. I didn't even know him, and I hated the hell out of him.[74]

Burglary, by contrast, is a victim-avoiding crime. More than anything else, this explains why residential burglars generally concentrate their offenses during times of the day when residents are least likely to be at home. When burglars screen potential targets, determining whether or not a home is occupied is in the forefront of their decisionmaking process. A burglar may, for example, telephone the victim's home from a nearby pay telephone and let it ring. Some indication of how aversive to violence burglars are can be gleaned from data on all household burglaries reported in the National Crime Victimization Survey. During the period 1973–1982, a household member actually saw the offender in 12.7 percent of the cases. An assault, rape, or robbery occurred in 4 percent of these incidents.[75] Burglary, moreover, is viewed as relatively safe. Burglars rarely are arrested while in the act; arrest, if it occurs at all, takes place in the area in which a burglary has been reported or while the burglar is engaged in disposing of stolen merchandise.[76] The clearance rate of 13.5 percent for burglary is the lowest for all the Index crimes.[77] Also, burglary holds little risk of harm to the offender or victims.

Men and women with a distinct preference for burglary often are afraid of the drama and uncertainty of armed robbery. They do not want to "have to shoot anyone," and they fear the risk of serious injury or death at the hands of the victim or the police. Equally feared are the long prison terms that this contingency would bring. Burglary for them represents a favorable compromise between safety and the quest for bigger money.[78] Malcolm X summarized these beliefs with this observation:

> Burglary, properly executed, though it had its dangers, offered the maximum chances of success with the minimum risk. If you did your job so that you never met any of your victims, it first lessened your chances of having to attack or perhaps kill someone. And if through some slip-up you were caught later, by the police, there was never a positive eyewitness.[79]

At heart, the majority of burglars are *sneaks*. And although many have committed or will commit armed robbery, generally they do not like to do so and can be lured into doing so only under highly promising or desperate circumstances.

It is interesting to note that "vastly more robbers have done burglary than burglars have done robbery."[80] Burglary is an offense that juveniles commit early in their criminal careers because it permits them to minimize the chances of violent confrontation. Looking back on their early burglaries, some young men describe them as "little, sneaky things I used to do when I was a kid."[81] Their progression to robbery occurs because robbery provides "a much faster source of cash" and also because of their increasing "capacity for violent encounters."[82] Consequently, as juveniles grow into young adults, there is some movement from crimes depending on stealth to those involving the use of force.

Although there is limited long-term specialization by persistent thieves, the existence of distinct crime preferences combined with "habit [and] familiarity with techniques ... [tends] to draw them back towards their 'main line'—the type of crime they [feel] most at home with." As opposed to rigid specialization, therefore, the more common pattern is "what might be called 'short-term specialization,' . . . periods in which they . . . become involved in a specific type of crime to the virtual exclusion of others."[83] Through experience, most eventually discover that some kinds of theft appeal to them, perhaps because they believe these are relatively safe or because they simply believe they are good at those types. Consequently, some tend to see themselves either as burglars or robbers and to restrict their criminal activities accordingly, at least for short periods of time. A self-described convicted burglar made this point while responding to a question about criminal hangouts:

Q: Is it unusual for stickup men to hang around the same places as burglars?
A: Well, I have trouble, how do you separate it, you know? Because if something [stickup] looks good, I'll go out on it. I don't *like* it, but I will go out. And it don't have to be nothing fantastic, it could be $1,000 or $1,500 for me to go. But if it's real easy, I'm going to go.
Q: You don't consider yourself a burglar, as a specialist?
A: Well, that's all I do, really. As far as crime is concerned, that's my preference.
Q: But you've done stickups too?
A: Yes, I don't prefer them. I wouldn't go to supermarkets, I wouldn't stick up a tavern. I wouldn't stick up a savings and loan. I don't like to deal with four or five or ten people.
Q: If a good opportunity comes along?
A: If a good opportunity comes along, [say] with two individuals coming from the bank with a bag of money, and it's a quick grab? I'm for it. I went on a couple of deals in my life where it was more or less of a tip, where maybe some secretary or funeral clerk would be carrying money to the bank for the store, [you] grab the purse. It's a snap.

Grounded both in personal crime preferences and past experience, thieves and hustlers tend to repeat what they are comfortable with that also has been successful in the past. Once they have identified and enjoyed success at a specific hustle, they tend to repeat it. This causes them to reduce severely their criminal versatility. Many remain uninterested in or intimidated by the prospects of committing other types of crime, even when they seemingly possess the requisite skills to do so.

The Contemporary Scene

The lesson gained from historical transformations of criminal offending is that the knowledge and skills needed to earn a good living from stealing probably do not differ greatly from those required for successful legitimate employment. Consider, first, the realm of manual labor. For more than a century, those who labored in America's foundries and factories performed labor-intensive work using hammers, prybars, wedges, and other such tools. When the United States was one of the world's major producers of manufactured goods, lucrative crime such as safecracking required similar tools and skills. Intelligence, commitment, hard work, and application of a common pool of skills could bring a decent return from the foundry, from the construction site, or from crime. A high school diploma was not necessary. However, the skills most in demand in legitimate industry have changed dramatically in recent decades, and the majority of Americans no longer need or employ manual skills to earn a living. Use of them in lucrative crimes such as safe burglary has declined also.

The criminal skills of yesterday are not equal to today's opportunities and challenges. Thieves now find it correspondingly difficult to defeat state-of-the-art alarms and safes. Most would not know even how to begin. It seems apparent that "the more sophisticated the prevention technology . . . , the more sophisticated criminals must become to maintain acceptable levels of success."[84] High school dropouts in most cases are not equal to the challenge. Today's successful thieves either must have a working knowledge of electronics, computers, and electronic records systems or else they must know someone who does. They have changed "from crackers to hackers."[85] As money safes and alarm systems became increasingly sophisticated, the gap between the skills and resources possessed by or accessible to most males in the general population and the arcane technical skills and equipment needed to defeat them increased also. A 1991 survey of U.S. state prison inmates shows, for example, that only 22 percent had completed high school and 12 percent had attended college for some period of time.[86]

We should not ignore the ways that the class and status background of thieves and hustlers both fails to provide them the social and interpersonal skills prerequisite for criminal success and also makes them uninterested in or unwilling to employ criminal skills more likely to pay off than traditional forms of theft. Those accustomed to subordination do not easily move into superordinate positions and employ successfully the organization and interpersonal skills this requires. Men who value egalitarianism do not adapt easily to hierarchical arrangements, even if they are the pathway to more lucrative and less risky forms of crime. Ill-prepared to take advantage of the new opportunities, most persistent thieves and hustlers must content themselves with financial returns barely adequate to sustain their lifestyle of choice. Thus, they must increase the number of offenses they commit, which brings repeated exposure to the "bitch of chance."[87] For those who know how to use the new technologies, the payoff can be substantial.

Whether products of urban underclass neighborhoods or rural poverty, those who are denied access by life circumstances to well-paying, respectable employment in the legitimate economy figure prominently among those who continually replenish the ranks of persistent thieves. Few of them are capable of pursuing or willing to pursue entrepreneurial criminal options, and they are increasingly unable to locate large sums of easily stolen cash. Slow to take advantage of the new criminal opportunities, the vast majority content themselves with modest criminal returns or engage in high-risk crimes.[88] The 1978 Rand Inmate Survey of 2,190 jail and prison inmates in Michigan, Texas, and California found that whereas 49.4 percent of respondents had committed at least one burglary and 43.8 percent had committed at least one robbery during the two years before incarceration, only 15.9 percent had committed fraud, the lowest rate of the eight crimes included in the survey.[89] Findings from the 1986–1987 Desistance Project, in which 60 persistent property offenders nearing release from prison were interviewed and surveyed regarding past criminal involvement, revealed that during their lifetime the subjects had committed an average of 100.6 residential burglaries, 43.4 business burglaries, and 21.9 armed robberies, but only 8.8 acts of credit card fraud.[90] In ethnographic research on 105 active urban burglars, subjects were asked about all the crimes they had committed during their lives. Fraud and crimes that require attention to appearance were low on the list of offense frequency:

> The range of money-making crimes from which the majority of the offenders could choose was fairly limited. By and large, they did not hold jobs that would allow them to violate even a low-level position of financial trust. . . . Similarly, few had the technical expertise required to disarm the sophisticated security systems protecting lucrative commercial targets or the interpersonal skills needed to commit frauds. It is not surprising, therefore, that, besides residential burglary, almost all of them stuck to a limited number of crimes requiring little skill, such as theft (mostly shoplifting), stealing cars, street-corner drug selling and robbery.[91]

Similarly, ethnographic interviews with 154 males randomly selected from the intake prison populations of three states (Washington, Nevada, and Illinois) found that most of the active offenders, despite the fact all were convicted of felonies, in fact had committed petty crimes. The investigators noted that "[a]ll of our data strongly suggest that . . . most were disorganized, unskilled, undisciplined petty criminals who very seldom . . . made any significant amount of money from their criminal acts."[92] The picture painted by these reports is one of substantial numbers of persistent offenders with limited skill and experience committing crimes of fraud. As their more intelligent and ambitious peers are lured away by more remunerative and less risky new opportunities or by entrepreneurial ones, those who persist at traditional forms of theft increasingly assume the form of a deskilled criminal *Lumpenproletariat*, a development noted by observers and thieves alike:

> When I started stealing, there were still plenty of legitimate thieves taking off proper scores; professionals who worked at their chosen specialties and adhered somewhat to a code of ethics. Or at least they exercised a degree of common sense. But the last few years have brought about a great change. The ranks of the professionals have been badly polluted by an influx of what might be called undeactivated sludge-muggers, strong-arm artists, and idiots who think the only way to pull an armed robbery is to shoot a cab driver or a grocery store clerk.[93]

It would be a mistake to endorse hastily or enthusiastically these remarks by a man who, by his own admission, engaged in a wide range of criminal activities during his larcenous career. If the discipline and operational intelligence of contemporary thieves fall short of what were commonplace traits a few decades ago—there is no way to assess this claim—the reason may lie not in the qualities of those who are drawn to robbery, burglary, and theft but in the kinds of offenders who *no longer are* drawn to it. Whatever the reason, a variety of evidence suggests that today's street thieves must settle for styles of theft that are pedestrian and returns that are paltry. Asked to describe a typical day in his life on the streets, an incarcerated offender said, for example:

> I'd probably get up about seven o'clock, then I'd get dressed and go to a restaurant and have some coffee. After that I'd go past my partner's house and wake him up. Then we might go and stand on the corner near the El tracks and watch the people. Maybe we'd see somebody we know who is leaving their house. If we did, we might go and break into the place while they're gone.

This operational style, regardless of what it displays in resourcefulness, surely cannot be called sophisticated. However, it is not uncharacteristic of contemporary offenders and the great majority of those who are subjects of this analysis.

There are exceptions. An example is an informant with experience in a variety of crimes, including burglary, robbery, and shoplifting. He also told of a time when he played the role of "injured passenger" in staged "accidents" with municipal buses. The informant received a lump-sum payment for filing a claim and retaining as counsel the attorney who organized the scheme, and he also received a portion of any financial settlement with municipal authorities or their insurance representative. Clearly, not all contemporary thieves are ignorant of new criminal opportunities and unable to exploit them because of the limitations caused by their class background or because they cannot improvise and maintain successfully the criminal organization they require.

Notes

1. Peter Crookston, *Villain* (London: Jonathan Cape, 1967), pp. 61, 64. See also John Landesco, "The life history of a member of the '42' gang," *Journal of Criminal Law, Criminology, and Police Science* 23(1933), pp. 964–998.

2. James A. Inciardi, *Careers in Crime* (Chicago: Rand McNally, 1975), p. 93.

3. James A. Inciardi, *Careers in Crime* (Chicago: Rand McNally, 1975), p. 94.

4. A generation of thieves learned to extract from dynamite the nitroglycerine used to blast open money safes. Dynamite was acquired in several ways, often stolen from construction sites. The process of extracting nitroglycerine is described in Lee Duncan, *Over the Wall* (New York: E. P. Dutton, 1936), especially pp. 160–163.

5. John Bartlow Martin, *My Life in Crime* (New York: Harper & Brothers, 1952), pp. 130–131.

6. Safe manufacturers distinguish and manufacture both money safes and record safes. The former presents to burglars a far more formidable challenge than the latter, which are constructed primarily to minimize potential loss from fire.

7. The thermal lance or "burning bar," which came into industrial use after 1960, was adopted quickly by burglars. One of the chief drawbacks to using it, however, is that the extremely high temperatures it generates often incinerate the contents of money safes. On the decline of safecracking generally, see James A. Inciardi, "Vocational crime," in *Handbook of Criminology*, edited by Daniel Glaser (Chicago: Rand McNally, 1974).

8. Billie Miller and David Helwig, *A Book About Billie* (Ottawa, Canada: Oberon, 1972), p. 140.

9. Simon Hakim and Andrew Buck, *Residential Security* (Bethesda, Md.: National Burglar and Fire Alarm Association, 1991).

10. See, for example, Ingo Walter, *The Secret Money Market* (New York: Harper and Row, 1990).

11. See, for example, the discussion in Peter Letkemann, *Crime as Work* (Englewood Cliffs, N.J.: Prentice-Hall, 1973).

12. Malcolm Braly, *False Starts* (New York: Penguin, 1976), p. 279.

13. Jay S. Albanese, "Tomorrow's thieves," *The Futurist* 22(September-October 1988), pp. 24–28.

14. Bureau of Justice Statistics, *Electronic Fund Transfer Fraud* (Washington, D.C.: U.S. Department of Justice, 1985); and James M. Tien, Thomas F. Rich, and Michael F. Cahn, *Electronic Fund Transfer Systems Fraud* (Washington, D.C.: U.S. Department of Justice, Bureau of Justice Statistics, 1986).

15. Federal Bureau of Investigation, *Crime in the United States, Uniform Crime Reports, 1983* (Washington, D.C.: U.S. Government Printing Office, 1984), p. 158.

16. *New York Times*, "One less thing to believe in: High-tech fraud at an ATM," May 13, 1993, pp. A1, A9. Two weeks after this incident, police announced arrests in the case. Convictions followed several months later. These subsequent developments in no way alter the fact that the thieves were successful in stealing a sizable sum of money.

17. Susan Shapiro, *Wayward Capitalists* (New Haven, Conn.: Yale University Press, 1984).

18. *U.S. News and World Report*, "Health care fraud," February 24, 1992, pp. 34–43.

19. *U.S. News and World Report*, "Health care fraud," February 24, 1992, pp. 34–43.

20. David Weisburd, Stanton Wheeler, Elin Waring, and Nancy Bode, *Crimes of the Middle Classes* (New Haven, Conn.: Yale University Press, 1991), pp. 182–183. See Jerome Jackson, "Fieldwork as a methodology to examine economic law-violators: The case of the fraud master" (presented at the annual meeting of the American Society of Criminology, New Orleans, November 1992).

21. David Weisburd, Stanton Wheeler, Elin Waring, and Nancy Bode, *Crimes of the Middle Class* (New Haven, Conn.: Yale University Press, 1991), p. 183.

22. U.S. Congress, Senate, Hearing before the Subcommittee on Consumer Affairs of the Committee on Banking, Housing, and Urban Affairs, *Credit Card Fraud*, 98th Congress, 1st session (Washington, D.C.: U.S. Government Printing Office, 1983).

23. U.S. Congress, Senate, Hearing before the Subcommittee on Consumer Affairs of the Committee on Commerce, Science, and Transportation, *Telemarketing Fraud and S. 568, The Telemarketing and Consumer Fraud and Abuse Protection Act*, 103d Congress, 1st session (Washington, D.C.: U.S. Government Printing Office, 1993).

24. *Knoxville News-Sentinel*, "Fraud ring gets rich by raiding trash bins," October 13, 1995, p. A13.

25. U.S. Congress, House of Representatives, Hearing before the Subcommittee on Regulation, Business Opportunities, and Energy of the Committee on Small Business, *Innovation in Telemarketing Frauds and Scams*, 102d Congress, 1st session (Washington, D.C.: U.S. Government Printing Office, 1991); U.S. Congress, House of Representatives, Committee on Government Operations, *The Scourge of Telemarketing Fraud: What Can Be Done Against It?* 102d Congress, 1st session (Washington, D.C.: U.S. Government Printing Office, 1991).

26. Richard M. Titus, Fred Heinzelman, and John M. Boyle, "Victimization of persons by fraud," *Crime and Delinquency* 41(1995), p. 65.

27. Federal Bureau of Investigation, *Crime in the United States, Uniform Crime Reports, 1964* (Washington, D.C.: U.S. Government Printing Office, 1965); Federal Bureau of Investigation, *Crime in the United States, Uniform Crime Reports, 1992* (Washington, D.C.: U.S. Government Printing Office, 1993).

28. Michael Levi, Paul Bissell, and Tony Richardson, *Prevention of Cheque and Credit Card Fraud* (London: Home Office, Crime Prevention Unit, 1991).

29. See, for example, U.S. Congress, Senate, *U.S. Government Efforts to Combat Fraud and Abuse in the Insurance Industry,* 102d Congress, 2d session (Washington, D.C.: U.S. Government Printing Office, 1992).

30. John H. Lindquist, *Misdemeanor Crime* (Newbury Park, Calif.: Sage, 1988), p. 88.

31. Richard M. Titus, Fred Heinzelman, and John M. Boyle, "Victimization of persons by fraud," *Crime and Delinquency* 41(1995), p. 54–72.

32. Michael Levi, "The victims of fraud" (paper presented at the second Liverpool Conference on Fraud, Corruption, and Business Crime, University of Liverpool, 1991); and Neal Shover, Greer Litton Fox, and Michael Mills, "Long-term consequences of victimization by white-collar crime," *Justice Quarterly* 11(1994), pp. 301–324.

33. Bureau of Justice Statistics, *Felony Sentences in State Courts, 1990* (Washington, D.C.: U.S. Department of Justice, 1993), p. 6; Bureau of Justice Statistics, *Forgery and Fraud-Related Offenses in 6 States, 1983–88* (Washington, D.C.: U.S. Department of Justice, 1990); and Bureau of Justice Statistics, *Sourcebook of Criminal Justice Statistics, 1992* (Washington, D.C.: U.S. Government Printing Office, 1993), p. 488.

34. Neal Shover, "Professional criminal: Major offender," in *Encyclopedia of Crime and Justice,* edited by Sanford H. Kadish (New York: Macmillan, 1983).

35. The drug trade has made available, particularly to ghetto youth, unprecedented financial incentives and rewards. The rewards of robbery and burglary pale by comparison, and some of the ablest and most ambitious young men have been integrated into drug-selling organizations. See Mercer L. Sullivan, *"Getting Paid"* (Ithaca, N.Y.: Cornell University Press, 1989); Thomas Mieczkowski, "Geeking up and throwing down: Heroin street life in Detroit," *Criminology* 24(1986), pp. 645–664; and Carl S. Taylor, *Dangerous Society* (East Lansing: Michigan State University Press, 1990).

36. A large body of research has linked heroin addiction and drug dealing by street-level users. An exemplary study, based on interviews with 279 male addicts in southern California, is Elizabeth Piper Deschenes, M. Douglas Anglin, and George Speckart, "Narcotics addiction: Related criminal careers, social and economic costs," *Journal of Drug Issues* 21(1991), pp. 383–411.

37. Nathan McCall, *Makes Me Wanna Holler* (New York: Random House, 1994), p. 123.

38. Thomas Mieczkowski, "Geeking up and throwing down: Heroin street life in Detroit," *Criminology* 24(1986), pp. 645–666.

39. David Halberstam, *The Fifties* (New York: Villard, 1993).

40. Stuart Henry, *The Hidden Economy* (London: Martin Robertson, 1978).

41. Charles H. McCaghy and R. Serge Denisoff, "Record piracy," in *Crime and Society,* edited by Leonard D. Savitz and Norman Johnston (New York: John Wiley & Sons, 1978).

42. *Billboard,* "RIAA domestic anti-piracy plan is paying off," March 27, 1993.

43. Recording Industry Association of America, *News,* February 14, 1994; *Billboard,* "RIAA domestic anti-piracy plan is paying off," March 27, 1993.

44. U.S. Congress, Senate, Committee on Governmental Affairs, Hearing before the Permanent Subcommittee on Investigations of the Committee on Governmen-

tal Affairs, *Professional Motor Vehicle Theft and Chop Shops, 1979,* 96th Congress, 1st session (Washington, D.C.: U.S. Government Printing Office, 1980).

45. See, for example, Pierre Tremblay, Yvan Clermont, and Maurice Cusson, "Jockeys and joyriders: Changing patterns in car theft opportunity structures," *British Journal of Criminology* 34(1994), pp. 307–321.

46. Mercer L. Sullivan, *"Getting Paid"* (Ithaca, N.Y.: Cornell University Press, 1989), p. 176.

47. U.S. Bureau of the Census, *Statistical Abstract of the United States: 1994* (Washington, D.C.: U.S. Government Printing Office, 1994), pp. 58 and 396.

48. U.S. Bureau of the Census, *Statistical Abstract of the United States: 1994* (Washington, D.C.: U.S. Government Printing Office, 1994), p. 396.

49. Lawrence E. Cohen and Marcus Felson, "Social change and crime rate trends: A routine activity approach," *American Sociological Review* 44(1979), pp. 588–608.

50. Federal Bureau of Investigation, *Crime in the United States, Uniform Crime Reports, 1963* (Washington, D.C.: U.S. Government Printing Office, 1964), p. 100; and *Crime in the United States, Uniform Crime Reports, 1992* (Washington, D.C.: U.S. Government Printing Office, 1993), p. 205.

51. Federal Bureau of Investigation, *Crime in the United States: Uniform Crime Reports, 1963* (Washington, D.C.: U.S. Government Printing Office, 1964), pp. 21 and 93; and *Crime in the United States, Uniform Crime Reports, 1993* (Washington, D.C.: U.S. Government Printing Office, 1994), p. 39.

52. George M. Camp, "Nothing to Lose: A Study of Bank Robbery in America" (Ph.D. thesis, Department of Sociology, Yale University, 1968); and James Francis Haran, "The Loser's Game: A Sociological Profile of 500 Armed Bank Robbers" (Ph.D. thesis, Department of Sociology, Fordham University, 1982).

53. National Association of Convenience Stores, *1992 Convenience Store Industry Factbook* (Washington, D.C.: Congressional Information Service, 1992), p. 2.

54. George Camp, "Nothing to Lose: A Study of Bank Robbery in America" (Ph.D. thesis, Department of Sociology, Yale University, 1968); Federal Deposit Insurance Corporation, Financial Reporting Section, *Data Book* (Washington, D.C.: U.S. Government Printing Office, 1992).

55. James A. Inciardi, "Vocational crime," in *Handbook of Criminology,* edited by Daniel Glaser (Chicago: Rand McNally, 1974).

56. See, for example, George F. Rengert and John Wasilchick, *Suburban Burglary* (Springfield, Ill.: Charles C. Thomas, 1985).

57. Federal Bureau of Investigation, *Crime in the United States, Uniform Crime Reports, 1963* (Washington, D.C.: U.S. Government Printing Office, 1964), p. 21; Federal Bureau of Investigation, *Crime in the United States, Uniform Crime Reports, 1993* (Washington, D.C.: U.S. Government Printing Office, 1994), p. 29.

58. Examples include Julian Roebuck, *Criminal Typology* (Springfield, Ill.: Charles C. Thomas, 1967); and Jan M. Chaiken and Marcia R. Chaiken, *Varieties of Criminal Behavior* (Santa Monica, Calif.: Rand Corporation, 1982).

59. Neal Shover, "Burglary as an Occupation" (Ph.D. thesis, Department of Sociology, University of Illinois, Urbana-Champaign, 1971).

60. Joan Petersilia, Peter W. Greenwood, and Marvin Lavin, *Criminal Careers of Habitual Felons* (Washington, D.C.: U.S. Department of Justice, National Institute of Law Enforcement and Criminal Justice, 1978).

61. Richard T. Wright and Scott Decker, *Burglars on the Job* (Boston: Northeastern University Press, 1994), p. 15.

62. Tony Parker and Robert Allerton, *The Courage of His Convictions* (London: Hutchinson, 1962), p. 93.

63. John MacIsaac, *Half the Fun Was Getting There* (Englewood Cliffs, N.J.: Prentice-Hall, 1968), p. 7.

64. Dermot Walsh, *Heavy Business* (London: Routledge & Kegan Paul, 1986), p. 65.

65. John Bartlow Martin, *My Life in Crime* (New York: Harper & Brothers, 1952), p. 42.

66. See, for example, John Irwin, *The Felon* (Berkeley: University of California Press, 1987), p. 8–12.

67. Nicholas Pileggi, *Wiseguy* (New York: Simon and Schuster, 1985), p. 203.

68. John MacIsaac, *Half the Fun Was Getting There* (Englewood Cliffs, N.J.: Prentice-Hall, 1968), p. 125.

69. Nathan McCall, *Makes Me Wanna Holler* (New York: Random House, 1994), p. 97.

70. Eugene Delorme, *Chief*, edited by Inez Cardozo-Freeman (Lincoln: University of Nebraska Press, 1994), p. 113. For an insightful discussion of the problems and uncertainty of robbery, see Jack Katz, "The motivation of persistent robbers," in *Crime and Justice: An Annual Review of Research,* vol. 14, edited by Michael Tonry (Chicago: University of Chicago Press, 1991).

71. David Luckenbill, "Generating compliance: The case of robbery," *Urban Life* 10(1981), pp. 25–46. For an autobiographical account, see John MacIsaac, *Half the Fun Was Getting There* (Englewood Cliffs, N.J.: Prentice-Hall, 1968), pp. 124–129.

72. Pete Earley, *The Hot House* (New York: Bantam Books, 1992), p. 82.

73. Jack Katz, *Seductions of Crime* (New York: Basic Books, 1988).

74. Nathan McCall, *Makes Me Wanna Holler* (New York: Random House, 1994), p. 134.

75. Bureau of Justice Statistics, *Household Burglary* (Washington, D.C.: U.S. Government Printing Office, 1985).

76. Jerome H. Skolnick, *Justice Without Trial* (New York: John Wiley & Sons, 1966); John E. Eck, *Solving Crimes* (Washington, D.C.: U.S. Department of Justice, National Institute of Justice, 1983).

77. Kathleen Maguire, Ann L. Pastore, and Timothy J. Flanagan, *Sourcebook of Criminal Justice Statistics, 1992* (Washington, D.C.: U.S. Government Printing Office, 1993).

78. John Bartlow Martin, *My Life in Crime* (New York: Harper & Brothers, 1952), p. 41.

79. Malcolm X, *The Autobiography of Malcolm X,* with the assistance of Alex Haley (New York: Grove, 1964), p. 140.

80. Dermot Walsh, *Heavy Business* (London: Routledge & Kegan Paul, 1986), p. 153.

81. Mercer L. Sullivan, *"Getting Paid"* (Ithaca, N.Y.: Cornell University Press, 1989), p. 135.

82. Mercer L. Sullivan, *"Getting Paid"* (Ithaca, N.Y.: Cornell University Press, 1989), p. 135.

83. Mike Maguire, in collaboration with Trevor Bennett, *Burglary in a Dwelling* (London: Heinemann, 1982), p. 41.

84. Jay S. Albanese, "Tomorrow's thieves," *The Futurist* 22(September-October, 1988), p. 25.

85. Jay S. Albanese, "Tomorrow's thieves," *The Futurist* 22(September-October 1988), p. 25.

86. Bureau of Justice Statistics, *Survey of State Prison Inmates, 1991* (Washington, D.C.: U.S. Department of Justice, 1993), p. 3.

87. Malcolm Braly, *False Starts* (New York: Penguin, 1976), p. 233.

88. William Julius Wilson, *The Truly Disadvantaged* (Chicago: University of Chicago Press, 1987); Ken Auletta, *The Underclass* (New York: Random House, 1982).

89. Jan M. Chaiken and Marcia R. Chaiken, *Varieties of Criminal Behavior* (Santa Monica, Calif.: Rand Corporation, 1982), p. 21.

90. This study is described in the Appendix.

91. Richard T. Wright and Scott Decker, *Burglars on the Job* (Boston: Northeastern University Press, 1994), p. 54.

92. John Irwin and James Austin, *It's About Time* (Belmont, Calif.: Wadsworth, 1994), p. 43.

93. John MacIsaac, *Half the Fun Was Getting There* (Englewood Cliffs, N.J.: Prentice-Hall, 1968), p. 23. This point is developed in Kenneth D. Tunnell, *Choosing Crime* (Chicago: Nelson-Hall, 1992).

4

Identity, Lifestyle, and Character

The personal and social consequences of disadvantage and disrepute function not only to reduce the number of options available to thieves from working-class backgrounds but also to shape the utilities they value and pursue. A distinction can be drawn between persistent thieves whose crimes in part spring from strong and enduring identification with crime as a means of livelihood and peers whose criminal identification and involvement are weak or intermittent. It is an important distinction, if only because career choices and decisions regarding participation in criminal acts are influenced by it. Identification with crime means the degree to which one sees it as an attractive and potentially bountiful source of income and livelihood or simply as a readily available means of resolving immediate problems. In the same way that some persons identify with and would like to become physicians, others see crime as either an attractive, if only short-term, occupational option or as a dependable and expedient source of income. Only offenders who identify with crime and see it as a desirable personal option will invest the requisite time and energy learning about it. The comments of an English burglar could not be more accurate:

> [T]echnical education by itself will never make a burglar. He must have many other qualities too which are inborn, but which are polished by practice. He must really want to be a screwsman [burglar]. He must not take it up just because he is too idle or incompetent to make a living of working, and thinks thieving is easier.[1]

To the young, thieves or hustlers who display the trappings of success can be objects of attention and admiration. Piri Thomas commented approvingly on "Johnny D," an adult in the New York barrio where he grew up:

> Johnny D . . . was about the hippest cat on Eighth Avenue, the slickest nigger
> in the neighborhood . . . Johnny did everything. He used to sell all the horse
> in the neighborhood . . . He was a pimp. He had all kinds of chicks hustling
> for him.[2]

Similarly, another man found the lifestyle appealing as an adolescent:

> [W]hen hanging on the corner, I tried to imitate the small-time hustlers who
> came to Turkey's house. I walked around, constantly shaking dice in my
> hands, waiting for the next crap game to get under way. I didn't know nearly
> enough about the hustling life to make a living at it, but it seemed glamorous
> and appealing enough to want to learn.[3]

Recall also the words of Robert Timmons, who was described in Chapter
1: "I wanted to be like Mr. Leon." Boys like him have little doubt that
crime will pay off for them.

All who persist at direct-contact theft do not identify with crime
equally, however. Persons may be arrested, convicted, and incarcerated
repeatedly in their lives, but this by itself does not demonstrate a high
level of identification with crime. Just as crime is an attractive and potentially lucrative source of livelihood and respect for some, for others it is a
personal and experiential aberration. A study of prison inmates in three
states estimated that fully 57 percent of the men neither were "into crime"
nor identified with it.[4] The 1978 Rand Inmate Survey of 2,170 U.S. prison
and jail inmates asked respondents to choose from a list of identities those
that they thought described them correctly in the months before they
were arrested. The list included 21 choices, of which 10 are unambiguously criminal: "burglar," "robber," "forger," "drug dealer," "car thief,"
"con man," "booster" "fence," "thief" and "drug user/addict." Each prisoner was asked to indicate which of the identities "best describe the way
you thought of yourself." Inmates were permitted to choose more than
one of the identities. Of the 1,199 men who were charged with or had been
convicted of robbery, burglary, motor vehicle theft, or larceny, 46 percent
did not choose any of the 10 criminal identities.[5]

Among men who *do* identify with crime, even if their identification
with it is weak or inconsistent, an array of criminal identities is represented. As the term is used here, *identities* are "the character . . . that an
individual devises for himself . . . [It] is his imaginative view of himself
as he likes to think of himself being and acting."[6] Adults generally have multiple identities grounded in the diverse settings of everyday life such as
the family, the workplace, and places of recreation and leisure. Although
most of our identities are conventional and legitimate, an individual's
repertoire of identities may include criminal ones as well.

Criminal Identities

Currently and to different degrees, five criminal identities are common among persistent thieves: *thief, hustler, dope fiend* and *crackhead, outlaw,* and *fuckup.*

Thief

A small and ever declining proportion of those who persist at crimes such as burglary and robbery identify with and aspire to be a *thief.* In the United States, this complex of criminal perspectives and normative system can be traced back more than a century. It developed from the frontier tradition of banditry and also from the impoverished ethnic neighborhoods of America's major cities. Although for decades its influence and dominance in the underworld were unrivaled, the thief identity probably sustained its last surge of appeal in the exploits of Depression-era outlaws.[7] Good thieves still can be found today, but they are a dying breed.

Major themes in the world of thieves are the "big score," the importance placed on "solid" character and norms of honesty and trustworthiness in dealings with one another, and the commission of crime with skill and pride of craft.[8] In the folklore and world of thieves, the big score is a highly lucrative crime that will enable one to retire from crime permanently. It is, in the words of one of them, the "great rock candy mountain that beckons us all."[9] The proceeds from the big score are fancied as a way to acquire a legitimate business to which the thief would retire to enjoy financial success, autonomy, and the respect of others. One man envisioned his big score as a step toward this goal:

> It would be about twenty thousand dollars, I figure—a bank job, or a really good drop. I'd put the money into drugs next. Drugs turn over fast. I'd have a hundred thousand pretty soon. Then I'd put the money into stocks. I'd have a big portfolio, and I would use my earnings to buy a store. It would be my place, and I would run it. That's where I would end up. I'd have my store and a lot of bread, and I would settle down. I'm looking for that sting now.[10]

The fact that very few thieves ever reach this objective or manage to hold onto their wealth when they do in no way diminishes its hold on their imagination.

Thieves are distinguished by their character as much as by their aspirations. They are honest in their dealings with one another, they will not cooperate with law enforcement officials or prosecutors, and they render assistance to peers and their families when the former are in prison.[11] They are disdainful of thieves who steal from ordinary citizens, suggesting by contrast that they only steal the money or property of victims "who can afford to lose it." This position probably stems less from a humane concern for crime victims than from recognition of the fact that one is unlikely to be financially successful at crime by stealing from the poor. Thus the position, expressed by one thief, that "if they ain't got a pot, piss on 'em."[12]

Thieves are known also for their verbal, organizational, or technical skills. They take pride in and they are respected for committing complex, financially rewarding crimes. Men who can defeat sophisticated security systems and avoid detection and arrest while doing so are respected. Crimes such as these are achievements. The safecracker, for example, who can locate, plan, and successfully carry out complex scores is much admired for his abilities, whereas thieves who employ crude and unsophisticated skills are derided as "knob knockers" or other equally scornful designations.[13] Their putative skills are one reason that prospects for taking off the big score generally are thought to be good. In the thief's world, success is measured by how much time one has done and the amount of money one has made from stealing. To be a successful thief is to earn well and spend little time in prison.

Thieves share a consciousness of kind and a respect for those who practice their craft successfully:

> Most people shy away from the word "thief" as if it were the dirtiest word in the language. In most circles it almost gives you the right to kill a man who calls you that. But it's not so among us thieves. That's what we call ourselves, "thieves." . . . Though we do have terms for the various specialties, the general term for anybody who makes his living from larceny, robbery or burglary is "thief." The highest praise you can hear during shoptalk and bull sessions in prisons or thieves' hangouts . . . is "he's a first-class thief" or "a damn good thief."[14]

In the early decades of the twentieth century, the place of dominance in the underworld enjoyed by thieves was reflected in the sub-rosa culture and social organization of prison inmates. In the wall-enclosed penitentiaries of that era, the "right guy" epitomized the ideals and style of the thief. He was loyal to and would not exploit other inmates, viewed with suspicion prison staff, and remained strong and resolute despite the problems of confinement.[15] Never mind that reality was different. A newly imprisoned thief described his surprise on discovering that "the very thieves of whom I had read as being desperate, daring, murderous, were cynical, morose, moody" and given to "squabbling amongst themselves."[16] The fact that the norms of the thief were honored in the breach as often as not did not diminish the collective support they received as ideals from thieves and convicts generally.

Although the thief identity described with varying accuracy the criminal perspectives and participation of many thieves in an earlier period of American history, its strength declined significantly in later decades. A host of factors explain this development, including the gradual decline of urban ethnic neighborhoods, the decline of the cash-based economy, improvements in police identification technology, and the professionalization of criminal justice. The thief's former place of dominance now is filled by a criminal identity more attuned to the world produced by these developments and by racial and ethnic shifts in the ranks of thieves and prisoners: the *hustler*.

Hustler

The designations *hustler* and *hustling* have been part of the argot of thieves for a century or more, but the clearest historical precedents and strongest contemporary appeal of hustling are among African Americans. As a style of illicit conduct, hustling emerged from and adapted historically to the conditions of their communities and lives. It "was picked up in the South from a variety of grifters, short-con men, flimflam men, pool hustlers, pimps, and gamblers, who regularly toured rural areas and, while 'beating' rural Negroes, were also imparting these forms of theft."[17] Hustling was carried from there by migrating blacks to America's urban centers where it took firm root in their ghetto communities.

Historically, two major constraints have operated to make hustling less rewarding financially than the crimes committed by the, now passing, thief. African Americans were denied tutoring in technically complex crime skills by white professional thieves, making it more difficult for them to employ these techniques. Just as important, they were unable to move freely in white neighborhoods where the largest number of potentially high-yield targets could be found without becoming objects of citizen and police scrutiny. African American hustlers as a result had little choice but to limit themselves to less remunerative crimes committed in or close to their home communities. These men, for whom the financially marginal return from their hustles and crimes virtually ensures that they must stay active if they are to make a living, are aptly named.

In the years after World War II, the proportion of officially processed offenders who were African American increased, and identities and styles once confined principally to them took on use and currency among thieves and drug users generally. This shift was apparent by the mid-1960s. In 1966, the President's Commission on Law Enforcement and Criminal Justice supported a study of 50 unincarcerated offenders "whose major source of income [was] from criminal pursuits and who [spent] a majority of their working time in illegal enterprises." Most were identified through police sources. Asked to describe what they did, the subjects gave revealing characterizations of their daily routines: "Over and over, ... [they] would answer 'I hustle.'"[18]

Hustling is a frenetic and full-time pursuit. This is captured in the response of a street hustler when he was asked by Studs Terkel to describe his normal day: "My day? I get up in the mornin', eat, I bathe, put my clothes out. And I come out and look for somethin' to steal."[19] It is hardly surprising, therefore, that Eliot Liebow described hustlers as men who "work hard at illegal ways of making money," who are "on the street to turn a dollar any way they can: buying and selling sex, liquor, narcotics, stolen goods, or anything else that turns up."[20] Malcolm X wrote of the period in his life when "I was a true hustler ... I considered myself nervy and cunning enough to live by my wits, exploiting any prey that presented itself."[21] Hustlers are prepared "to do almost anything for money—except work hard at a regular job."[22]

These comments highlight the high degree of alert opportunism and versatility characteristic of hustlers' pursuits. *Hustling* "may refer to anything from robbing and sticking up others to gambling, fencing, and 'sellin' dope.'"[23] Based on their interviews with active hustlers, investigators supported by the president's commission concluded that to hustle "is to be persistently on the lookout for an opportunity to make an illegal buck. A criminal 'on the hustle' will do pretty much whatever is required; he will consider whatever comes up."[24] Hustlers may be into a "million things," with a "hundred schemes in a day."[25] A man who engaged in crime for most of his adult life does not quarrel with this description:

> [W]hen you're stealing, you can't just be a burglar, you've got to be a burglar, stickup man, twenty different things. Burglary in the long run is safer. You'll get away with a hundred burglaries where you'll get away with five stick-ups. But if there's a place over here where there's a lot of money and the only way to get it is go in and stick him up, you're a hell of a thief if you don't stick him up.[26]

As a day-to-day activity, hustling has the flavor conveyed by this informant when he was asked to describe the hustler:

> A hustler is a person who is running all the time. He doesn't have a job where he has to punch a clock—and he doesn't have any other kind of position where he has to stay in one place all the time—like the guy who owns his own business. He doesn't stay stationary.

There are diverse styles of and approaches to hustling. Generally, the highest prestige goes to hustlers who employ verbal and sartorial "sharpness," which is evidenced by their ability to outwit, outfox, dupe, or "take" others for their money or valuables.[27] In contrast to these "smooth" hustlers, "rough" hustlers generally use physical skills or the threat or use of force. Where separating others from their valuables is concerned, the former are respected for their ability to "talk it off," whereas rough hustlers are known for "ripping it off" or "tearing it off." Regardless of one's hustling style, however, success in the world of street-level hustling is based on one's ability to maintain the *appearance* of success, particularly over a long period of time.

The influence of the hustler identity on the styles and behavior of thieves from all racial and ethnic backgrounds is a clear indication of how its influence has moved beyond the African American experience, but there remain areas in which black and white variants of hustling differ. One is the high level of commitment to sharpness and personal appearance by African American hustlers as compared with its lesser importance among whites. A black hustler said simply, "The main reason we hustled and stole so hard was to pick up money to buy clothes."[28] An observer of black hustlers commented: "Self-aggrandizement consumes his whole being and is expressed in his penchant for a glamorous life-style, fine clothes, and fancy cars. On the corner he attempts to influence others by displaying the trappings of success."[29] In America's urban ghettos, he is viewed by some residents, particularly the young, as the "epitome of this phenomenon and an idol of the 'cool' world."[30] In the words of one hustler, "People on the street . . . look up to me because I dress good, I keep cash, I've got women, and I don't work."[31] This style has become more common in recent years as legitimate opportunities have diminished and "old heads" who succeeded legitimately have distanced themselves from street life and have become, therefore, less visible.[32]

In contrast to norms of loyalty and mutual assistance that receive strong verbal support from thieves, hustlers can be more pragmatic about these matters. A hustler thus commented on his reactions after calling the police station and being told that his crime partner had been arrested:

> I just hang up. I hang up on Frank. There's nothing I can do for him, nothing at all. I ain't got no big money; he's busted; and that's the way it goes. He was a fine crime partner while it lasted, but now he is wasted and I gotta look out for me.[33]

Nor do norms of honesty in their dealings with one another receive strong support from hustlers:

> There wasn't no honor amongst us. If we stole something at night, didn't sell it that night, and hid it until next morning, any one of us was likely to go out there and take it. They called it gettin' burnt. You'd burn the rest of the guys,

or maybe two of us would go out there and take it, and we'd burn the other two. Say we robbed a paper boy and made some money. If I went in his pocket and got twenty-five dollars. I'd say I got ten.[34]

In recent decades, as the proportion of black inmates in America's prison population increased, hustlers played an important part in reshaping the social organization and culture of prisoners as well as the prisoners' underground economy. Production and distribution of contraband goods and services have been endemic features of the prison's underlife since its historical emergence. The reality of imprisonment is such that hustling is ubiquitous:

> Everybody in prison has to have a little hustle. The guys that work in the kitchen steal food and sell it. The guys that work in the laundry steal sheets, and that kind of stuff. The guys that work on the pants, they do alterations, but you pay for that. Some guys have people outside that send them money for cigarettes, commissary, this and that.[35]

The perspectives and styles of hustlers found already fertile soil, and as their numbers grew, so did their cultural influence. To a degree that may be unprecedented, hustlers have identified and exploited opportunities for making money in the prison world. Gambling, loan-sharking, and drugs are major sources of income for them. In some prisons they manage by extortion to control even the distribution of state-provided day-to-day amenities such as food and toilet tissue. One result is that doing time in the contemporary American prison can be an expensive enterprise, particularly for the vulnerable with resources.[36]

Dope Fiend and Crackhead

The use of drugs is nearly universal among unsuccessful persistent thieves and hustlers, and many are addicted to heroin, alcohol, or cocaine. This plays an important part in their lives and in their criminal activities. A high proportion of addicts, for example, engage from time to time in low-level drug sales, chiefly as a means of ensuring a supply for their own use, and a much larger number commit crime to finance their habit.[37] In doing so they exact a very heavy toll from their victims and from the wider community.[38]

It should come as no surprise that a strong relationship exists between drug use and criminal activity.[39] Someone using heroin or crack cocaine regularly is more likely to be involved in crime. One reason for this relationship is the high cost of purchasing the drug. For most, the only way to support their habit is through illegal means. One must not assume a causal relationship, however. Research determining the onset of addiction and crime shows that drug users often begin their criminal career before they become addicted to drugs. These studies indicate that drug use may not cause crime but heavy use does increase the prevalence of criminal activity.

Research on street-level drug users and crime consistently shows that periods of high drug use are associated with an increase in the number of crime days per year and also the users' income from crime.[40] The intensity of criminal participation declines as drug use decreases. Interviews with heroin addicts in Harlem, for example, found that the number of nondrug crimes committed per year ranged from 116 for irregular users to 162 for regular users to 209 for daily users.[41] Dope fiends and crackheads commit many crimes, if only because the return from most is small. Data collected from crack and heroin abusers in New York City found that the average monetary return from a robbery was $79 and from a burglary $112.[42] The average return for thieves whose crimes, unlike those committed by these men, are not restricted to poor neighborhoods surely is higher, but no one seriously disputes that the returns from street crime at best are modest. For most men they are considerably less.[43]

Preoccupation with fixing and with securing funds to purchase drugs are major concerns of dope fiends: "The addict who hustles for his daily fixings has his eye on one thing alone, the dope and getting it into his veins. He knows he's gotta steal to score to fix, . . . It's a fact of living, like breathing."[44] It is hardly surprising, therefore, that a high proportion of the gains from criminal activity immediately is spent on illegal substances. A study of New York City addicts who admitted committing at least one offense in the preceding 24 hours found that 71 percent of the income they received from their crimes was spent on illicit drugs.[45] Days when the addict is desperate are times when he is liable to engage in high-risk crimes.

> There's nothing, *nothing*, motivates you more than needing a shot of dope. And you go to any lengths, really. You crash through windows, just take outrageous goddam chances to grab something. And when you get desperate and the end of the day is coming and you see you've got to hit, then if you haven't got enough during the day to cop, you know, to get the stuff, that's when you start doing dumb things. You get a little desperate.[46]

This partially explains why addicts frequently are arrested and confined in jails and prisons.

Because of the exigencies and pressures of their drug use and lifestyle, addicts are regarded almost universally as untrustworthy and potentially treacherous. This unflattering description is endorsed even by former addicts: "You can't trust a dope fiend. Man, I can't tell you that too many times. You can't trust dope fiends! . . . When you're a dope fiend there's no rules, no regulations, no system of buddy-buddy or friendship that counts."[47]

In a belated dialogue with his brother, a former addict, imprisoned for participation in a fatal robbery, confessed:

> You know that TV of youall's got stolen from Mommy's. Well, I did it. Was me and Henry took youall's TV that time and set the house up to look like a robbery. We did it. Took my own brother's TV. Couldn't hardly look you in the face for a long time after we done it. . . . No way I was gon confess though. Too shamed. A junkie stealing from his own family. . . . See but where it's at is you be doing any goddamn thing for dope.[48]

Another man commented on how relations within his group of young males changed: "The deeper we got into the drug thing, the more paranoid and ruthless we became. Guys who'd been the best of hanging partners since way back when started turning on each other and ripping each other off."[49] Norms of loyalty to one another and to sparing as victims those who are poor or emotionally close have little meaning to dope fiends.

Although heroin users may be accorded low status in the underworld, many of them dispute this assessment. Unlike thieves and many hustlers, dope fiends are less inclined to dismiss as unsuccessful peers who endure repeated sentences in jails or prisons while achieving limited financial success from crime. An imprisoned dope fiend said, for example:

> I think, in order for a man to live out there in the streets by his own wits, and his own initiative, and his own ingenuity takes more than a notion, you know. It's not easy. . . . It's a pretty hard road, you know.
>
> Q: I detect a certain feeling on your part that [it is unfair to label the] addict . . . a petty thief.
>
> A: Well, it is unfair, because you have to look at the position that an addict is in. I mean, he doesn't have the time to sit back and plan something. . . . The average one doesn't have the money to rent a truck or, say if there was some equipment that he needed, he doesn't have the money to finance the necessary operations. So he resorts to other things. But I'll say this—the mind of an addict, I mean the drive, the things that he will come up with because there is a steady drive there, you have to have money every day, all day, and the things that he will do, it's just such a strong thing behind him that is motivating him. And his mind is so keen. . . . I would say, as far as ingenuity and in the things that he thinks of and ideas and whatnot, I wouldn't say that he is inferior to any other thief. It's just that most everything he does is on a small scale.

Dope fiends distinguish between the cool or hip and the square.[50] Many of those who use heroin see themselves as part of a hip or cool minority who are superior experientially to those who do not use drugs. The heroin addict is often concerned with his outward appearance and goes to great length to develop the proper speech, walk, and dress style. Others see the heroin addict as sick and weak, enslaved to his drug to escape from life; however, this is not accurate. The heroin addict, or "cool cat,"[51] is always on the move, looking for a hustle, or "taking care of business."[52] The "real hustling dope fiend" is afforded high status by his peers. At the same time, they disparage addicts who hang around begging for money and small amounts of heroin.[53]

The appearance of crack cocaine has changed the moral hierarchy of street-level drug users. Crack quickly acquired a reputation for stripping users' self-esteem and forcing them into treacherous and unpredictable behavior.[54] Even more than dope fiends, crack users are seen as capable of doing anything, even robbing "their own momma"[55] to satisfy their drug needs. The physical appearance and dress of crackheads often deteriorate as their drug use increases. More reclusive than dope fiends, many engage in solitary drug use.[56] Crackheads are less inclined than heroin addicts to dispute the low regard in which they are held by thieves and hustlers. Many are aware of the risks of regular drug use and dislike the adverse effects of crack.[57] Crackheads generally have displaced heroin addicts at the bottom of the moral hierarchy of drug users.

Outlaw

The decline of the thief and the ascendance of hustling are major changes in the underworld since World War II. Another change, more recent in origin, is the increasing appeal of the outlaw as a criminal identity. Although outlaws compose but a small proportion of persistent thieves, the attention they receive from the media and from criminal justice apparatchiks is enormous. They account for a disproportionate share of violent predators, offenders who use violence, often to commit armed robbery.[58]

In the worldview of outlaws, humanity can be divided into two principal groups: the strong and the weak. Life is a process of struggle and conflict in which only the strong can hope to prosper. Inevitably they prey upon the weak who, they believe, are destined and even *deserve* to be victims. Since it is their refusal or inability to employ violence that invites victimization, victims have no one to blame but themselves. Outlaws demonstrate resolve not to be a victim principally by ritualistic action meant to communicate to others that they are ruthless, a "gangster" or a "monster." A gangster "will appear ready to back his intentions violently and remorselessly."[59] The badass and monster want to be seen by others as men who will do absolutely anything to accomplish their objectives. He "scorns the disapproval of society, reveals no mercy or compassion for others, and remains ready to use violence to protect himself or achieve his ends."[60]

The ranks of outlaws are filled primarily by young adults who are products of urban gangbanging and by men hardened from spending their youthful years in confinement. Even among the "state-raised," however, the outlaw identity is uncommon. Whatever the source of exposure to the outlaw identity, those who embrace it are quick to employ violence as a vehicle for managing their personal affairs and as a basis for ordering one another. The convict writer Jack Henry Abbott defined the identity:

> The model we emulate is a fanatically defiant and alienated individual, who cannot imagine what forgiveness is, or mercy or tolerance, because he has no *experience* of such values. His emotions do not know what such values are, but he *imagines* them as so many "weaknesses."[61]

Along with the ascendance of hustling and hustlers, the influence of outlaws also has helped transform the inner world of jails and prisons in recent decades. When challenged or "disrespected" by other inmates, the outlaw is determined to be "a total brute" for whom the only language he understands, respects, or could be persuaded by is violence. To be prepared for anything less, the outlaw believes, only invites disrespect and exploitation.[62] Consequently, "the old 'hero' of the prison world—the 'right guy'—has been replaced by outlaws and gang members," a development that has "raised toughness and mercilessness to the top of prisoners' value systems."[63]

Fuckup

Fuckups are men whose identification with and commitment to crime and criminal lifestyles are far less organized and consistent than in the case of thieves and hustlers.[64] Whether this is principally because of limited exposure to criminal identities or because of their personal limitations and shortcomings cannot be said, but their identity is incoherent and does not fit neatly into any of those described thus far. Although they may embrace a criminal identity occasionally, they are men of unstable and erratic nature who have difficulty following any consistent path. Not surprising, they are prone to waiver in commitment to crime and to all that it entails.

"Fucking up" and "trouble" are major themes in the worldview of fuckups. They have a devil-may-care attitude and often see themselves as men who are prone to do "stupid things." The distinguishing characteristic of "stupid" behavior is that it results in "trouble"—usually in the form of "unwelcome or complicating involvement with official authorities or agencies of middle-class society."[65]

The crimes committed by fuckups generally show poor planning and execution. The experience of a man who was interviewed several months after release from his second prison sentence shows these elements. The informant, his nephew, his sister, and an acquaintance spent the better part of a day drinking and doing illicit drugs. Toward evening, the males began talking about the need to "make some money." They considered various criminal options before they decided to rob a convenience store located in a nearby city. Their choice of this target was based on intelligence that can only be called flimsy. Intending to drive to the target and rob it, the informant and his nephew tried to cut themselves loose from their two companions. When this failed, the informant decided to take the entire group, sister and all, on what proved to be an ill-fated robbery:

Wouldn't nobody get out of the car [so] I said, "well man, you know, if they don't want to get out, then take them with us," you know. "I'm quite sure they ain't going to tell it on me, you know, if something was to happen." . . . So they just went. So we goes by this place, we drive by once so I said, "well, look, we can't hardly tell who's in there or not." . . . I send [my nephew] in, I give him a dollar and I said, "just go in, buy something and look it over." So he goes in and when he comes back out he says, "man, the place is sweet," you know. By him being my nephew, I know him and I trust him. . . . So me and this guy, we gets out. . . . On the way walking up to this place [we saw] a fellow go in. So he said, "well, what are we going to do?" And I said "there ain't nothing but two in there. We'll take him too." So about the time we get right to the place I ask him, I said "have you ever did any robberies?" And he said, "yeah, man, I do them all the time." We didn't have but one pistol and . . . I said, "well, you let me hold the pistol then, you let me go in with the pistol." So I've got this ski mask rolled up to about this far and see, he don't have on nothing. . . . When we go in, we go to the back so they really ain't paying no attention to us. So we're back there for about two or three minutes and I said, "well, are you ready?" And he said, "yeah." When he say that, I pull the ski mask down and about the time we get up by the counter [the clerk] sees me with this ski mask and this gun. So when we get to the counter he goes up under the counter and throws the money bag up on the counter. When he does that, the guy that I'm with he grabs the money bag and runs clean out of the store and leaves me. I'm knowing I can't run out behind him because, you know, they'll have plenty of time to call the police or watch us or something. So by me being an experienced robber, I don't go out, because after he run out the door, the fellow that went in to buy something, he said, "well I'm leaving too." And I said "no, you can't leave" and I grabs him from behind and, you know, tells him to come back in. I lays him down on the floor beside the counter. I takes his wallet, his jewelry and in the meantime while I'm doing that I've got my eye on this person here behind the counter, I make him step away from the counter while I'm doing this. After I do that, I goes to the counter and I make him take all the money out of the cash register and put it in a sack, plus his money. . . . I snatched the phone out of the wall. I takes them and puts them in the cooler. . . . Then when I get back down to where we was parked at, you know, they've got the motor running and everything. . . . It's done got so dark I said, "do you know where you're going?" and he said, "no." So we had to turn around and come back. By the time we come back and go past the store it's police swarming everywhere, you know. . . . So everybody is cool until they see a sign that says thirty miles to Nashville and everybody gets happy because they, they must have done seen the money bag. Because it was fat. So they turns on the music, fires up weed but I'm steady looking out the rearview mirror on this side because I see a car . . . back there. I tell everybody, I said, "now look, don't nobody turn around or nothing but the police is behind us." About that time they put that big spotlight on the back window. They ain't stopped us or nothing, they're just following us. Everybody turned around, so my guess is it might make the police suspicious. . . . On the side of the road I'm looking for somewhere I can throw this money bag out and remember where I threw it and come back and get it. I let them get beside us, they've still got this big light on us but they can't see me over here by the door. So I lets down the window—this here was real dumb, what I done—and I forgets to zip the money bag up and I throws the money bag out of the window and money flows all in the air. So they pulls us over. They make each one of us get out one at a time and lay on the interstate, . . . just lay flat. They stopped traffic and everything.

The ineptitude displayed in virtually every facet of this undertaking is not unusual for fuckups. When they are not incarcerated, fuckups often spend their time hanging out in bars and taverns that cater to those on the margins of society. As Malcolm Braly described them, these establishments are patronized by "a trickle of youngsters outgrowing the juvenile gangs, and another trickle of older men out on parole."[66] There, fuckups drink and socialize with other patrons while remaining open to consider any options that arise.[67]

Noncriminal Identity

In contrast to thieves, hustlers, dope fiends, crackheads, outlaws, and fuckups, many persistent thieves do not have a criminal identity, and their crimes therefore generally are not motivated by the desire to establish their criminal credibility. The majority of them are *lower-class men*, whose perspectives are products of their working-class life experiences. Lower-class men do not see themselves as criminals, and they eschew criminal identities. They see the world as a place that is rigged by those who have money and power, and they experience an abiding sense of unfairness. Joseph Howell noted what the white blue-collar families he lived among for a time believed:

Society was no damn good. It was controlled by the rich and the powerful who made decisions to help themselves, not the common man. But the world was just this way, most people agreed. There wasn't much you could do to change it. Of course, you could fight it as an individual; and most people . . . did. But few expected things to change or be any different.[68]

The lower-class man's alienation "is expressed in hostility toward college students and other groups who [appear] to 'have it made' or [are] 'making it'—the boss, white-collar workers in general, 'rich folks.'" The lower-class man "believes things are determined for him and that he doesn't have much control over the direction of his life."[69] He sees himself as a victim of fate.

Major themes in the beliefs of lower-class men include pursuit of manliness and masculine ideals, which are equated with toughness and courage. These men are judged by how they respond to challenges of one kind or another. The ability to take care of oneself in a world where challenge and adversity are thought to be inevitable counts as a prime virtue. Thus the patrons of a tavern frequented by white construction workers believed that in childrearing "a boy has to learn to fight, to defend himself, and to give back at least as much punishment as he takes. If a boy doesn't learn this, he will be weak and tend to be 'victimized' all his life, not only by men, but also by women."[70]

The ideal male has heart. This is "an insistence on receiving respect, without weighing alternatives, envisioning consequences, or even systematically organizing the precise execution of a combative plan."[71] A person with heart is ready for any situation or any fight, despite the odds of defeat.[72] It is a sign of good character, one that shows others they are not someone to "play" with or someone who can be ripped off without a fight.[73] An ethnographic study of the Hallway Hangers, a group of 18- to 21-year-old white males who resided in public housing, noted that their world is one of paradox:

> To be "bad" is literally to be good. . . . [T]his emphasis on being bad is inextricably bound up with the premium put on masculinity, physical toughness, and street wisdom in working-class culture. . . . To be bad is the main criterion for status in this subculture; its primacy cannot be overemphasized, and its importance is implied continually by the boys.[74]

And a study of the "extended primary group" of African American men who spent their leisure time in another tavern noted that "everyone . . . likes to see himself as being 'as tough as the next guy.'"[75]

In the world of lower-class males, respectful treatment by others is expected. When it is not forthcoming or, worse, when one is insulted or "disrespected," a violent response is condoned if not expected. It is ironic perhaps that men and women aware of how they are denied dignity and respect elevate it to utmost importance among one another. This amounts to "fighting for recognition from each other of their own worth."[76] The importance attached to manliness and interpersonal respect makes for a certain *disputatiousness* on the part of many men. This is the tendency, when a person has experienced a negative interactional outcome, to (1) blame the other for it and (2) express the grievance to and demand reparation from him or her.[77] One must be ready to fight or to use violence to secure it or to demonstrate other valued personal qualities or behaviors:

> You know, fighting ain't a good thing. It ain't a good thing, but goddammit, you got to stick up for yourself, and you got to take care of yourself, and you can't let nobody push you around. Once you start letting somebody push you around then other people are going to start pushing you around. You got to stick up for your rights.[78]

Simply put, throughout much of the working class, "You are not respected if you do not show some toughness; if people can step all over you and you do nothing about it, you are nothing but a punk."[79] In the most extreme of circumstances, when a man permits another to treat him improperly without readiness to employ violence, it signals to others that "People could get *next* to him with impunity and on their own terms. If he had it and they wanted it, they could take it."[80]

Coupled with the emphasis lower-class males attach to manliness and respect is their interest in excitement and risk-taking behaviors:

> The quest for excitement finds what is perhaps its most vivid expression in the highly patterned practice of the recurrent "night on the town." This practice, designated by various terms in different areas ("honky-tonkin'"; "goin' out on the town"; "bar hoppin'"), involves a patterned set of activities in which alcohol, music, and sexual adventuring are major components. A group of individuals sets out to "make the rounds" of various bars or night clubs. Drinking continues progressively throughout the evening. Men seek to "pick up" women, and women play the risky game of entertaining sexual advances. Fights between men involving women, gambling, and claims of physical prowess, in various combinations, are frequent consequences of a night of making the rounds.[81]

When the emphasis on manliness is coupled with the pursuit of excitement, an evening's outcome can be very unpredictable. Making the rounds and other leisure pursuits of lower-class men places them in potentially volatile settings and situations where decisions made hastily or carelessly, perhaps while drunk, can spill over and erode entirely one's already precarious legitimate rewards and commitments. It is in this context that their commitment to and their pursuit of personal styles and values endorsed by working-class males occasionally bring them into conflict with the law.[82] They are often present, for example, at

> crimes being committed by friends or relatives, and, under special circumstances—such as when they are in the company of more criminally oriented acquaintances, saving face in front of peers, intoxicated, or trying to take advantage of an opportunity for financial gain—they are drawn into the commission of a crime.[83]

Roger Morton, who was described in Chapter 1, exemplifies the lower-class man.

Life as Party

To understand better the choices made by persistent offenders, it is useful to examine the worlds in which much of their time is spent. If we want to know why individuals choose to commit crime, we could do worse than to examine the contextually anchored purposes and utilities of their criminal decisions and acts. We should try to see their options and risks through their eyes. Where persistent thieves are concerned, this inevitably calls for examination of *life as party*, the principal lifestyle that frames and influences their decisionmaking. It is the context also in which they pursue various identities and character projects.

As the concept is used here, *lifestyles* are socially shared values and tastes that are reflected primarily in leisure and consumption patterns.[84] They are the structurally grounded animus and patterns of daily activity. It is instructive to examine the behavior of persistent thieves in the context of the lifestyle that is characteristic of many of them at some time. This lifestyle embodies and selectively emphasizes values and tastes recognized and endorsed by many males, particularly those from working-class backgrounds.[85]

The hallmark of life as party is enjoyment of "good times" with minimal concern for obligations and commitments external to the person's immediate social setting. Those who pursue life as party are determined to suspend concern for serious matters in favor of enjoying the moment. It is a lifestyle distinguished in many cases by two repetitively cyclical phases and correspondingly distinctive approaches to crime. When offenders' efforts to maintain the lifestyle are largely successful, crimes are committed in order to continue a pattern of activities they experience as pleasurable. Under these circumstances, as Dermot Walsh put it, they are "part of a continuing satisfactory way of life."[86] By contrast, when offenders are less successful at party pursuits, their crimes are committed in hopes of forestalling or reversing circumstances experienced as threatening, precarious, or unpleasant. Corresponding to each of these two phases of party pursuits are distinctive utilities and risk assessments.

Persistent thieves spend much of their criminal gains on alcohol and other drugs.[87] The proceeds of their crimes "typically [are] used for personal, non-essential consumption (e.g., 'nights out'), rather than, for example, to be given to family or used for basic needs."[88] Interviews with 30 active Texas burglars revealed, for example, that they "stressed need for money to fulfill expressive needs as the primary motivation for their criminal behavior. Only one informant reported a primary need for money to purchase something other than alcohol or drugs or for 'partying.'"[89] Echoing these findings, one thief has written that the life

> is mostly a party. I don't think people understand that it's quite like that, but it is. In other words, you don't work. . . . When you get your money, you usually get it real fast and you have a lot of time to spend it. You can sleep all day if you want to and you can go out and get drunk, get high—you don't have to get up the next morning to go to work. The women that you have around you, their moral standards is the same as yours so you have a lot of fun and get a lot of cock.[90]

Thieves and hustlers spend many of their leisure hours enjoying good times, albeit there is a decidedly frenetic and always precarious quality to the way these times are lived. For example,

> I smoked an ounce of pot in a day, a day and a half. Every other day I had to go buy a bag of pot, at the least. And sometimes I've went two or three days in a row. . . . And there was never a day went by that I didn't [drink] a case, case and a half of beer. And [I] did a 'script of pills every two days.

A substantial proportion of the money earned by thieves is consumed by the high cost of drugs, but some is used also for ostentatious consumption and enjoyment of luxury items and activities that probably would be unattainable on the returns from the minimum-wage jobs that increasingly characterize working-class employment.

Life as party is enjoyed in the company of others and typically includes shared consumption of alcohol and other drugs. In bars and lounges, on street corners, or while cruising in automobiles, party pursuers celebrate and affirm values of spontaneity, independence, and resourcefulness. Spontaneity means that rationality and long-range planning are eschewed in favor of enjoying the moment and permitting the day's activities and pleasures to develop in an unconstrained fashion. This may mean, for example, getting up late, usually after a night of partying, and then setting out to contact and enjoy the company of friends and associates who are known to be predisposed to partying:

> I got up around about eight-thirty that morning. . . .
>
> Q: Eight-thirty? Was that the usual time that you got up?
>
> A: Yeah, if I didn't have a hangover from the night before. . . .
>
> Q: What kind of drugs were you doing then?
>
> A: I was doing . . . Percodans, Dilaudids, taking Valiums, drinking. . . . Anyway, I got up that morning [and I] . . . decided to walk [over to my mother's home]. This particular day, . . . my nephew was over [there]. . . . We was just sitting in the yard and talking and drinking beer, you know. . . . It was me, him, and my sister. . . . And this guy that we know, . . . he came up, he pulled up. So my nephew got in the car with him and they left. So, you know, I was sitting there talking to my sister. . . . And then, in the meantime, while we was talking, they come back about thirty minutes later with a case of beer, some marijuana and everything, . . . and there was another one of my nephews in the car with them. Me, two of my sisters, and two of my nephews, we got in the car with this guy here and we just went riding. [Eventually] we went back out [toward my mother's home] but instead . . . we went to this little joint [tavern]. Now we're steady drinking and smoking weed all during this day. So when we get there, we park and get out and see a few friends. We [were] talking and getting high, you know, blowing each other a shotgun [sharing marijuana].

Party pursuits also appeal to offenders because they permit conspicuous display of independence.[91] This generally means avoidance of the world of routine work, freedom from being "under someone's thumb," and freedom to avoid or to escape from restrictive routines:

> I just wanted to be doing something. Instead of being at home, or something like that. I wanted to be running, I wanted to be going to clubs, and picking up women and shooting pool. And I liked to go to [a nearby resort community] and just drive around over there. A lot of things like that. . . . I was drinking two pints or more a day. . . . I was doing Valiums and I was doing Demerol. . . . I didn't want to work.

Misfits in a world that values precise schedules, punctuality, and disciplined subordination to authority, party pursuers relish the independence and autonomy to structure time and daily routines as they wish. Although they have adapted to the class and status handicaps of their backgrounds by embracing a lifestyle that may seem aimless and short-sighted, it nevertheless permits them to highlight freedoms valued not just by street-corner peers but by working-class men generally.

The proper pursuit and enjoyment of life as party entail major expense, largely because of the cost of drugs: "We was doing a lot of cocaine, so cash didn't last long, you know. If we made three thousand, two thousand of it almost instantly went for cocaine." Given the substantial expenses involved, life as party requires continuous infusions of money, and no single method of generating funds allows enjoyment of it for more than a few days. Consequently, the emphasis on spontaneity and independence by those who pursue this lifestyle is matched by the importance attached to financial resourcefulness, as evidenced by the ability to sustain it over a period of time. One of the most important consequences of the value afforded resourcefulness and respect for those who demonstrate it is that criminal acts, as a means of sustaining life as party, generally are not condemned by the offender's peers. Some celebrate successful crimes as victories.

Consumption of alcohol and other drugs often precedes discussion of criminal opportunities and decisions to exploit or to turn away from them. In their ten-state survey of prison inmates, University of Massachusetts investigators found that 55 percent of the 1,038 respondents sentenced for robbery, burglary, automobile theft, or theft were either "drunk" or "high on drugs" when they committed the crime(s) for which they were serving time.[92] Significantly, this drug use often occurs in an interactional context of like-minded others. Although the individuals may know one another only casually outside of the immediate setting, the group and relationships among its members assume considerable importance for them. After a few hours together consuming alcohol or smoking marijuana, men who scarcely know one another may come to feel they are the best of friends and be willing to do nearly anything to ensure that the camaraderie and good feelings do not end prematurely. Alternatively, this contact can generate exaggerated and stylized identities that cause members to attach great importance to matters usually treated as secondary, including claims and imputations about participants' character.[93] The experience is encapsulating, meaning that it tends to push members' extrasituational identities and concerns to the background of attention.[94]

When the possibility of crime is raised in group context, individuals may try to involve the others, usually by "gassing them up." This is accomplished by exaggerating either the likely financial return from a proposed crime or the ease of committing it successfully. Both the effects of drugs and the social-psychological effects of group participation and identity constrain members' reasoning abilities and their willingness to decline participation in group pursuits.[95] They generally "focus on the proximate reward of group cohesion and [are] less aware of the longer-term negative consequences."[96] Describing a burglary he and a friend committed, an informant said, for example:

Well, it all started, you know, I was running around and drinking a little bit heavy, you know. I went to Mt. Vernon . . . and run into a friend of mine. He was down, he was out of work and stuff. . . . I told him, I said, "man, if you want to, I'll run down here tonight and we'll drink a coupla beers and we'll talk about it." So everything was cool, his wife was gone, and everything, you know. So I went down there and his wife was at home. So he wanted to go out to the car and get drunk. And I said, "we'll go out there and drink a sloe gin," you know. We drunk that sloe gin and everything, and got drunk as a dog. I told him, "I know a little place" that I thought might be easy to hit, you know. And we went over [there], and I parked my car. . . . I walked over to the Amoco station there and knocked the window out and crawled in there and handed him all kinds of cigarettes out of there. Money, guns—there was a .25 automatic in there. And as I was coming out of the place—I was so drunk that I didn't care, you know. Inside, I just knew that I couldn't get caught, but when I came out, I fell right in the arms of two deputies, you know. They took me straight to jail.

The interaction preceding criminal decisions generally is distinguished by circumspection and the use of linguistic devices that relegate risk and fear to the background of attention. Thus the act of stealing may be referred to obliquely but knowingly as "doing something" or as "making money." The reasoning process employed in these situations, dubbed "argument by contradiction,"[97] is one of pursuing an option unless or until a problem is encountered that causes the decisionmaker(s) to reject it. Potential obstacles to employing criminal solutions to the need for funds are approached blithely but confidently in the same spontaneous and playful manner as are the rewards of life as party:

[After a day of partying,] I [got] to talking about making some money, because I didn't have no money. This guy that we were riding with, he had all the money. . . . So me and him and my nephew, we get together, talking about making some money. This guy tells me, he said, "man, I know where there's a good place at."
Q: Okay, so you suggested you all go somewhere and rob?
A: Yeah, "make some"—well, we called it "making money."

Q: Okay. So then you and this fellow met up in the bar . . . Tell me about the conversation.
A: Well, there wasn't much of a conversation to it, really . . . I asked him if he was ready to go, if he wanted to go do something, you know. And he knew what I meant. He wanted to go make some money somehow, any way it took.

Recall from Chapter 3 that in the crimes they commit, as in the drugs they consume, party pursuers are anything but narrow specialists.

To the external observer, inattention to risk at moments of crime-commission decisionmaking may seem to border on irrationality. For the offender engaged in party pursuits, however, it is but one aspect of behaviors that are rational in other respects. It opens up opportunities to enjoy life as party and to demonstrate commitment to values shared by peers.

Resourcefulness and disdain for conventional, middle-class rationality affirm personal qualities and styles that are respected and admired in the world of party pursuers.

Paradoxically, pursuit of life as party can be appreciated and enjoyed in the long term only if participants moderate their involvement in it. Doing so, however, requires an uncommon measure of discipline and forbearance. Extended and enthusiastic enjoyment of life as party threatens constantly to deplete irrevocably the resources needed to sustain it. How does this happen? Some offenders become ensnared increasingly by the chemical substances and drug-using routines that are common in the lifestyle. In this case, the pleasures and meaning of drug consumption change. Once the party pursuer's physical or psychological tolerance increases significantly, drugs are consumed not for the high they once produced but instead to maintain a sense of normality by avoiding sickness or withdrawal. Enter desperation: "See, I was doing drugs every day. It just wasn't every other day, it was to the point that after the first few months doing drugs, I would have to do 'X amount' of drugs, say, just for instance, just to feel like I do now. Which is normal."

Party pursuits also erode legitimate fiscal and social capital. They cannot be sustained by legitimate employment, and they may in fact undermine both one's ability and inclination to hold a job. Even if offenders are willing to work at the kinds of employment available to them, and evidence suggests that some offenders are not, the physical demands of work and party pursuits conflict.[98] Few men past young adulthood can spend their nights drinking and playing in bars and routinely arise and go to work just a few hours later. The best times of the day for committing many types of property crime are the times when offenders would be at work. Days spent searching for suitable businesses to rob or homes to burglarize cannot be spent at work, and it is nearly impossible to do both consistently and well. Besides, it is the display of independence at precisely the times when others are working that boosts the appeal of life as party. For party pursuers, legitimate employment often is forgone or sacrificed.[99] The absence of income from noncriminal sources thus reinforces the need to find it elsewhere.

Determined pursuit of life as party also may affect participants' relationships with legitimate significant others. Many offenders manage to enjoy the lifestyle successfully only by exploiting the concern and largesse of family and friends.[100] This may take the form of repeated requests for and receipt of personal loans that go unreturned, occasional thefts, or other forms of exploitation:

> I lived well for a while. I lived well ... until I started shooting cocaine real bad, intravenously. . . . And then everything, you know, went up in smoke, you know. Up my arm. The watches, the rings, . . . the car, you know. I used

to have a girl, man, and her daddy had two horses. I put them in my arm. You know what I mean? . . . I made her sell them horses. My clothes and all that stuff, a lot of it, they went up in smoke when I started messing with that cocaine.

Eventually, friends and even family members may come to believe that they have been exploited or that continued assistance will only prolong a process that must be terminated: "Oh, I tried to borrow money, and borrow money and, you know, nobody would loan it to me. Because they knew what I was doing." After first refusing further assistance, persons who formerly provided support may avoid social contacts with the party pursuer or sever ties altogether:

Q: Besides doing something wrong, did you think of anything else that you could do to get money? . . . Borrow it?
A: No, I'd done run that in the ground. See, you burn that up. That's burned up, right there, borrowing, you know. . . . Once I borrow, you know, I might get $10 from you today and, see, I'll be expecting to be getting $10 tomorrow, if I could. And then, when I see you [and] you see me coming, you say, "no, I don't have none." . . . As the guys in the penitentiary say, "you absorb all of your remedies," you see.

Last, when party pursuits are not going well, feelings of shame and self-disgust are not uncommon.[101] When offenders find themselves in these straits, they often take steps to reduce these feelings by distancing themselves voluntarily from conventional others:

Q: You were married to your wife at that time?
A: Yeah, I was married . . .
Q: Where was she living then?
A: I finally forced her to go home, you know . . . I made her go home, you know. And it caused an argument, for her to go home to her mother's. I felt like that was the best thing I did for her, you know. She hated me . . . for it at the time, didn't understand none of it. But, really, I intentionally made her go. I really spared her the misery that we were going to have. And it came, it came in bundles.

Regardless of why or how estrangement occurs, when party pursuers sustain severe losses of legitimate income and social resources, they grow increasingly isolated from conventional significant others. This in turn reduces interpersonal constraints on their behavior and their readiness to decline participation in illicit activities.

As pursuit of life as party increasingly assumes qualities of difficulty and struggle, offenders' motivations, utilities, and risk perceptions also change. Increasingly, crimes are committed not so much to enhance or sustain the lifestyle as to forestall further erosion of already unpleasant personal circumstances. Those addicted to alcohol or other drugs, for example, must devote increasing time and energy to the quest for money to purchase their chemicals of choice. Both their drug consumption and the frequency of their criminal acts increase. For them and for others, inability to draw on legitimate or low-risk resources eventually may precipitate a crisis. For example, a heroin addict facing a court appearance on a burglary charge needed funds to hire an attorney:

> I needed some money bad or if I didn't, if I went to court the following day, I was going to be locked up. The judge was going to lock me up. Because I didn't have no lawyer. And I had went and talked to several lawyers and they told me . . . they wanted a thousand dollars, that if I couldn't come up with no thousand dollars, they couldn't come to court with me. . . . So I went to my sister. I asked my sister, I said, "look here, what about letting me have seven or eight hundred dollars"—which I knowed she had the money because she . . . had been in a wreck and she had gotten some money out of a suit. And she said, "well, if I give you the money you won't do the right thing with it." And I was telling her, "no, no, I need a lawyer." But I couldn't convince her to let me have the money. So I left . . . I said, shit, I'm fixin' to go back to jail. . . . So as I left her house and was walking—I was going to catch the bus—the [convenience store] and bus stop was right there by each other. So I said I'm going to buy me some gum. . . . And in the process of me buying the chewing gum, I seen two ladies, they was counting money. So I figured sooner or later one of them was going to come out with the money. . . . I waited on them until . . . one came out with the money, and I got it.

Confronted by crisis and preoccupied increasingly with relieving immediate distress, the offender may experience and define himself as propelled by forces beyond his control. Behavioral options are dichotomized into those that hold out some possibility of relief, however risky, and those that promise little but continued pain. Legitimate options are few and are seen as unlikely solutions; a criminal act may offer some hope of relief, however temporary. The criminal option may be imbued with almost magical prospects for reversing or ending the state of discomfort:

> I said, "well, look at it like this"—if I don't do it, then tomorrow morning I've got the same [problems] that I've got right now. I could be hungry. I'm going to want food more. I'm going to want cigarettes more. I'm going to want everything more. [But] if I do it, and if I make it, then I've got all I want.

Acts that once were the result of blithe unconcern with risk can over time come to be based on a personal determination to master or reverse what is experienced as desperately unpleasant circumstances. The blithe inattention to risk characteristic of decisionmaking when the party goes well now gives way to the offender's perception that he has *nothing to lose:*

> It . . . gets to the point that you get into such a desperation. You're not working, you can't work. You're drunk as hell, been that way two or three weeks. You're no good to yourself, and you're no good to anybody else. Self-esteem is gone [and you're] spiritually, mentally, physically, financially bankrupt. You ain't got nothing to lose.

Desperate to maintain or reestablish a sense of normality, the offender pursues emotional and physical relief with a decision to act resolutely, albeit in the face of legal odds recognized as narrowing. By acting boldly and decisively to make the best of a grim situation, one gains a measure of respect, if not from others, then at least from oneself.[102]

> I think, when you're doing . . . drugs like I was doing, I don't think you tend to rationalize much at all. I think it's just a decision you make. You don't weigh the consequences, the pros and the cons. You just do it.
> You know, all kinds of things started running through my mind. If I get caught, then there, there I am with another charge. Then I said, well if I don't do something, I'm going to be in jail. And I just said, I'm going to do it.

The fact that sustained party pursuits often cause offenders to increase the number of offenses they commit and to exploit criminal opportunities that formerly were seen as risky should not be interpreted as meaning they believe they can continue committing crime with impunity. The opposite is true. Many offenders engaged in crimes intended to halt or reverse eroding fortunes are aware that eventually they will be arrested if they continue their course:

> Q: How did you manage not to think about, you know, that you could go to prison?
> A: Well, you think about it afterwards. You think, "wow, boy, I got away with it again." But you know, sooner or later, the law of averages is gonna catch up with you. You just can't do it [commit crime] forever and ever and ever. And don't think you're not gonna get caught, 'cause you will.

The "law of averages" is recognized in the abstract by nearly all thieves; a majority of them endorse the premise that they will be caught "eventually" if they continue committing crime.[103] The cyclical transformation of party pursuits from pleasant and enjoyable to desperate and tenuous is one reason they are able to continue committing crime despite awareness of inevitable and potentially severe legal penalties. Although the path to this point is not uniform for alcoholics, heroin addicts, and cocaine users, it is their common experience.

The threat posed by possible arrest and imprisonment, however, may not seem severe to some desperate offenders. In the context of their marginal and precarious existence, even prison holds out the promise of some relief:

> [When I was straight], I'd think about [getting caught]. I could get this, and that [penalties].. . . . And then I would think, well, I know this is going to end one day, you know. But, you know, you get so far out there, and get so far off into it that it really don't matter, you know. But you think about that. . . . I knew, eventually, I would get caught, you know. . . . I was off into drugs and I just didn't care if I got caught or not.

> When I [got] caught-and they caught me right at the house—it's kind of like, you feel good, because you're glad it's over, you know. I mean, a weight being lifted off your head. And you say, well, I don't have to worry about this shit no more, because they've caught me. And it's over, you know.

In sum, as a result of offenders' eroding access to legitimately secured funds, their diminishing contact with and support from conventional significant others, and their efforts to maintain drug consumption habits, crimes that once were committed for recreational purposes increasingly become desperate attempts to forestall or reverse uncomfortable or frustrating personal fortunes. To offenders pursuing the short-term goal of maximizing enjoyment of life, legal threats can appear either as remote and improbable contingencies when party pursuits fulfill their recreational purposes or as an acceptable risk in the face of continued pain, isolation, and failure.

Identity and Character Projects

Numerous investigators, using survey and ethnographic methods alike, have shown that criminal acts that are indistinguishable on legal or other grounds can have diverse subjective meanings and can result from a variety of motivations. Interviews with 113 California robbers, for example, revealed that although most were intent on securing money when they robbed, more than 40 percent of the subjects were motivated by nonmonetary reasons. They robbed because of anger, a desire for excitement, to impress friends, or to recover money that was owed them.[104] These men took cash or other valuables in the process of robbery, but the money was of secondary importance in their motivations.

Although a high proportion of stealing by persistent thieves takes place in the context of life as party, much of it has less to do with securing money to keep the party going than with matters of identity and character. The criminal identities sketched earlier are normative and evaluative touchstones for some persistent thieves. For those wanting to be a "good hustler," for example, their choices are constrained by their understanding of what this requires.

Why do some working-class males pursue criminal identities or identities that carry with them increased risk of involvement in crime? Why do men choose to pursue a reputation as a "good thief" or a "badass"? The answer, I suggested at the outset of this chapter, is that it appeals to them—they identify with it. Men who identify with crime typically want to do well in terms of the standards and norms of their criminal peers.

> [I]n my mind I was Superfly. I'd drive up slow to the curb. My hog be half a block long and these fine foxes in the back. Everybody looking when I ease out the door clean and mean. Got a check in my pocket to give Mom. Buy her a new house with everything in it new. Pay her back for the hard times. . . . Wasn't no way it wasn't gon happen. [I] was gon make it big. I'd be at the door, smiling with the check in my hand and Mommy'd be so happy she'd be crying.[105]

For men such as this, successful crime commission reinforces a sense of personal competence and occupational success. One of the inescapable ironies of stealing and most illicit activities, however, is that success cannot be relished and celebrated publicly without risking uncontrolled dissemination of information about a person and his activities.[106] Peer respect is extremely important to some thieves, but it must be sought and enjoyed in a circumspect fashion. Many, however, simply cannot resist boasting or dropping hints about their criminal exploits:

> One great failing of the thief is that when he gets money he immediately makes tracks for some hangout where he throws a few dollars on the bar just to "give the house a tumble" and let them guess where he "scored" and how much he got. He looks wise, says nothing, spends a few dollars, and goes out. Then the guessing begins and it's surprising what good guessers some poor thieves are.[107]

Refusal or inability to keep silent about one's activities, in short to manage one's personal front, is one of many personal shortcomings separating most persistent thieves from their more successful criminal contemporaries.[108]

One of the more common projects for which crime is the vehicle springs from the drive to be a successful person and to have the admiration and respect that come with it. Some persistent thieves hope to distinguish themselves by achieving long-term monetary success, generally via the "big score" or the "big sting." This fantasized, highly lucrative crime not only would serve as testament to their intelligence and sharpness but would also enable them to become legitimate and respectable business-men. As one of them expressed it: "If I make it through, I will *really* have gotten over; I'll be right up there with the Rockefellers!"[109] Proportion-ately, no more than a handful of persistent thieves and hustlers are suc-cessful in these endeavors. On top of the liabilities and self-imposed restrictions of their class, few have sufficient control over their ego, tem-perament, or drug habit either to locate and pull off a big score or to make a go of entrepreneurial crime. Their access to the social connections needed to be successful at crime are equally limited.[110] Virtually none manage to keep their eye on the goal of monetary success, to avoid the temptations and excesses of "life in the fast lane"[111] and to emerge from their criminal career with financial security. The fundamental truth is that "[i]t's hard to move slow with fast money."[112] The autobiographies of thieves and hustlers contain many expressions of amazement at how effortlessly and quickly ill-gotten funds are spent and how carefully hon-est money is managed.

> I had saved several hundred dollars while working at the mill and, curiously, was loath to spend it in the reckless fashion in which I had spent stolen money at other times. The money I had now represented hard labour. I could almost see the parts of the hours I had worked for each fifty-cent piece that I laid on a tobacconist's counter.[113]

The way money is acquired is a powerful determinant of how it is defined, husbanded, and spent.

As the term is used here, *character* is the combination of qualities or traits of individuals that are thought to be "essentializing," in the sense that they "fully color our picture of the person so characterized."[114] Thus the esteemed traits or qualities of persons of good character contrast sharply with the qualities of persons of poor character. Keep in mind here that the standard for these matters is not the local Parent-Teacher Associ-ation but the underworld and the street corner. Not uncommonly, in the diverse and numberless venues where the party takes place, men who identify with crime openly embrace criminal identities of the kind out-lined in this chapter. Others plot or engage in behaviors calculated to show that they possess esteemed character traits, ruthlessness perhaps. For these men at these times, money is an afterthought. Their crimes are best seen as *projects* meant to impress and win deference from others.

The importance of matters of reputation and respect is clear particularly in crimes of interpersonal violence, where the goal is to be recognized as "bad" or, perhaps, as a "crazy nigger."[115] There is an element of identity or character display in many types of crime, and stealing is no exception:

> Ain't everybody in the street crazy. We see what's going down. We supposed to die. Take our little welfare checks and be quiet and die. That ain't news to nobody. It's what's happening every day . . . Them little checks and drugs. What else is out there? The streets out there. The hard-ass curb. That's why the highest thing you can say about a cat is he made his from the curb. That's a bad cat. That's a cat took nothing and made something. When a dude drive up in a big hog and goes in the bar with a fox on his arm and drops a yard on the counter, he's bad. Got to be bad. What else he be but bad if he made all his shit from the hard rock?
>
> Don't matter if it's gone tomorrow. If he's dead tomorrow. The cat was bad. He made it the only way he could.[116]

Recounting an evening of gambling, a former street hustler described a setting in which he wanted to gain the respect of other players. His efforts failed:

> We went to this house in Brooklyn. It was full of people and they said, good, come on in, we've got new blood. They invited me to roll the dice. That was cool; I stepped up and I put a hundred on the table, and wow, everybody got quiet. I thought they were impressed, you know?. . .
>
> Then . . . Jeff's dad came up to the table, and I looked to see what he was gonna throw—and he starts with *fifteen hundred dollars!* I couldn't believe it! Everybody got noisy again, and I realized what was happening. I had really chumped . . . it good.
>
> I couldn't believe the things Jeff's old man did. He kept throwing the bread down, and he was smilin' and drinking and it mean *nothin'* to him. He lost fifty—five hundred. . . . He didn't even blink. He went out to the car afterward, and he was feelin' just fine. He went to this bar, and you know he bought everybody in the house a drink. . . .
>
> Wow, that is showing something—a dude who has really got *his.*[117]

For some men, crime is an opportunity to test themselves and to show that they are capable and therefore worthy of respect. The example of an informant, a businessman who spent only six months in confinement despite a lifetime of hustling, is instructive. Although he has supported himself and his family with several kinds of work as an adult, he always hustled on the side. At the time he was interviewed, he owned a construction company and occasionally sent street-level thieves to building sites to steal equipment and materials needed for his own jobs. Asked whether he ever would give up hustling entirely, he responded: "I don't know. Hustling is fun. We test ourselves sometimes, you know. We test ourselves against the system." Successful and unusually rational in his approach to hustling, he is an exception to the pattern of failure typical of most persistent hustlers.

The quest to be successful generally is not a quest for monetary success alone. Rather, money is valued largely because it stands as evidence of personal qualities and character. An informant interpreted his display of success as a way of compensating for earlier misfortune that may have been interpreted characterologically: "Really, what it was was impressing everybody, you know. 'Here Floyd is, and he's never had nothing in his life, and now look at him—he's driving new cars, and wearing jewelry,' you know." Many are intent on winning a respected reputation.

> It ain't the money or the cars or the women. It's about all that but that ain't what it's deep down about. . . . The money ain't nothing. You just use the money to make your play. To show people you the best. Yeah. Look at me. I got mine. . . . You out there to show your ass. To let people know you're somebody. . . . Straight people don't understand. I mean, they think dudes is after the things straight people got. It ain't that at all. People in the life ain't looking for no home and grass in the yard and shit like that. We the show people. The glamour people. Come on the set with the finest car, the finest woman, the finest vines. Hear people talking about you. Hear the bar get quiet when you walk in the door. . . . See. It's rep. . . . That's what it's about. . . . You make something out of nothing.[118]

The extreme importance of interpersonal respect, particularly to men who almost certainly are denied it based on their location in class and moral hierarchies, cannot be minimized.

For men whose crimes are identity or character projects, the *way* they are committed can be as important as completing them successfully. Robberies committed with cruel indifference to victims, for example, can do much to cement the identity of outlaw or badass. Careful preparation, an emphasis on use of proper skills, and, more generally, qualities of professionalism may be seen as indicators of competence and probable success. An informant whose criminal repertoire included stealing removable fiberglass tops from sports cars recounted with pleasure and pride how he and his crime partner organized and prepared for trips to nearby cities to locate and steal them. Their preparations included renting an automobile with a trunk large enough to hold several car tops as well as collecting equipment

they would need. After reaching their destination, they searched the park-
ing lots at large apartment complexes to identify and note cars with the
appropriate removable tops before returning at night to steal them. The
informant was proud of techniques he and his partner developed to break
car windows quietly and quickly, unfasten car tops, and load them into the
trunk of the rental car. For him as for most, criminal participation is challenging. A successful outcome means they have bested an implacable
adversary. When crimes require offenders to employ terror and lethal
weapons in crime commission, the enjoyment of success is heightened further by knowledge they avoided potentially fatal consequences.[119]

Thieves and hustlers for whom monetary concerns are secondary motivations sometimes see life as a string of challenges or obstacles in which
the objective is to triumph or at least to show evidence of proper character. Successful crime commission is a challenge par excellence, one that
requires courage and gameness. Gameness is the determination to prevail
or at least *not to be seen as loser* in any contest or situation in which character or identity is at stake.[120] It is evidenced by pressing the issue boldly
or in dogged refusal to relent or withdraw until a favorable outcome has
been reached. Crime is an outstanding medium for character projects precisely because it belongs to a category of behavior in which "the individual has the risk and the opportunity of displaying to himself and sometimes to others his style of conduct when the chips are down."[121]

Issues of character are imbued with considerable importance in the
world of working-class males. Consequently, character disputes are not
uncommon, particularly during party times. In any of countless ways,
one or more participants may impugn or challenge another's character.
This can range from angry, aggressive shouts that another is "light-
weight" to stealing from him. When these incidents occur, they silently
evoke in all who are present the potentially damning question, What kind
of man would let himself be treated like that? Determination not to be
treated disrespectfully or exploited in other ways occasionally finds
expression in criminal acts that are projects for demonstrating manly
character. When, for example, crime is employed as social control, it
becomes a moralistic expression of disapproval meant to achieve com-
pensation or restitution for a harm that is viewed as intolerable. An informant told, for example, how he burglarized the home of an acquaintance:

> I was mad. . . . When I was in the penitentiary, my wife went to his house for
> a party and he give her a bunch of cocaine. . . . It happened, I think, about a
> week before I got out. . . . I just had it in my mind what I wanted to do—I
> wanted to hurt him like I was hurt. . . . I was pretty drunk when I went by
> [his home], and I saw there wasn't no car there. So I just pulled my car in.

The response to disrespectful treatment or imputation of weak character may follow the harm by weeks, months, or even years, or it may occur immediately.[122] Another informant described a series of events that resulted in his decision to break into and steal from an automobile:

> We got evicted from our apartment, for bein' two days late on our rent. It was on Friday, and our rent come due on Wednesday. We were drawin' our payday on a construction site, and Steve was my buddy. I was livin' with him and his wife. She come over and said "they throwed our stuff out on the street." And we're over there pickin' up our paychecks! Well, we shoot back over there, and they done kicked us out of the apartment. And there we are with the money, tryin' to pay' em. The guy picked up a stereo that I bought when I was in the army, one of those nice, big old stereos. And they stole it. It was in the apartment complex, and they had it. So we went out drinkin' that night, tryin' to figure out what we was gonna do. And Steve come in and said, "hey, your stereo's out there in a car, outside." Went out there, it looked just like mine. And it *was* mine! So I broke the windows out of the car and took the stereo and left. When I drove away, there was a security guy. So they got me for that. Now, I shouldn't have broke that guy's window out, but he shouldn't have took my stereo. But that's not burglary, not the way I look at it. That was *justice,* the way I look at it, 'cause he shouldn't of had my stuff.

Experiences like these are common in the worlds and lives of persistent thieves.[123]

As previously discussed, cyclical transformations of life as party can produce increasing isolation and desperation. Those for whom crime is an identity or character project also risk distinctive emotional changes as they either rise or fall. At crime and other high-risk ventures, "success typically produces an enormous increase in feelings of self-determination and self-actualization, a pronounced sense of their own competence."[124] Indeed, crime "may create more powerful feelings of competence than other types of . . . activities because it offers the right mix of skill and chance, a combination that maintains the illusion of controlling the seemingly uncontrollable."[125] The danger here is arrogance, the danger of equating with character willingness to risk rapidly increasing odds of failure. Disdain or apparent indifference to the potentially serious consequences of one's acts can be a powerful display of gameness for those bent on showing that they are distinguished in some way.

Fundamental to the notion of crime as identity and character project is the understanding that these matters cannot be taken for granted long; once gained they can be lost. A favorable outcome and judgment one time do not guarantee a lifetime of respect. It is precisely the potential for gaining or restoring character that makes crime appealing to some. It is a means of transforming yesterday's knave into today's prince. An informant told how he and two crime partners mulled over various crime options before deciding to burglarize a store that was believed nearly impregnable:

> I said "hell," I said, "there ain't no, there ain't nothing the motherfuckers make that can't be hit." . . . That's when, you know, I got to thinking about it. And the drunker I got, the more I got to thinking about it, you know. They say this motherfucker can't be hit. Well, . . . they ain't had Mike Stevens there. Let me show them, you know, I can do it.

For him and others like him, however, a successful project brings only short-term deference and respite. Inevitably proof of character must be offered again. The future holds the need for more high-risk projects, which increases the chances of arrest.

Just as happens with the dynamics of life as party, the dynamics of identity and character projects can transform and distort the criminal calculus of those who pursue them. The importance to thieves and hustlers of identity issues and concerns invites consideration of how they shape decisionmaking. Prospective actions are evaluated not only in terms of the amount of trouble they may bring but also for what success at them would suggest to others about one's identity or character. These matters can be extremely important, particularly for men whose investments in legitimate identities and lines of action are shallow and unrewarding.

Lifestyle and Identity as Choice

The question of choice can be redirected from why offenders choose to commit discrete criminal acts to why they choose indolent or risky lifestyles. Among the varying answers to this question, one emphasizes how social factors such as family disorganization can push men into lifestyles with high potential for criminal involvement. A complementary answer highlights the attractiveness and seductions of high-risk lifestyles and the pull they exert on the individual.[126] The importance and influence of these "pull factors" have been employed particularly in analyses of illicit markets. Where manufacture, distribution, and use of illicit drugs are concerned, many believe that enforcement efforts are doomed to failure. Arresting and confining individual offenders accomplish little in the way of reducing drug supplies because the promise of profits means that new entrepreneurs will step in and take the place of those who are incapacitated. A similar process may be at work in the choice of lifestyles that place their pursuers at increased risk of criminal participation. Rooted in their class and status background, their cultural inheritance may predispose them to select high-risk lifestyles despite efforts to arrest and incapacitate those who commit common-law property crimes.

The choice of life as party, which reflects widely held subterranean values, may be a response to occupational prospects and experiences in which workers are required to subordinate themselves to the dictates of others, often while performing physically tiring, unpleasant, or dirty work. Party pursuits may appeal particularly to males whose only legitimate occupations have these characteristics. This analysis goes part of the way toward making understandable the big-score fantasies of so many thieves and hustlers, but it is important to recognize its class origins also. In the words of Alan Sillitoe, the English novelist of working-class origin, "[t]he outspoken ambition of our class was to become one's own boss."[127] Success at party pursuits earns for offenders a measure of respect from peers for their demonstrated ability to "get over," which translates into "self-esteem . . . as a folk hero beating the bureaucratic system of routinized dependence."[128]

Men for whom life as party is the backdrop for identity or character projects are responding not only to these same conditions but also to the routinization and monotony characteristic of modern labor. The world of legitimate employment increasingly is a bureaucratized and impersonal one in which employees are denied opportunities to exercise creativity in their work. Increasingly, people dedicate heart and soul to maintaining role patterns associated with social structures that they themselves had no part in creating. In this world, crime can be a form of *edgework*, voluntary behavior that carries with it "a clearly observable threat to one's physical or mental well-being or one's sense of an ordered existence."[129] Edgework is voluntary behavior to which serious risks are attached. Like other types of edgework, crime permits the person to break free of alienative and restrictive bonds and routines. An English persistent thief articulated the perspective:

> I'll willingly gamble away a third of my life in prison, so long as I can live the way I want for the other two-thirds. After all, it's my life, and that's how I feel about it. The alternative—the prospect of vegetating the rest of my life away in a steady job, catching the 8:13 to work in the morning, and the 5:50 back again at night, all for ten or fifteen quid a week—now that really does terrify me, far more than the thought of a few years in the nick.[130]

Another former thief put it this way:

> There are few enough places in the world today where a man can find real frontiers and sure-enough adventure, where he can gamble his wits and freedom against a powerful and implacable authority; few enough ways to lift himself above the banality of a commuter culture.[131]

Nevertheless, stealing in the contemporary world requires use of skills street-level thieves have little knowledge of or experience with. They know little or nothing about entrepreneurship, the ability to organize personnel and resources for productive purposes. The same is true of their knowledge of managing hierarchical work organizations. Inability or refusal to discipline themselves, to assume an entrepreneurial posture, or to rationalize their stealing through organization, careful planning, and assessment of changing criminal opportunities marks and handicaps them. Successful stealing over any appreciable period of time requires the same skills needed for success in legitimate occupational pursuits. Those who cannot or will not employ these skills are destined for the correctional netherworld.

Crime control policies that narrowly focus on the decision to commit crimes ignore the attractiveness of lifestyles and identities that obscure both the boundary and the passage between legal and illegal conduct and that thereby conduce to criminal participation. At times when we conjure and contemplate "the criminal decisionmaker," it probably is helpful to keep in mind that his decisions are made in a world of drug using, display, and competition that is populated predominantly by young males. Bars, dope houses, and gambling joints are settings in which interaction can range from easygoing and playful to intense and deadly serious. Those present may like and respect one another, or they may harbor simmering grudges. Their pockets may be full of money, or their most pressing problem may be securing some. These contexts, identities, and interactions can distort severely participants' calculus and decisionmaking process. The decision to commit robbery may be indistinguishable theoretically from the decision to purchase a television set. This does not change the fact that the former typically is made in a context of hedonism in which the costs of alternative actions can be blurred or easily discounted; the latter is not. Reviewed in Chapter 6 is what is known about the way these men make decisions, particularly the degree to which they are sensitive to the risk of arrest. First, however, we turn to an examination of how the crimes of persistent thieves change over the life course and, for most, lead eventually to desistance from serious criminal participation.

Notes

1. Peggie Benton, *Peterman* (London: Arthur Barker, 1966), p. 169.

2. Piri Thomas, *Down These Mean Streets* (New York: Signet, 1968), pp. 108–109.

3. Nathan McCall, *Makes Me Wanna Holler* (New York: Random House, 1994), p. 81.

4. John Irwin and James Austin, *It's About Time* (Belmont, Calif.: Wadsworth, 1994), pp. 40–49.

5. Mark Peterson, Jan Chaiken, and Patricia Ebener, *Survey of Jail and Prison Inmates, 1978: California, Michigan, Texas* (Ann Arbor, Mich.: Inter-University Consortium for Political and Social Research, 1984). This is based on my secondary analysis of the Rand Inmate Survey data.

6. George J. McCall and J. L. Simmons, *Identities and Interactions* (New York: Free Press, 1966), p. 67.

7. The classic description of professional criminals is Edwin Sutherland, *The Professional Thief* (Chicago: University of Chicago Press, 1937). For an excellent, if romanticized, fictional depiction of thieves and their perspectives, see Clyde B. Davis, *The Rebellion of Leo McGuire* (New York: Farrar and Rinehart, 1944). For a firsthand account of the convict code circa 1940, see Nathan Leopold, *Life Plus 99 Years* (New York: Doubleday, 1958). For an excellent description and interpretation of inmate normative systems circa 1960, see John Irwin and Donald R. Cressey, "Thieves, convicts, and the inmate subculture," *Social Problems* 10(1962), pp. 142–155.

8. John Irwin, *The Felon* (Berkeley: University of California Press, 1987), pp. 8–12.

9. Tony Parker and Robert Allerton, *The Courage of His Convictions* (London: Hutchinson, 1962), p. 188.

10. James Willwerth, *Jones* (New York: M. Evans and Co., 1974), p. 185.

11. Edwin Sutherland, *The Professional Thief* (Chicago: University of Chicago Press, 1937).

12. John MacIsaac, *Half the Fun Was Getting There* (Englewood Cliffs, N.J.: Prentice-Hall, 1968), p. 5.

13. Burglary skills are discussed in Neal Shover, "Burglary as an Occupation" (Ph.D. thesis, Department of Sociology, University of Illinois, Urbana-Champaign, 1971); and in Peter Letkemann, *Crime as Work* (Englewood Cliffs, N.J.: Prentice-Hall, 1973).

14. James (Big Jim) Morton, with D. Wittels, "I was king of the thieves," *Saturday Evening Post* (August 5, 1950), pp. 18–19.

15. Gresham M. Sykes and Sheldon L. Messinger, "The inmate social system," in *Theoretical Studies in Social Organization of the Prison*, edited by Richard A. Cloward, Donald R. Cressey, George H. Grosser, Richard McCleery, Lloyd E. Ohlin, Gresham M. Sykes, and Sheldon L. Messinger (New York: Social Science Research Council, 1960).

16. Ernest Booth, *Stealing Through Life* (New York: Alfred A. Knopf, 1929), p. 259.

17. John Irwin, *The Felon* (Berkeley: University of California Press, 1987), p. 12.

18. Leroy Gould, "Crime as a Profession" (New Haven, Conn.: Department of Sociology, Yale University, 1967), photocopy, p. 25.

19. Studs Terkel, *Race* (New York: Anchor Books, 1993), p. 244.

20. Eliot Liebow, *Tally's Corner* (Boston: Little, Brown, 1966), pp. 32–33. See also John Hagedorn, with Perry Macon, *People and Folks* (Chicago: Lake View Press, 1988), especially pp. 101–103.

21. Malcolm X, *The Autobiography of Malcolm X*, with the assistance of Alex Haley (New York: Grove, 1965), p. 108.

22. Elijah Anderson, *A Place on the Corner* (Chicago: University of Chicago Press, 1978), p. 130.

23. Elijah Anderson, *A Place on the Corner* (Chicago: University of Chicago Press, 1978), p. 134.

24. Leroy Gould, "Crime as a Profession" (New Haven, Conn.: Department of Sociology, Yale University, 1967), photocopy, p. 25.

25. Nicholas Pileggi, *Wiseguy* (New York: Simon and Schuster, 1985), pp. 51–55.

26. John Bartlow Martin, *My Life in Crime* (New York: Harper & Brothers, 1952), p. 41.

27. For a discussion of the importance of these qualities in African American ghetto communities, see Ulf Hannerz, *Soulside* (New York: Columbia University Press, 1969), especially pp. 110–113.

28. Nathan McCall, *Makes Me Wanna Holler* (New York: Random House, 1994), p. 90.

29. Elijah Anderson, *Streetwise* (Chicago: University of Chicago Press, 1990), pp. 103–104.

30. David Schulz, *Coming Up Black* (Englewood Cliffs, N.J.: Prentice-Hall, 1969), p. 80.

31. James Willwerth, *Jones* (New York: M. Evans and Co., 1974), p. 100.

32. Elijah Anderson, *Streetwise* (Chicago: University of Chicago Press, 1990).

33. Richard P. Rettig, Manual J. Torres, and Gerald R. Garrett, *Manny* (Boston: Houghton Mifflin, 1977), p. 160.

34. Henry Williamson, *Hustler*, edited by R. Lincoln Keiser (New York: Avon, 1965), pp. 35–36.

35. Stuart L. Hills and Ron Santiago, *Tragic Magic* (Chicago: Nelson-Hall, 1992), p. 133.

36. See, for example, the hustle described in Pete Earley, *The Hot House* (New York: Bantam, 1992), pp. 156–158.

37. Peter Reuter, Robert MacCoun, and Patrick Murphy, *Money from Crime* (Santa Monica, Calif.: Rand, 1990). For evidence on drug dealing by street-level crack-cocaine users, see James A. Inciardi and Anne E. Pottieger, "Crack-cocaine use and street crime," *Journal of Drug Issues* 24(1994), pp. 273–292.

38. Elliott Currie, *Reckoning* (New York: Hill and Wang, 1993).

39. Edward Preble and John J. Casey, "Taking care of business: The heroin user's life on the street," *International Journal of the Addictions* 4(1969), pp. 1–24; Bruce D. Johnson, Paul Goldstein, Edward Preble, James Schmeidler, Douglas S. Lipton, Barry Spunt, and Thomas Miller, *Taking Care of Business* (Lexington, Mass.: Lexington Books, 1985); Charles E. Faulpel and Carl B. Klockars, "Drugs-crime connections: Elaborations from the life histories of hard-core heroin addicts," *Social Problems* 34(1987), pp. 54–68; Marcia R. Chaiken and Bruce D. Johnson, *Characteristics of Different Types of Drug-Involved Offenders* (Washington, D.C.: National Institute of Justice, 1988); Bruce D. Johnson, Kevin Anderson, and Eric D. Wish, "A day in the life of 105 drug addicts and abusers: Crimes committed and how the money was spent," *Sociology and Social Research* 72(1988), pp. 185–191; James Q. Wilson, "Drugs and crime," in *Drugs and Crime*, edited by Michael Tonry and James Q. Wilson (Chicago: University of Chicago Press, 1990); Elizabeth P. Deschenes, M. Douglas Anglin, and George Speckart, "Narcotics addiction: Related criminal careers, social and economic costs," *Journal of Drug Issues* 21(1991), pp. 383–411; Bureau of Justice Statistics, *Drugs, Crime, and the Justice System* (Washing-

ton, D.C.: U.S. Department of Justice, 1992); James A. Inciardi and Anne E. Pottieger, "Crack-cocaine use and street crime," *Journal of Drug Issues* 24(1994), pp. 273–292.

40. This in no way contradicts the fact that an undetermined number of drug users manage their habit successfully without resorting to stealing. Results from an American study are reported in Dan Waldorf, Craig Reinarman, and Sheigla Murphy, *Cocaine Changes* (Philadelphia: Temple University Press, 1991). Similar findings are reported in a Canadian study: Yuet W. Cheung, Patricia G. Erickson, and Tammy C. Landau, "Experience of crack use: Findings from a community-based sample in Toronto," *Journal of Drug Issues* 21(1991), pp. 121–140.

41. Bruce D. Johnson, Paul J. Goldstein, Edward Preble, James Schmeidler, Douglas S. Lipton, Barry Spunt, and Thomas Miller, *Taking Care of Business* (Lexington: Lexington Books, 1985).

42. Bruce Johnson, Kevin Anderson, and Eric Wish, "A day in the life of 105 drug addicts and abusers: Crimes committed and how the money was spent," *Sociology and Social Research* 72 (1988), pp. 185–191.

43. Compare, for example, Bruce D. Johnson, Paul J. Goldstein, Edward Preble, James Schmeidler, Douglas S. Lipton, Barry Spunt, and Thomas Miller, *Taking Care of Business* (Lexington: Lexington Books, 1985).

44. Richard P. Rettig, Manual J. Torres, and Gerald R. Garrett, *Manny* (Boston: Houghton Mifflin, 1977), p. 42.

45. Bruce D. Johnson, Eric D. Wish, and Kevin Anderson, "A day in the life of 105 drug addicts and abusers: Crimes committed and how the money was spent," *Sociology and Social Research* 72(1988), pp. 185–191.

46. Eugene Delorme, *Chief,* edited by Inez Cardozo-Freeman (Lincoln: University of Nebraska Press, 1994), p. 111.

47. Richard P. Rettig, Manual J. Torres, and Gerald R. Garrett, *Manny* (Boston: Houghton Mifflin, 1977), pp. 88–89.

48. John Edgar Wideman, *Brothers and Keepers* (New York: Holt, Rinehart and Winston, 1984), p. 94.

49. Nathan McCall, *Makes Me Wanna Holler* (New York: Random House, 1994), p. 127.

50. Harold Finestone, "Cats, kicks and color," in *The Other Side,* edited by Howard S. Becker (New York: Free Press, 1964). For a discussion and interpretation of "coolness," the "cool cat," and hustling in the worlds of African American males, see Richard Majors and Janet Mancini Billson, *Cool Pose* (Lexington, Mass.: Lexington, 1992).

51. Richard Stephens and Stephen Levine, "The street-addict role: Implications for treatment," *Psychiatry* 34(1971), pp. 351–357.

52. Edward Preble and John J. Casey, "Taking care of business: The heroin user's life on the street," *International Journal of the Addictions* 4(1969), pp. 1–24.

53. Edward Preble and John J. Casey, "Taking care of business: The heroin user's life on the street," *International Journal of the Addictions* 4(1969), pp. 1–24.

54. Yuet W. Cheung, Patricia G. Erickson, and Tammy C. Landau, "Experience of crack use: Findings from a community-based sample in Toronto," *Journal of Drug Issues* 21(1991), pp. 121–140.

55. Eloise Dunlap, Bruce Johnson, Harry Sanabria, Elbert Holliday, Vicki Lipsey, Maurice Barnett, William Hopkins, Ira Sobel, Doris Randolph, and Ko-Lin Chin, "Studying crack users and their criminal careers: The scientific and artistic aspects of locating hard-to-reach subjects and interviewing them about sensitive topics," *Contemporary Drug Problems* 17 (1990), pp. 121–144.

56. Yuet W. Cheung, Patricia G. Erickson, and Tammy C. Landau, "Experience of crack use: Findings from a community-based sample in Toronto," *Journal of Drug Issues* 21(1991), pp. 121–140.

57. Yuet W. Cheung, Patricia G. Erickson, and Tammy C. Landau, "Experience of crack use: Findings from a community-based sample in Toronto," *Journal of Drug Issues* 21(1991), pp.121–140.

58. Jan Chaiken and Marcia Chaiken, *Varieties of Criminal Behavior* (Santa Monica, Calif.: Rand Corporation, 1982).

59. Jack Katz, *Seductions of Crime* (New York: Basic Books, 1988), p. 218.

60. John Irwin and James Austin, *It's About Time* (Belmont, Calif.: Wadsworth, 1994), p. 85.

61. Jack Henry Abbott, *In the Belly of the Beast* (New York: Random House, 1981), p. 13.

62. Kody Scott, *Monster* (New York: Atlantic Monthly Press, 1993), p. 295.

63. John Irwin, *The Felon* (Berkeley: University of California Press, 1987), p. vii. For an example of this process, see Kody Scott, *Monster* (New York: Atlantic Monthly Press, 1994), pp. 292–301.

64. This discussion borrows heavily from John Irwin, *The Felon* (Berkeley: University of California Press, 1987), pp. 23–26.

65. Walter B. Miller, "Lower-class culture as a generating milieu of gang delinquency," *Journal of Social Issues* 14(1958), p. 7.

66. Malcolm Braly, *On the Yard* (Boston: Little, Brown, 1967), p. 233.

67. The men recruited to kill labor leader Jock Yablonski, his wife, and his daughter were small-time thieves who spent their leisure time in this type of establishment. See Trevor Armbrister, *Act of Vengeance* (New York: Saturday Review Press, 1975).

68. Joseph T. Howell, *Hard Living on Clay Street* (Garden City, N.Y.: Anchor, 1973), p. 322.

69. John Irwin, *The Felon* (Berkeley: University of California Press, 1987), p. 31.

70. E. E. LeMasters, *Blue-Collar Aristocrats* (Madison: University of Wisconsin Press, 1975), p. 111.

71. Jack Katz, *The Seductions of Crime* (New York: Basic Books, 1988), p. 124.

72. Jack Katz, *The Seductions of Crime* (New York: Basic Books, 1988), p. 125.

73. Jack Katz, *The Seductions of Crime* (New York: Basic Books, 1988), pp. 183–184.

74. Jay MacLeod, *Ain't No Makin' It* (Boulder, Colo.: Westview, 1987), p. 26.

75. Elijah Anderson, *A Place on the Corner* (Chicago: University of Chicago Press, 1978), p. 157.

76. Richard Sennett and Jonathan Cobb, *The Hidden Injuries of Class* (New York: Alfred A. Knopf, 1972), p. 148.

77. David F. Luckenbill and Daniel P. Doyle, "Structural position and violence: Developing a cultural explanation," *Criminology* 27(1989), pp. 419–436.

78. Joseph T. Howell, *Hard Living on Clay Street* (New York: Anchor, 1973), p. 296.

79. Ulf Hannerz, *Soulside* (New York: Columbia University Press, 1969), p. 80.

80. Dan Rose, *Black American Street Life* (Philadelphia: University of Pennsylvania Press, 1987), p. 222.

81. Walter B. Miller, "Lower-class culture as a generating milieu of gang delinquency," *Journal of Social Issues* 14(1958), p. 11.

82. Walter B. Miller, "Lower-class culture as a generating milieu of gang delinquency," *Journal of Social Issues* 14(1958), pp. 5–19.

83. John Irwin and James Austin, *It's About Time* (Belmont, Calif.: Wadsworth, 1994), p. 45.

84. Benjamin D. Zablocki and Rosabeth Moss Kanter, "The differentiation of life-styles," in *Annual Review of Sociology*, vol. 2, edited by Alex Inkeles, James Coleman, and Neil Smelser (Palo Alto, Calif.: Annual Reviews, 1976), pp. 269–298.

85. David Matza and Gresham Sykes, "Juvenile delinquency and subterranean values," *American Sociological Review* 26(1961), pp. 712–719; Walter B. Miller, "Lower-class culture as a generating milieu of gang delinquency," *Journal of Social Issues* 14(1958), pp. 5–19.

86. Dermot Walsh, *Heavy Business* (London: Routledge & Kegan Paul, 1986), p. 15.

87. Joan Petersilia, Peter W. Greenwood, and Marvin Lavin, *Criminal Careers of Habitual Felons* (Washington, D.C.: U.S. Department of Justice, National Institute of Law Enforcement and Criminal Justice, 1978); John J. Gibbs and Peggy L. Shelley, "Life in the fast lane: A retrospective view by commercial thieves," *Journal of Research in Crime and Delinquency* 19(1982), pp. 299–330; Figgie International, *The Figgie Report Part VI—The Business of Crime* (Richmond, Va.: Figgie International Inc., 1988); Paul Cromwell, James N. Olson, and D'Aunn Wester Avary, *Breaking and Entering* (Newbury Park, Calif.: Sage, 1991).

88. Dermot Walsh, *Heavy Business* (London: Routledge & Kegan Paul, 1986), p. 72. See also Jack Katz, *Seductions of Crime* (New York: Basic Books, 1988), especially pp. 215–218.

89. Paul F. Cromwell, James N. Olson, and D'Aunn Wester Avary, *Breaking and Entering* (Newbury Park, Calif.: Sage, 1991), p. 21.

90. Bruce Jackson, *A Thief's Primer* (New York: Macmillan, 1969), pp. 146–147.

91. M. Persson, "Time-perspectives amongst criminals," *Acta Sociologica* 24(1981), pp. 149–165.

92. James Wright and Peter Rossi, *Armed Criminals in America* (Ann Arbor, Mich.: Inter-University Consortium for Political and Social Research, 1985). My calculations. See the Appendix for a discussion of the larger study.

93. See, for example, Leon R. Jansyn, Jr., "Solidarity and delinquency in a street corner group," *American Sociological Review* 31(1966), pp. 600–614.

94. Edwin Lemert, "An isolation and closure theory of naive check forgery," in *Criminal Behavior Systems*, edited by Marshall B. Clinard and Richard Quinney (New York: Holt, Rinehart and Winston, 1967); and Richard T. Wright and Scott Decker, *Burglars on the Job* (Boston: Northeastern University Press, 1994).

95. Paul F. Cromwell, James N. Olson, and D'Aunn Wester Avary, *Breaking and Entering* (Newbury Park, Calif.: Sage, 1991), pp. 52–71. A brief description of the types of hard drugs commonly used by street-level thieves can be found in Elliott Currie, *Reckoning* (New York: Hill and Wang, 1993), pp. 333–344.

96. Ann Cordilia, "Alcohol and property crime: Exploring the causal nexus," *Journal of Studies on Alcohol* 46(1985), p. 170. See also Ann Cordilia, "Robbery arising out of a group drinking context," in *Violent Transactions*, edited by A. Campbell and J. Gibbs (New York: Blackwell, 1986).

97. Paul F. Cromwell, James N. Olson, and D'Aunn Wester Avary, *Breaking and Entering* (Newbury Park, Calif.: Sage, 1991), pp. 37–40.

98. Paul F. Cromwell, James N. Olson, and D'Aunn Wester Avary, *Breaking and Entering* (Newbury Park, Calif.: Sage, 1991).

99. George F. Rengert and John Wasilchick, *Suburban Burglary* (Springfield, Ill.: Charles C. Thomas, 1985).

100. See the discussion of this phenomenon in Elijah Anderson, *Streetwise* (Chicago: University of Chicago Press, 1990), especially pp. 86–87.

101. Charles E. Frazier and Thomas N. Meisenhelder, "Criminality and emotional ambivalence: Exploratory notes on an overlooked dimension," *Qualitative Sociology* 8(1985), pp. 266–284.

102. Jack Katz, *Seductions of Crime* (New York: Basic Books, 1988), pp. 124–125.

103. Trevor Bennett and Richard Wright, *Burglars on Burglary* (Aldershot, U.K.: Gower, 1984).

104. Floyd Feeney, "Robbers as decision makers," in *The Reasoning Criminal*, edited by Derek B. Cornish and Ronald V. Clarke (New York: Springer-Verlag, 1986). See also Jack Katz, *Seductions of Crime* (New York: Basic Books, 1988), especially pp. 183–184.

105. John Edgar Wideman, *Brothers and Keepers* (New York: Holt, Rinehart and Winston, 1984), pp. 89–90.

106. An outstanding discussion of this and other fundamental problems of street-level stealing can be found in Mike Maguire, in collaboration with Trevor Bennett, *Burglary in a Dwelling* (London: Heinemann, 1982).

107. Jack Black, *You Can't Win* (New York: A. L. Burt, 1926), p. 191.

108. For an elaboration of this point, see Mike Maguire, in collaboration with Trevor Bennett, *Burglary in a Dwelling* (London: Heinemann, 1982).

109. James Willwerth, *Jones* (New York: M. Evans, 1974), p. 24.

110. See the discussion in Neal Shover, "The social organization of burglary," *Social Problems* 20(1973), pp. 499–514. A revealing autobiographical description of these connections is Frank Hohimer, *The Home Invaders* (Chicago: Chicago Review Press, 1975).

111. John J. Gibbs and Peggy L. Shelley, "Life in the fast lane: A retrospective view by commercial thieves," *Journal of Research in Crime and Delinquency* 19(1982), pp. 299–330.

112. Nathan McCall, *Makes Me Wanna Holler* (New York: Random House, 1994), p. 131.

113. Ernest Booth, *Stealing Through Life* (New York: Alfred A. Knopf, 1929), p. 280.

114. Erving Goffman, *Interaction Ritual* (Garden City, N.Y.: Anchor, 1967), p. 218.

115. Nathan McCall, *Makes Me Wanna Holler* (New York: Random House, 1994), p. 53. See also Jack Katz, *Seductions of Crime* (New York: Basic Books, 1988), pp. 88–90.

116. John Edgar Wideman, *Brothers and Keepers* (New York: Holt, Rinehart and Winston, 1984), p. 132.

117. James Willwerth, *Jones* (New York: M. Evans and Co., 1974), p. 216.

118. John Edgar Wideman, *Brothers and Keepers* (New York: Holt, Rinehart and Winston, 1984), p. 131.

119. John McVicar, *McVicar, by Himself* (London: Hutchinson, 1974), p. 164.

120. An example is John McVicar, *McVicar, by Himself* (London: Hutchinson, 1974), p. 198.

121. Erving Goffman, *Interaction Ritual* (Garden City, N.Y.: Anchor, 1967), p. 237.

122. Donald Black, "Crime as social control," *American Sociological Review* 48(1983), pp. 34–45.

123. See, for example, Paul F. Cromwell, James N. Olson, and D'Aunn Wester Avary, *Breaking and Entering* (Newbury Park, Calif.: Sage, 1991), p. 22.

124. Stephen Lyng, "Edgework: A social-psychological analysis of voluntary risk taking," *American Journal of Sociology* 95(1990), p. 872.

125. Stephen Lyng, "Edgework: A social-psychological analysis of voluntary risk taking," *American Journal of Sociology* 95(1990), p. 872.

126. Jack Katz, *The Seductions of Crime* (New York: Basic Books, 1988).

127. Alan Sillitoe, *The Loneliness of the Long-Distance Runner* (New York: Signet, 1959), p. 142.

128. Dermot Walsh, *Heavy Business* (London: Routledge & Kegan Paul, 1986), p. 16.

129. Stephen Lyng, "Edgework: A social-psychological analysis of voluntary risk taking," *American Journal of Sociology* 95(1990), p. 857.

130. Tony Parker and Robert Allerton, *The Courage of His Convictions* (London: Hutchinson, 1962), p. 88.

131. John MacIsaac, *Half the Fun Was Getting There* (Englewood Cliffs, N.J.: Prentice-Hall, 1968), pp. 19–20.

5

Career Changes and Termination

One of the most striking characteristics of those who commit much of the robbery, burglary, and theft that occur in contemporary America is their youth.[1] Adolescents and young adults swell the ranks of thieves; children and those who are middle-aged or older are represented at a level far below their proportionate share of the general population.[2] In 1990, for example, 59.7 percent of all persons arrested for the crimes of robbery, burglary, theft, and motor vehicle theft in the United States were age 24 or younger; only 36.5 percent of Americans were this young.[3] Whereas 16.1 percent of those arrested for property crime in 1990 were age 35 or older, 46.1 percent of the general population were this old.[4] Use of arrest statistics to document the youthful age of thieves understandably is open to challenge because the tallies omit the characteristics of offenders who were not arrested. The same age imbalance is found, however, in the reports of street-crime victims who are confronted by or otherwise chance to see their offenders. The perpetrators were age 20 or younger in 50 percent of the 14 million personal robberies reported to the National Crime Victimization Survey between 1973 and 1984.[5] The fact that these data provided by victims reflect a stage of the crime-and-response process that precedes the decision whether or not to report to police strengthens confidence in the overall picture of street-level thieves as predominantly juveniles and young adults.

Of all male juveniles who *ever* engage in serious delinquency, most do so infrequently and do not persist at it more than a few months or years. Few are or become chronic offenders. Put differently, the age when they begin committing crime is followed quickly by the age when they cease such activity. Investigators from the University of Pennsylvania used school, police, and court records to examine the delinquency histories of all boys who were born in Philadelphia in 1945 who also resided there from ages 10 to 18. Analysis showed that only 6 percent of the boys and 18 percent of those with a record of delinquency accumulated five or more police contacts before becoming adults.[6] In a subsequent study of all boys born in Philadelphia in 1958, the same investigators found that 7.5 percent of the entire cohort and 23 percent of those with official delinquency records were chronic offenders.[7]

Although they are prime candidates for participation in robbery and theft when they become adults, even most of these chronic delinquents eventually drop out of serious crime. This is one of the principal findings from a study of young thieves in Toronto, Canada. Members of the sample, who ranged in age from 15 to 23 years, were observed and interviewed over a period of four years. The investigator found that they practiced theft for an average of 28 months before most discontinued stealing.[8] Similar findings are reported in a study of young-adult males in three neighborhoods of Brooklyn, New York. Although there were some important differences in crime and delinquency in the three areas, individual involvement in economic crime was similar in all of them:

> [M]ost members . . . moderated their economic crime involvement as they grew older and began to work more steadily. More often than not, they were in the labor market and working by their late teens. Some ceased engaging in economic crime altogether at this point; others shifted to less severe, risky and frequent crime, though this process was much slower in the two poorer neighborhoods.[9]

The overall pattern is clear: By their early to mid-20s, many young chronic offenders cease accumulating serious criminal charges. "Stanley," the street mugger whose early life was chronicled in one of criminology's classic studies, exemplifies those who persist at crime despite repeated confinements only to desist from it later.[10] Stanley first came to the attention of Chicago juvenile court officials at age 10 and later served three terms in the state juvenile training school, a sentence in the state reformatory, and two sentences in the Chicago House of Correction. More persistent than many thieves, Stanley did not stop committing burglary and robbery until age 26.[11]

Careers and Career Variation

The concept *criminal career* figures prominently both in textbook analyses of crime and in public-policy debates over what can and should be done about it. Both the concept and its utility are matters of considerable if arcane scholarly controversy. As the term is used here, criminal careers are patterned changes in offenders' behavior and perspectives during the period bounded by their first and final serious criminal acts.[12] That offenders do change over the course of their criminal careers is beyond question.

One result of sustained involvement in stealing and hustling, for example, is that many offenders develop skill at spotting cash or other "stealables" as opportunities that others remain unaware of:

> An underworld education makes a lot of difference to a man. In every way. Say you're a legitimate businessman and you're taking a ride in an automobile with a man that's a loser, that's been in the rackets for years. Like me. We see a group of men walking down an alley in a steady stream. That means they're going to a temporary book as the regular book on the main street is closed up. But to you it's just people walking down the alley. And we're riding along, I see an attractive young woman stepping out of a big restaurant. It's about one-thirty in the afternoon. She has a thick envelope under her arm and she's walking toward the bank. That doesn't mean anything to you. But to me it means she's bringing money to the bank, I'm gonna get back and check on her, see if she does that every day, it might be worth grabbing. As we ride along for eight or ten blocks, I've seen a half dozen things that are not legitimate and you have seen nothing but the ordinary street scenes. A man that's a thief, whenever he's moving around, will recognize a hundred opportunities to make a dollar.[13]

Sustained participation in crime sensitizes the thief to stimuli and meanings he was unaware of previously. It also causes him to see and appreciate criminal opportunities that do not exist for those without criminal experience.[14] Crime changes the thief's perceptual templates.[15]

The notion that offenders have "careers" in crime is beguiling but potentially misleading. Borrowed from both the world and the analysis of work and occupations, the career concept is an analytic tool. It should not be construed or applied literally.[16] For one thing, not all persistent thieves see or approach crime or their activities as an occupation. And for those who do, there are not the formalized career lines and well-defined career-progression markers that are common in legitimate occupations. Moreover, the criminal careers of most thieves show little evidence of advancement or progression. They "start at the bottom and proceed nowhere."[17] The career concept also suggests a great deal more planning, intentional choice, and persistence than most street-level thieves ever muster. One of the attractions of the criminal-career concept is that it sensitizes us to look for change over the period of offending, the diverse but finitely numbered forms it assumes, and the apparent reasons for it. Questions about the patterning of criminal careers and why they change are at the core of contemporary criminology.

The matter of whether and why desistance from crime eventually occurs is one of the most important of these questions. *Desistance* is the voluntary termination of serious criminal participation. The concept neither builds upon nor requires assumptions that most or any thieves eventually stop committing crime entirely. And the fact that a large proportion of them *do* abandon crime does not mean that the process always is accomplished abruptly and cleanly. Many, particularly those with criminal identities, may reduce the frequency of their offenses but continue committing crime for months or even years:

> I done got a little *softer*, you know. I done got, hey man, to the point, you know, where, like I say, I don't steal, I don't hustle, you know. But I don't pass the opportunity if I can get some free money. I'm not gonna pass. . . . I don't hustle, you know, I don't make it a everyday thing. I don't go out *lookin'* for things, you know.

Perhaps the most visible consequence of age-linked changes is that the average monthly offense rate of men who persist at stealing and hustling decreases as they get older.[18] The rationale for reducing the frequency of their offenses was put clearly by an informant:

> When you're younger, you can . . . steal to pay the rent, you know. Hell, you can go out and steal seven days a week. And sooner [or later] . . . you learn that—to me, it's *exposure time,* you know—you don't want to get "exposed" too much.

It is not an uncommon pattern among men like him as they age that

> they refrain from the repeated commission of felonies of which society is especially intolerant. They discontinue being what *they* believe is a threat to society. However, they often continue to commit some felonies—felonies which they perceive as safe, such as receiving stolen property and marijuana use—and many misdemeanors, such as shoplifting.[19]

Generally, however, thieves shift from the high-visibility and confrontational crimes of their youth to lines of criminal endeavor they judge to be less risky.[20] Armed robbery is the prototypical highly visible, highly confrontational, and risky crime; shoplifting or selling marijuana represents the other extreme. The rationale for this change was described by Michael Preston:

> I caught one number—that 10 years, all them robberies—and then, you know, everything I did then was more like a finesse thing. . . . I'm not gonna stick no pistol in nobody's face, man, you know. I'm not gonna strong-arm nobody, you know. I'm not gonna go in nobody's house. You understand what I'm sayin'? I'm not gonna do that.

Q: You figure as long as you don't do those things you won't go to the penitentiary?
A: Hey, you better believe it.

An imprisoned burglar shared with me his plans after release to devote
more of his time and energies to shoplifting:

> You know, it's funny but there's only a few things that a man goes to the pen-
> itentiary for—burglary or robbery or something like that. But how many
> ways of making money are there that you don't have to revert to robbery or
> burglary? Thousands. I mean [where you're] between being legit and being
> crooked. You're skating on thin ice, and if that ice breaks it's not going to
> break bad. You might get your foot wet, you might get a fine or something.
> What they're [police, prosecutors, courts] really concerned with are these vi-
> olent cases, man, these people who are causing these headlines and stuff. . . .
> If I am going to be a thief I might as well be the one who is skating on that
> thin ice. And a person who is skating on thin ice is less likely to go to the pen-
> itentiary. . . . 'Cause if you get arrested boosting [shoplifting] it is generally a
> fine. If worse comes to worst, you're going to have to do a year in the county
> jail—in some places, nine months.[21]

Another informant, despite a lengthy record of burglary, was incarcerated
for manufacturing illicit drugs when he was interviewed. Shifting to this
new offense because he believed the chances of being arrested for it were
slim, he abandoned burglary but he did not give up crime.

Changing their frequency of offending or their criminal line is not the
only illicit pathway open to aging persistent thieves reluctant or slow to
abandon their criminal ways. Some move into crime-commission roles as
background operators rather than frontline participants.[22] An example is
provided by a youth who was heavily involved in an automobile theft organization:

> [The older guys] showed us the tricks of the trade. Sometimes the old guys
> put the young guys to drive the cars. The old guys already have records. If
> they get caught they know they get in more trouble, they got families or they
> know the consequences are gonna be worse. Now the courts know a young
> fella might have made a mistake, give him a break. Not the older person.
> They don't give you no break.[23]

A burglar-turned-fence commented that he left the penitentiary thinking,
"Damn, I'm tired. I'm going to quit crawling in these fucking windows.
So I quit crawling in windows but, you might say, I had someone else

crawling in windows for me."[24] Instead of playing a direct role in burglaries, those who are older may work to acquire information about worthwhile targets that can be passed along to burglars. Others settle into lives of dereliction and persistent petty offending. Typical is an informant with a history of several prison terms who earns small sums of cash from tending the door at an illicit gambling house and running errands for players. His sleeping arrangements were uncertain, and he spent most days drinking wine and congregating around the fire barrels used for winter warmth by the homeless and others down on their luck. A small proportion of thieves, principally those who have known some success at crime, abandon it only when forced to do so by the infirmities of age.

The proportion of offenders who follow these various pathways is unclear, primarily because the later stages of criminal careers have been neglected by investigators. For the most part, the desistance phenomenon has been approached inferentially. The limited research in this area generally does not extend beyond a focus on recidivism or the *failure to desist* from renewed criminal participation. Whether knowledge about criminal careers might be used to reduce recidivism rates or in other ways modify them and thereby reduce the toll taken by persistent thieves is an important policy issue.

Contingencies and Transitions

One of the keys to understanding criminal-career variation lies in identifying significant *career contingencies.* These are changes in offenders or in their objective circumstances that have the effect of maintaining them on a crime path, of changing their criminal behaviors, or of switching them to noncrime. Understanding significant contingencies in the careers of thieves helps us interpret and explain why, for example, some males have little more than a flirtation with crime while others devote decades to it. The search for contingencies requires no assumptions about the empirical nature or duration of criminal careers, only that some conditions cause a turning away from crime while others cause the opposite.

As persistent thieves get older, two classes of contingencies have significant impacts on their lives and criminal careers: (1) the development of conventional social bonds, activities, and rewards and (2) strengthened resolve and determination to abandon crime entirely or in other ways restrict their criminal participation.

Conventional Bonds, Activities, and Rewards

During World War II, the U.S. armed forces absorbed large numbers of males from the civilian labor force just as the demand for industrial production increased enormously. The nation faced a major labor supply shortage. To meet this need, thousands of American women took factory jobs and helped produce armaments needed for the war effort. Former prison inmates were another source of badly needed manpower. During the years 1940 through 1947, thousands of prisoners were paroled to the military, thereby releasing other citizens for civilian work. In Illinois, for example, 2,942 parolees served in the U.S. Army, and although most of these men were first offenders at the felony level, many were recidivists.[25] In the period 1951–1953, the Illinois Felon Study examined the military and civilian adjustment of the World War II military parolees. Five hundred men living in northern Illinois were located, contacted, and interviewed. Investigators compared the postmilitary situations of those who had put their crime years behind them and the experiences of members of the sample who had relapsed into crime. The greatest difference between the two groups was in the strength and stability of their immediate social environment. Specifically, those who had managed to avoid repetition of their earlier mistakes were found to be employed at work "related to [their] capacities and interests" and to be integrated into "law abiding communities."[26]

A decade later, investigators from the University of Illinois reached similar conclusions after studying 145 men released from federal prisons. The study focused on problems parolees encounter and the conditions and experiences that facilitate or impede successful avoidance of serious criminal conduct. Interview data collected from the men over a period of 3–9 months showed that "releasees who did not return to crime seemed generally to be distinguished by their achievement of economic self-sufficiency and satisfaction in primary group relationships not requiring or encouraging disorderly or criminal activity."[27] These results were confirmed again in Thomas Meisenhelder's interviews with 20 convicted and incarcerated thieves. Although the men were incarcerated, during earlier periods of freedom all had "abandoned criminal behavior for some more or less significant period of time."[28] Research interviews focused on circumstances that produced these periods of albeit temporary desistance. Meisenhelder's analysis showed that successful exiting from crime was contingent upon "acquisition of some type of tie to conformity. Most often this stake or investment in being conventional was actualized when, and if, the respondent obtained what he perceived as a good job. . . . [They] also were able to form positive interpersonal relationships with conventional others."[29] Since Meisenhelder completed his study, confidence in the validity of this finding has been strengthened by statistically refined reanalysis of data collected by Sheldon and Eleanor Glueck in their classic study of the development and persistence of criminal participation in a sample of Boston, Massachusetts, males.[30] Reanalysis of the Gluecks' data caused the investigators to conclude that "job stability and marital attachment in adulthood were significantly related to changes in adult crime—the stronger the adult ties to work and family, the less crime and deviance occurred among both delinquents and controls."[31] In short, successful establishment of bonds with conventional others and participation in conventional activities are major contingencies on the path that leads to termination of a criminal career.[32]

The consequences of these conventional ties and activities are clear and undisputed, but the specific forms they assume vary considerably. The establishment of a mutually satisfying relationship with a woman is one of the most common and experientially important forms:

> When I reached the age of 35 it just seemed like my life wanted to change. I needed a change in life, and I was tired of going to jail. I wanted to change my life and stay out here. And by meeting the woman that I met it just turned my life completely around. . . . When I met her it just seemed like something in my life had been fulfilled.

An informant who still engaged occasionally in "light hustling" told why, at an earlier time in his life, he had stopped committing crimes entirely:

> I started living with this woman, you know, and my life suddenly changed. . . . I was contented, you know, bein' with her. . . . I cared about her, you know. I wanted to be with her, you know. That was it. . . . And, hey, I just found enjoyment there.

Interviewed more than 10 years after his final arrest, a man who had traveled the circuit from juvenile crime and confinement to many years in the penitentiary pointed to his spouse's influence on him during earlier periods of unemployment and stress:

> I loved my wife—I love her still—and she talked to me a lot. . . . And if it wouldn't been for her, no tellin' where I'd be at, 'cause I'd most likely had a gun in my hand and robbed a bank or something. Or took something from somebody to get some food, you know. . . . She helped me along.

Immersion and successful involvement in any of several legitimate activities can function much like establishment of a close relationship with another person. Religious experiences and the attendant close social relationships resulting from them are an example.[33] An informant who earned a baccalaureate degree following his final parole told how the experience affected him:

I was learning things I didn't know anything about. And I'm not saying I liked all of it, you know, but I worked at it. And I think for the first three quarters I had a 4.0, and that made me feel good, the whole self-concept, you know, kind of thing. . . . Plus, some of the classes I really enjoyed. . . . And so I kind of got into it. I liked it.

For many, however, it is acquisition of a satisfying job, alone or combined with other experiences, that has a significant conventionalizing influence on their lives. An informant recalled, for example, nearly two decades earlier when he secured employment with a beauty and barber supply company: "The guy liked me from the jump. And that's when I hooked up with him. And I went straight a long time *without the intentions of going straight.* . . . That was one turning point in the later part of my life." Not all types of employment are equally likely to moderate offenders' criminal involvement, but there is little surprise about the kinds that do. They return a decent income, enable the individual to exercise intelligence and creativity, and allow for some autonomy in structuring the day's activities.[34] Of course, staggeringly few jobs of this type in the legitimate economy are available to men who persist at stealing and hustling for any length of time.

Why are conventional bonds and employment important career contingencies for persistent thieves? They offer a secure social niche and a source of support during what can be a rocky passage to a life without serious crime.[35] They provide both a reason to change and "social capital" for doing so.[36] The result can be a pattern of routine activities—a daily agenda—that conflicts with and leaves little time for the daily activities associated with crime. I asked an informant if his former associates ridiculed him after he "squared up."

No. See, I spent very little time with these people anyway. By me working during the week, I might see them on the weekend. . . . Everybody knew that I was a bricklayer, that I was making good money, and that I didn't have to [commit crimes].

Stable employment and supportive social relationships with noncriminals also provide legitimate rewards:

Through [his girlfriend] I met a whole lot of straight people, you know, that I enjoyed bein' around, you know. Like her people, her parents, her sisters and brother, you know, her mother. I enjoyed bein' around them. And they was straight, you know, never been incarcerated, never been affiliated with the law, and shit like that. I enjoyed bein' around them, because they did some things—like, we played cards, played little games, you know. I like sports, you know; we'd sit down and talk about sports, and do things of that nature.

Even as they leave little time for contact with former or potential crime partners, such experiences reinforce a noncriminal identity. A former heroin addict told me,

> [At] one time, man, I used to come down the street, right? All right, dudes run to me and hold conversation, you know. "Hey, John," so and so. They gonna talk about something. . . . At one time we could always, they'd see me and they'd talk about what, you know, happened the night before, or what party, or what crap joint we'd been in. But now, man, all they do is speak, because like we don't be together. We don't go to the crap games. We don't be with the hos and shit together.

The importance of integration in conventional social circles can be appreciated particularly by considering how its absence exacerbates ex-offenders' problems and leaves them with too much time on their hands. Failure to secure family and neighborhood acceptance by paroled thieves contributes to

> the reorientation of their behavior around a new view of themselves as disillusioned, baffled, and defeated men. Such a sense of defeat tended to initiate a process of personal demoralization . . . and . . . progressive withdrawal from their already attenuated conventional ties. They now had little choice but to consort with others of similar background. . . . Once such ties were formed, however, contingencies were likely to arise in which they were subject to procriminal pressures.[37]

Success at conventional pursuits by contrast strengthens prosocial identities and enables ex-offenders to avoid or resist criminal forces. Moreover, when aging men are tempted to revert to crime, fear of the negative consequences for their relationships with family and friends should they be arrested weighs heavily in their deliberations.[38]

Despite apparent or even abundant opportunity, however, many men are unsuccessful securing employment or at creating close ties with conventional others. The fact is that regardless of age or past experience, not all appreciate or make effective use of whatever opportunities are available to them. When they are young, most persistent thieves try their hand at legitimate employment for varying periods of time. When they get older, they often acknowledge and lament that they held potentially rewarding and satisfying jobs earlier in their lives but could not see or appreciate this at the time. As a youth, one informant secured work at the U.S. Government Printing Office, where an older employee wanted to teach him how to mix and to use inks: "I said to myself [that] I didn't even want to be there. As much as possible, I went into the men's restroom and went to sleep. . . . I was glad to get out of there when it was time to get off, and I wound up resigning the job." With the benefit of hindsight, he said that it was a good opportunity, one that he squandered.

The experiences of persistent thieves with women and others are similar to their experiences in the world of employment. From adolescence onward, most have close involvements with girlfriends, lovers, or spouses. For young thieves, these often are exploitative relationships of convenience and not important influences on their behavior.[39] Just as they do when recounting youthful error in failing to appreciate and exploit the payoffs from legitimate employment, retrospective acknowledgment of their failings in and responsibility for earlier, failed relationships with women is common:

> I remember one time, man, if a broad couldn't get no money—I'm gonna show you how stupid people used to think—if a girl couldn't get no money, you know, or wasn't sellin' no pussy, bringin' me some money, hey man, she couldn't have me. Isn't that a hell of a thing for a motherfucker to say, "she couldn't have me"?

In much the same way, the meaning of family ties also changes as many offenders get older:

> I have a daughter-in-law [and] a pretty fair son. He's never been arrested. I think I owe, I have a debt, you know, owe these people a debt, you know. . . . I feel that I should be dedicated to try to erase some of this bullshit that's been, . . . what you call it? Negative thinking.

Successful creation of bonds with conventional others and lines of legitimate activity indisputably is the most important contingency that causes men to alter or terminate their criminal careers. At all ages and potential turning points, those who fail to secure satisfying employment or to create bonds with conventional others often return to their former lifestyles and the risk of criminal involvement this brings.[40] Failure at early stages of their criminal careers does not condemn them irretrievably to a life of crime, however. Other contingencies, the probable occurrence of which increases with age and the lessons learned from hard experience, also increase the odds that offenders will turn away from or change their criminal careers. These contingencies reshape offenders' orientational stance not only toward crime but also toward a range of everyday situations and problems. In doing so, these orientational contingencies strengthen their resolve and determination to behave differently.

Resolve and Determination

Whereas establishing conventional social bonds and becoming involved in legitimate experiences are objective changes in offenders' lives that function to pull men away from deviant lifestyles and crime, other, subjective contingencies function principally to weaken the attractions of crime.[41] These subjective contingencies can occur at any age, but conditions are favorable particularly as offenders reach their late 30s and early 40s. Regardless of when they occur, however, they cause thieves to modify their assessment of the likely consequences of continued criminal participation and to resolve to avoid repeating the mistakes of the past.

A follow-up study of thieves released from nine English prisons is instructive. One of the principal objectives of the research was to learn what distinguishes former prisoners who do not commit new crimes from those who do. The investigators began by identifying from prison records a group of 130 male property offenders, aged 21 to 45. The men in the sample had from 3 to 14 previous criminal convictions, and 81 percent had served one or more previous prison sentences. The group, in short, was composed of persistent thieves. Each man was interviewed for the first time shortly before his prison discharge date, 90 men were interviewed a second time 1–6 months after release, and 67 men were interviewed again 7–20 months after release. In addition to the finding, which was not unexpected, that one of the most important reasons some of the former prisoners were able to turn away from a life of crime was establishment of strong family or interpersonal ties with conventional others, the investigators found that

> [m]ore of those who desisted stated unequivocally at both the pre-release and post-release stages that they wanted to desist. The persisters were increasingly more likely, across the three interviews, to express reservations about giving up crime. . . . And [the former] were increasingly more likely to express confidence in their ability to "go straight," while persisters were more likely to be either equivocal or dubious.[42]

To a substantial degree, men who are most determined to avoid crime are more successful doing so than their equivocating peers, even allowing for the possible influence of other factors.

Orientational, resolve-enhancing contingencies are produced by both advancing age and by the crime and confinement experiences of persistent thieves. To begin, there is evidence that aging increases offenders' interest in employment and in supportive and satisfying social relationships. Just as important, aging improves their ability and inclination simply to calculate more precisely and carefully the results of past and prospective criminal involvement. Aging, with its accumulating stock of experience, makes men less audacious and more capable of acting rationally.[43] Three additional social-psychological contingencies that often accompany aging cause men to turn away from crime: (1) a new perspective on the self; (2) a growing awareness of time; and (3) changes in aspirations and goals.

As they get older, persistent thieves and hustlers develop and employ a critical, detached perspective toward their earlier years, their youthful behavior, and the personal identity they believed it exemplifies. They gain a vantage point from which they can view and critique their youthful behavior and self. What they experience is nothing less than development of a separate, evaluative, judgmental perspective:

> I saw myself for what I really was. I saw what I was. I saw it. With my own eyes I saw myself. I could see it just as plain as I'm looking at you now. And I know that what I looked at was a sorry picture of a human being. . . . I was a self-made bastard, really.

A former English thief described a similar experience:

> I realized that the thoughts that were going through my mind were the thoughts of another person, and I began to look inwards at myself. I began to see the change that was taking place in me. . . . It was as if I was looking at someone I had known, someone who had been a habitual criminal.[44]

Parenthetically, acquisition of an altered perspective on their youthful self and activities can make it difficult for ex-offenders to answer questions without first qualifying their answers. Asked, for example, if there was anything he could recall that he liked about doing time, an informant responded by saying,

> Maybe I did. There's some things I might've liked, because I got a lot of recognition. I was, you know, accepted. Maybe I liked that part about it . . . but, see, I'm tryin' to put two things together. In my thinking *now*, I can't see *nothing* that I can say I enjoyed. But probably then I did.

Another man echoed these comments:

> In retrospect I would say I wasted [my earlier years]. But during that time I thought that, for me, it was productive. But now I can look back and say it's

wasted, 'cause all I gained from those years is experience and knowledge on how not to act no more, you know, how to keep out of trouble. But during that particular time, anything somebody say, boom, I'm ready to go, you know.

Employing their new perspective, aging offenders gradually come to see their youthful self as "foolish" or "dumb":

Hey man, everybody got the nature to want to live good, you know, a desire to live good. And I thought that was the best way to do it, you know, by stealing, you know. I could get things that I ordinarily couldn't get by working. But, man, now I don't look at it that way. I think I was stupid.

This new perspective symbolizes a watershed in their lives. They decide that their earlier identity and behavior are of limited value for constructing the future.

Some men are bedeviled by an inability to account for this change, but others point to several experiences that they believe facilitated its eventual arrival: "I was making comparisons between myself and those who was around me. You see, it's like looking in a looking glass when you see someone else like you. And I had a whole lot of them around that was like me." Others speak, sometimes poignantly, of the availability of dead time in prison as a vehicle they utilized to construct this new perspective.[45] A former dope fiend said,

I had a lot of time to think. Every time you go to jail—all right, all day long I'm running around playing with dudes—but think about them nights, man. I'd be in them cells, I got to be by myself and can't go to sleep. I got to think, and if you sit down and think enough, something's going to come to you. . . . First thing, you going to start trying to figure out things.

The aging process of persistent hustlers and thieves, then, includes a redefinition of their youthful criminal identity as self-defeating, foolish, or stupid.

In addition, persistent thieves as they get older eventually become acutely aware of time as a diminishing, exhaustible resource. As one man said, "I did not observe the value of time until I was damn near 46 or 47 years old." After achieving this new perspective, he began constructing plans for how to use the remainder of his life. The future now becomes increasingly valuable, and the possibility of spending additional time in prison especially threatening. A thrice-imprisoned parolee said he did not want to serve any more time. Asked if he was "afraid of doing time now," he replied,

No, I'm not really afraid of it. I don't know, I just don't want to do it. . . . It's just knocking time out of my life.

Q: Are you trying to say that the years you have left are more precious to you?

A: True. And they're a lot more precious to me than when I was 25 or 30. . . . I guess you get to the point where you think, well . . . you're getting old, you're getting ready to die and you've never really lived, or something. You don't want to spend it in the joint, treading water.

Similar comments were made by a man who was interviewed in prison:

I'm older [now] and I don't have much time. I guess you start looking at how much time you have left, and what to do with that time. . . . I'm 42 now. I got 20 years left and I'm sitting here doing this dead time, you know, nothing out of my life but dead time. . . . Every year that goes by, it seems like it's quicker, you know. Life, before you're 21 it seems like it's forever, before you turn 21. And after you do, time seems like it's flying by.

Increasingly aware now that the remaining years of their lives are passing, aging men dread receiving a long prison sentence even as they fear that, because of their previous convictions, any prison term they might receive will be lengthy. Not only would this subject them to the usual deprivations, but it would expropriate their few remaining, potentially productive years. They fear losing their last remaining opportunity to accomplish something and to prepare financially for old age. Michael Preston said he did not want to spend any more time in prison because "when I come out of there, that's *it*." Asked what he meant, Michael replied:

I'd be old, you know. . . . The whole world be done passed me by, man. . . . Hey, I'm 47, you know. And if I get one of them big numbers [long sentences] now, hey, I'm through bookin', you know. I'm through bookin'. . . . One of them big numbers, man, would do me in, you know. And I could not stand it.

The growing awareness of time as a limited resource intensifies fears of dying inside prison:

Man, the time, I didn't pay no attention to time [when I was younger]. They give me time, man, I just went in there and did the time and come on right out. And man, didn't give it no thought. I'd go right back and [commit crime]. . . . [Now] I'm gettin' older. Hey man, I ain't *got* to make it. See what I'm saying?

Q: No, I don't know what you mean. You "haven't got to make it."
A: I'm gettin' *older!*. . . As a young man I had a better chance of livin' and gettin' out. . . . I've seen dudes die in the penitentiary. . . . I don't know what
it is, something make me think about things like that now.

Aging thieves often lower their aspirations and goals, and this too reduces the attractiveness of crime. Eventually they no longer feel they
want or need to strive for the same level of material fulfillment and recognition they sought when younger. An ex-offender noted:

I've got to a point where things that were important to me twelve, fifteen
years ago aren't important now. I used to have a lot of ambitions, like everybody else has—different business ventures, stuff like that. But today, why,
with what I have to buck up against, why, I could be just as happy and just
as satisfied with a job that I'm getting by on, where I knew I wasn't going to
run into trouble or anything.[46]

And a 46-year-old former heroin addict who served three prison sentences expressed a similar view:

Hey man, . . . I like fine things, you know. I'd like to have me a nice automobile and—see, I don't have no automobile, man, you know. At one time I
used to dress, man I used to love fine clothes and things, you know. I don't
have that shit no more. . . . It's not going to worry me . . . because me
throwin' bricks at the penitentiary to obtain this? I'll never have it.[47]

Just as important, aging men revise their aspirations. Times spent partying and carousing now can seem tiresome or even irritating. These men
begin assigning higher priority to goals that formerly were less important:

The things I like to do, they don't require having a million dollars. I like to
do things, I like to walk. Many times, down by the Tidal Basin, Jefferson
Memorial, I see people walking. I see people out there fishing. These are
things I like to do. . . . Just like the song says, "the best things in life are free."

An interest in such things as "contentment," "peace," and harmonious interpersonal relationships becomes more important to them:

I've thought about having a lot of things tangible. But I know these things
will not really make me happy. . . . I've been over in Crystal City . . . a coupla
days in the past week. You look at those structures [buildings], and they are
very beautiful, you know. But . . . what is it if people are not at peace with
themselves?

Referring to his earlier participation in crime and also to the years he spent in some of America's most backward and brutal prisons, a 56-year-old man said:

> I don't want to live that kind of life no more. I want peace. I want joy and har-mony. I want to be with my children and my grandchildren. I got a bunch of grandkids, and I want to be with them. I want to be with my mother. And when she passes on—I was in prison when my daddy died, I got to come home for five hours in handcuffs to see him—and when my mother passes on, I want to be there with her.

This man's newly kindled interest in family members is not unique. Others experience similar sentiments, which develop only as they approach or attain middle age. Released from prison in their 30s or early 40s, men such as this experience a heightened sense of urgency about securing gainful employment:

> It's a little late in life to accomplish something now. About the only thing I can hope for now is that I'll be able to get a little social security built up. And try to get something saved up for old age.
> Q: Do you feel like life's passed you by?
> A: No, I don't feel like it's passed. But I'm feeling like it's catching up with me awful quick, and I haven't got anything to show for it.

Consider too the remarks of an imprisoned thief:

> I've had some good jobs in my life, but I could never get one again. I'm get-ting too old now. When I was a kid, I had some real good jobs, but if I could get a good job with a future to it, I'd probably square up. But now when I get out, I'm going to be forty years old—I'm thirty-seven now—and when I get out, I can't wander around from filling station to filling station. I've got to get out and make me some money.[48]

Those who manage to find secure legitimate work begin to appreciate the advantages of a job with benefits such as sick leave and a pension. A former Alcatraz prisoner, employed as a packer for a large moving company, told how much he enjoyed the challenge of designing and constructing ship-ping containers for unusual or custom items. He went on to say:

> I'm satisfied now, you know. There ain't nobody can get me to do nothin' [commit a crime]. Not now. Not the way I'm goin' now. . . . Every year I go away on vacation. I got three weeks now. Next year I get four weeks. Yeah, so I'm happy, you know, right now.

Those who continue their criminal activities often are content with committing less hazardous offenses, even if this means accepting smaller economic rewards.

One of the most interesting and important aspects of these changes reported by aging thieves is that they bear a striking resemblance to age-related changes reported by nonoffenders. Development of an evaluative perspective on the self certainly is not confined to aging offenders. Many aging nonoffenders also develop a detached, sometimes wistful, perspective toward their youth. Bernice Neugarten's research on a sample of males from the general population showed that they consistently changed their time orientation as they aged, restructuring life in terms of time-left-to-live rather than time-since-birth.[49] Her subjects also developed a new perspective on the self as they got older. Findings from a study of middle-aged males are consistent with the experiences of aging offenders. As they got older, the men became increasingly introspective. They began unmasking illusions about themselves and evaluating their lives in terms of relative success or failure. Increasingly, they became future oriented and thought about the inevitability and approach of death.[50] Aging, in sum, appears to increase the odds that a number of subjective contingencies will occur and dampen the criminal proclivities of persistent thieves.

There is more to the process of increasing resolve than the changes caused by aging. Other social-psychological changes aging thieves experience seem peculiar to men like them who have devoted substantial interest and time to crime and imprisonment. Sustained involvement in criminal activity and the jail and prison terms that typically follow demand much of the offender. One obviously must live with the fear of arrest and long-term confinement, but there are other problems as well. The commission of some crimes exposes one to the risk of serious personal injury or death. One also must deal routinely with other people who may prove unreliable or treacherous for one reason or another. Persons who are known as thieves or hustlers, for example, frequently are targets of the criminal designs of others. This necessitates constant vigilance. Duplicitous and predatory conduct by those who know or assume that one earns money illicitly is extremely common:

> At the gambling houses [Jake] knew all sorts of people. Show people, gamblers, criminals and even guys on the legit . . . [He] would go to a gambling place and if he saw someone there that he was sure would be good for a nice haul, he'd call me at my room and tell me where the guy lived. I'd hurry over there and break in. If the guy left the gambling house, Jake would call me at the place I was prowling and I'd get out fast. Most of these people were "sports" and they usually kept quite a bit of cash around their apartments.[51]

Added to the risk of victimization by other predators is the fact that acquaintances may talk too much or to the wrong people:

> Anxious to the point of imbecility that he shall be given full credit for his accomplishments, [a thief's friends] will mention his name in connexion with some crime. Their intent is to show his cleverness. Their accomplishment is to show the police the way to him.[52]

If arrested, crime partners may bargain with the prosecutor, giving up others in return for more lenient treatment. Over a long period of time, contending with all these problems takes its toll on offenders: "[Y]ou get tired. You get tired trying to be a tough guy all the time. People always expecting this and that."[53] Asked why he had abandoned crime, an informant answered succinctly: "Being tired, you know. Just collapsing, that's all. I'd say age made me weak, made me tired, you know. That's all."

With the benefit of experience, some offenders develop a detached analytic view of the entire criminal justice system.[54] They come to see it as an apparatus that clumsily but relentlessly engorges offenders and wears them down:

> [A]t 8 a.m. [on the day of my release], one of my keepers yelled, "McGregor, get your shit and get out, we need your cell." "What the hell do you need my cell for?" I cracked. "It's just like the other twenty-two hundred here." The "answer" was standing right outside my bars, wearing oversized coarse prison grays and a scared-to-death expression. I said hello to the new nigger waiting to take my place. . . . I could see the young brother's eyes jump with the same kind of hatred that used to keep my ass in the box, so I spoke to him, man-to-man. . . . "I ain't even gone yet, and already they got you to take my place. . . . It's taken me twenty-seven years of jailin' to learn that I am needed to do more than fill a shitbowl in some damn institution."[55]

A 57-year-old informant said that he never committed and would never again attempt the big score. Asked why he had given up this dream, he said, "Because I know how the system is. . . . The system is bigger than me." Similarly, another man said, "I got tired of doing time for little small things and serving such a long period of time. I got tired."

It is clear that aging offenders begin to experience the criminal justice process, especially imprisonment, as an imposing, irksome accumulation of aggravations and deprivations. They grow tired of the problems and consequences of criminal involvement: "I really don't know why I went straight. I just decided that after I got out. It wasn't fear of the law, it isn't fear of the penitentiary, 'cause I've sat down and thought it out very seriously, but I just had enough of it, that's all."[56] The lesson learned belatedly by these men is that they have been "swaggering in defiance of a machine that isn't paying the slightest attention, its meter simply adding the years, implacably."[57]

Occurrence of one or more of the four subjective contingencies I have discussed is consequential for thieves because it makes them increasingly ready and determined to "give something else a try." Now there is an interest in, a readiness for, and the resolve to make fundamental changes in their lives:

> All I want to do is just be happy and, you know, be content. Try to stay in the street, you know, try to get me a job. 'Cause I know—[age] 51—I ain't got too much longer to be here. I hope I'll be here until my hair gets white as this paper. But I know, at 51, I can't be runnin' in an' out of those penitentiaries.

At this point the offender experiences, simultaneously, a sense of liberation and apprehension—the former because it signals a break with the past, the latter because many subjects remain uncertain whether they can construct a satisfying life free of criminal involvement. The greater their resolve, the better their chance of success.

Desistance as Choice

Until recently, there was surprisingly little research on criminal careers and even less interest in theoretical explanations for career change. The explanations that were offered were for the most part conceptually imprecise and theoretically crude. *Maturation*, for example, was pointed to as the cause of desistance, although the meaning of this was not specified. The vagueness led one observer to note that this is "one of the—unhappily not infrequent—occasions on which a label has been mistaken for an explanation."[58]

The shortcomings of the maturation explanation cannot obscure the fact that some age-related biopsychosocial factors surely contribute to crime desistance as offenders get older.[59] I have suggested that aging makes offenders more interested in the rewards of conventional lifestyles and also more rational in decisionmaking. It makes them "less audacious" and therefore less interested in crime and other high-risk pursuits.[60] Biological, psychological, and social changes that accompany the aging process are only part of the reason men turn away from direct-contact property crime, however. It is equally clear that experiences unique to men who have devoted years to theft and other forms of crime play an important part in the process.

Analysis of data from his study of federal parolees led Daniel Glaser to conclude that for most offenders shifts from noncrime to crime or vice versa are determined largely by the expected payoffs. In a nutshell, when the expected payoffs from legitimate behavior exceed those expected from criminal behavior, men are more likely to choose law-abiding conduct. Expectations in turn are influenced by the degree of success one has enjoyed at straight and criminal pursuits in the past. To the extent offenders meet with self-defined success from crime, they will be optimistic about the potential payoffs from continued criminal participation and will be unlikely to desist; to the extent they meet with failure from crime, they will be unlikely to expect a reversal of this pattern and will be more likely to desist. Logically, this explanation is consistent with the fundamental assumptions of crime-as-choice theories.

In the metric of thieves and hustlers, those who earn well from crime while serving little time in prison are successful.[61] Despite whatever short-term monetary success they may enjoy, however, very few street offenders attain long-lasting financial success illegally. Instead nearly all the money they earn from crime is dissipated quickly on life as party. Their performance avoiding imprisonment is no better: Aging and criminal experience do not improve their odds of avoiding conviction and confinement. For the overwhelming majority of street offenders, then, extended involvement in crime brings only penury interspersed with modest criminal gains that are depleted quickly in sprees of partying, and repeated imprisonment.[62] This is the most important reason persistent thieves eventually lose confidence in prospects for achieving success by committing street crimes.[63] Repeated failure causes most eventually to see that the expected monetary returns from criminal involvement are paltry, both in relative and in absolute terms. "It was only with encroaching middle age . . . that Honk began to understand how small a stage he had played on, and how fleeting were its rewards."[64] Men like him also assume that any future prison sentence they receive, given the length of their previous criminal record, will be long. In sum, as offenders age, their expectations of the potential outcome of criminal acts change. Their perception of the odds narrows, and the perceived risks of criminal behavior loom larger.[65] Little wonder, then, that Robert Timmons, who had spent more than one-half of his life in institutions, expressed this view:

> I realized that, even though in crime, even though you might get away, let's say 99 times, the one time eliminates your future. You don't have no future. Regardless of what you have gained, you lost all of that. A rabbit can escape 99 times and it only takes one shot to kill him. So, I was a rabbit. . . . I want to enjoy life. But I know I can't do it successfully by committing crimes.

Another offender noted:

> [Y]ou get to thinking as you get older, you get wiser. You get to thinking there's no percentage in stealing because you can't constantly keep it up without getting caught and if you get caught, you're back in the penitentiary. And who wants to go back for five more years?... [N]ow no amount of money is worth my freedom because too many things can happen, plus you're losing all the luxury of being free. You're locked up.[66]

This does not mean that men cease *thinking* about crime altogether, only that they develop a more complex set of reasons for avoiding it in most situations.[67] However, in more advantageous circumstances, some believe they still are capable of resorting to crime:

> Now, I'm not going to tell you that if you put $100,000 on that table and I saw an opportunity, that I felt that I could get away with it, that I wouldn't try to move it. But there's no way, even now, there's no way that I would endanger my freedom for a measly four, five, ten thousand dollars. I make that much a year now, you know. And I see the time that I wasted—well, I figure I wasted four or five years when I was younger.
> Q: What do you mean, you "wasted" it?
> A: In and out of jail.

The fact that the criminal calculus changes with age helps explain why crime countermeasures that work quite well with older men are much less likely be effective with adolescents or with young adults.

What is true of most offenders' criminal performance is also true of their past performance in legitimate roles and employment: The degree of success they have known in the past determines their estimates of the likely payoff from more of the same. Most street offenders, however, have known little success in the legitimate work world, in part because it is difficult to manage sustained criminal involvement and the demands of a 40-hour workweek. Confinement further expropriates their young, energetic years and leaves them ill-prepared and demographically mismatched for many conventional occupations and career timetables. Coupled with their working-class backgrounds and employment experiences, this development causes most street offenders eventually to scale down their legitimate expectations to less ambitious levels. Growing disenchantment with criminal life leads to alternative, noncriminal lifestyles becoming increasingly apparent and attractive to street offenders as they get older. This does not mean, however, that the *expected* rewards of noncrime increase, since aging offenders come to have a very accurate assessment of their legitimate prospects. Prospects can be bleak particularly for those who spend many years in prison. Too late they see how repeated confinement severely constrains their prospects for a successful and rewarding straight life. Most do see this, even if it occurs too late for them to regain and find success on the straight pathway.

As they get older, men who have failed to desist from direct-contact property crime are likely at some point to take stock of their lives and their accomplishments. In the process, most confront the realization that crime has been an unproductive enterprise and that this situation is unlikely to change. In short, they realize that direct-contact theft is a dead end:

> I was thinking about it not too long ago. And it seems like you reach a certain age, and you look back, and it seems like all your life you were chasing that pot of gold at the end of the rainbow. And you reach a certain age, and when you look back, there ain't no pot of gold, really. And the *rainbow* is gone. And then where to from here?

This growing disenchantment with the criminal life causes offenders to lower their expectations for achieving success via criminal means. The allure of crime diminishes substantially as they get older:

> The impetus to think seriously about [desistance] seems to come in many cases from a gradual disenchantment with the criminal life in its totality: the inability to trust people; the frequent harassment by the police; the effects on wives and children when the offender is in prison; and [other hassles]. As people grow older such a process can become more painful and depressing and the optimistic outlook can give way to a feeling of being caught in a trap.[68]

No one seriously disputes the contribution that the risk of arrest and imprisonment makes to offenders' estimates of the likely consequences of and payoff from further criminal participation.[69] As noted by Cusson and Pinsonneault, "it is clear that, with age, criminals raise their estimates of the certainty of punishment."[70] Fear of reimprisonment was the "primary motive" of self-defined desisters in Thomas Meisenhelder's sample of imprisoned thieves.[71] Paul Cromwell and his colleagues stated that "for most of the desisters we interviewed, . . . the final decision to terminate a criminal lifestyle was primarily the result of their increasing fear of punishment."[72] The point was affirmed in a 1992 British study of 130 paroled thieves. The investigators reported that "a wish to avoid imprisonment and its ramifications was the most frequently mentioned reason for wanting to 'go straight,'"[73] and one of the explanations most frequently given for desisting was "to avoid another term of imprisonment."[74] It would be a mistake, however, to interpret this phenomenon as fear alone because most men who have been incarcerated have learned they can do time without the experience breaking them. Instead, it is growing realization of the futility of time spent in prison.

It is important to reiterate that just because most offenders eventually desist from direct-contact property crime is not to say that all do. I noted earlier that thieves who have enjoyed success are less likely than their unsuccessful peers to abandon crime until the infirmities of old age cause an involuntary retirement. Moreover, they also have internalized subcultural definitions of their criminality that blunt feelings of shame or guilt about their theft. Nor is it to say that they or any persistent thieves ever become indistinguishable from their fellow citizens who lack experience with crime and punishment. For many years, if not perhaps for the remainder of their lives, some will remain aware of and feel different from their peers. For these men,

> as years go by the criminal identity does not disappear but submerges to a latency stage. As it submerges, deviant activities which are common among criminal ex-convicts, even those who have straightened up their hand, subside. . . . This final latency stage of the criminal career is still quite different from "reformed" as conceived by penologists, sociologists, and the public at large. For instance, there is no denial of, or regret for, the past. In fact, [for some] the past criminal life is looked back upon with pleasure and excitement.[75]

Men such as these, who often insist they have not and never will "square up," are men who devoted most of their adult years to crime and also enjoyed a measure of success at it. Long past the point when they have stopped "working," they claim, "Why should I fool myself? I can still be tempted." Another group of ex-offenders, those who manage to overcome the handicaps of years spent in crime and prison, in fact may come to see them as a blessing. They believe it did little permanent damage. A twice-imprisoned informant said:

> Well see, the idea sticks out in my mind that it took what happened, it was necessary for what happened to me to get to where I am at now, you know. With the outlook I have. And so, if I regret that—what happened—you understand, then I regret being where I'm at. And that might be an academic thought, but I don't feel that it was a great loss, you know.

This man is one of the exceptional and fortunate few. Others will nurse deep regrets over the years they spent in crime and in penal institutions, particularly if they fail to achieve stability and happiness after putting these experiences behind them. Often they compare themselves with siblings or other contemporaries who pursued more conventional lives and who have supportive family ties and a measure of material comfort. Reflecting on the costs of 17 years spent in various penal institutions, a thief, dope fiend, and alcoholic noted:

> I'd like my life to be better. . . . It just seems that I missed so darn much growing up. One thing I missed is the work ethic. That's a handicap now, a real handicap. I don't generally go after something like people do. They work hard. They buy their little toys, their little campers and boats, and it just seems I'll never have it like that. I know it's material things, but it means that person is adult whoever owns it. He's adult and he's worked hard for it. It means more than he just has it. I see the person with things like that and I think, Why can't I be like that? No, it can't be. It's been so long I've been out of it.[76]

An informant who was living in public housing when I interviewed him said:

> Hey man, I just look at how successful and things that my brothers and sisters have been. And I thought at one time that I was really, you know, the one that was gonna be successful. Because I was gettin' the money. . . . Hey man, at one time I thought I was sure enough slick. . . . [But] I think I was stupid, man, because I give up all them years, you know, and I didn't get nothin', man.

The result can be a deep sense of futility and despair, as exemplified in the words of a middle-aged British thief:

> Looking back on my life, I suppose my ambitions were too fast for the normal ways of making money. I took what I thought was the easiest way and it's turned out to be the hardest really. If I'd had an honest job I don't think I'd have earned the money I've earned, but then I wouldn't have had the aggravation to put up with, like prison and all that. I wouldn't be as grey and bald-headed as I am. I've got nothing in the future really.[77]

Harry King, a career burglar who spent many years in prison, took his life after failing to find a place for himself in the straight world.[78] Certainly he is not the only aging persistent but unsuccessful thief who has done so.

Career Change as Interaction

Regardless of how or when offenders' criminal careers end, and despite the individualistic bias and tone of the foregoing description, the change process, like the process of juvenile involvement in crime, is a social and interactional one. It is something that each generation of persistent thieves "works out" in their experiences and contacts with one another.

To young men, the criminal life can be glamorous, appealing, and deceptively enjoyable. Some are captivated by its allure and the self-indulgent lifestyles that surround it. They identify with the criminal life and are confident they can succeed at criminal pursuits. Employing the standards of the street corner and the underworld, they want to succeed on its terms and to be recognized as a success by their criminal peers. When they are incarcerated, as most eventually will be, they are surrounded by others of similar age and aspirations. Those who may have doubts about the wisdom of the criminal path are reluctant to acknowledge this openly. Instead, convicts collectively maintain their resolve and a public faith that their setbacks are only temporary. Invariably, as will be discussed in Chapter 6, they exaggerate the ease of reversing their criminal fortunes. Nevertheless, most weather their initial penitentiary experience reasonably well, with their dreams intact or even strengthened.

Young men pay little attention to the few older men they encounter during their early years in prison. Occasionally, however, older convicts seek out their younger peers:

> Getting older in the penitentiary, you get a good chance to try to rectify some of the mistakes that you've made, man. You see a young guy, you know he's going down the wrong path. I mean, you sit down and talk to him, especially if they like you. . . . And you can sit a guy down and tell him, . . . go on and tell him how foolish you was and things. If he make the mistake, then he make it. But as a person, you've done your duty to him, that young guy. Because I definitely wouldn't want to see any young guy go through life as I have gone through.

Young men ignore these efforts by older convicts to present a less optimistic picture of the criminal life:

> No matter how you try to help some of the younger [inmates], they have this dream, that we may have had at one time in our lifetime, that they're smarter and wiser, and to hell with this old man, and so forth or so on. And when you try to help, to pull their coats to things, they'll tell you to kiss their butt, or so forth and so on.

Surely, the "youngsters" believe, the hard experiences of the older men contain no worthwhile lessons for them. The writer and ex-convict Malcolm Braly described a man he met in the Nevada state prison when he was young and his reactions to the man:

> Elmer . . . had served over thirty years in one institution or another . . . and I
> never doubted, though he still talked hopefully, he would serve thirty more.
> I came to know many like Elmer, but the time when I would compare them
> to myself was still far in the future.[79]

As men fail at crime and begin seriously to take stock of their lives and accomplishments, the standards and norms of thieves and hustlers gradually lose their appeal. They recall the warnings of older men, perhaps offered years earlier, not to be fooled by the apparent ease of committing crime successfully. As they get older and this process continues, the desire or need to demonstrate competence and success in the world of thieves and hustlers also becomes less important to them. As he began to change his perspectives, an English thief wrote that "[I] no longer felt anxious to prove that I was a pro, or that my form was respected and that I was somebody to be looked up to because I knew my way around."[80]

Older men find it less important than previously to show that they can stand up to the prison experience in the subculturally required fashion. Whereas younger men may feel compelled to demonstrate that they can do time and still maintain resolve to live life their way, with the crime that can be an integral part of this, older men begin to feel released from this obligation:

> When I was younger, I felt it was *something* being [in prison]. It really felt like
> that you finally prove yourself in some way. You finally prove your manhood
> in some way, or you finally prove your acceptance by going, doing the bit.
> But now, that is no longer the case. I ain't tryin' to prove myself to do no bit.

Having reached this point in the change process, men begin to acknowledge openly their doubts about crime and the penalties it can bring. Young men often are reluctant to talk openly about their misgivings, but aging offenders lose these reservations. Increasingly, they see and acknowledge their arrogant youthful estimates of the prospects for criminal success and the foolishness of using crime to "get even with" or to command attention from remote, uncaring others. They begin to see and to appreciate similar changes in their convict peers. Interacting with like-minded others reinforces their changing perspectives. They experience a new resolve at least to try an alternative and less risky way of supporting themselves. The degree of success they eventually enjoy varies enormously, but for many it will be marginal at best. Prospects can be bleak particularly for those who have no substantial fiscal or social capital to draw upon, which describes a high proportion of men who have spent many years in prison. "Most of those who stay out of prison are 'successes' in only the narrowest, most bureaucratic meaning of the term *non-recidivism*. Most ex-convicts live menial or derelict lives and many die early of alcoholism or drug use, or by suicide."[81]

Notes

1. Equally striking is the fact that they overwhelmingly are male. Gender variation in crime is beyond the scope of this book, but suffice it to say the reasons for it are an important explanatory problem for criminologists. See, for example, James W. Messerschmidt, *Masculinities and Crime* (Lanham, Md.: Rowman & Littlefield, 1993).

2. This is evident in self-report studies also. See, for example, Alan R. Rowe and Charles R. Tittle, "Life cycle changes and criminal propensity," *Sociological Quarterly* 18(1977), pp. 223–236.

3. Federal Bureau of Investigation, *Crime in the United States, Uniform Crime Reports, 1990* (Washington, D.C.: U.S. Government Printing Office, 1991), p. 184; U.S. Bureau of the Census, *Statistical Abstract of the United States, 1994* (Washington, D.C.: U.S. Government Printing Office, 1994), p. 14.

4. Federal Bureau of Investigation, *Crime in the United States, Uniform Crime Reports, 1990* (Washington, D.C.: U.S. Government Printing Office, 1991), p. 185; U.S. Bureau of the Census, *Statistical Abstract of the United States, 1994* (Washington, D.C.: U.S. Government Printing Office, 1990), p. 14.

5. In robberies committed by multiple offenders, they were of mixed ages. See Bureau of Justice Statistics, *Robbery Victims* (Washington, D.C.: U.S. Department of Justice, 1987).

6. Marvin E. Wolfgang, Robert M. Figlio, and Thorsten Sellin, *Delinquency in a Birth Cohort* (Chicago: University of Chicago Press, 1972).

7. Paul E. Tracy, Marvin E. Wolfgang, and Robert M. Figlio, *Delinquency Careers in Two Birth Cohorts* (New York: Plenum, 1990). These findings are confirmed by similar studies in Racine, Wisconsin. See Lyle D. Shannon, *Criminal Career Continuity* (New York: Human Sciences Press, 1988).

8. W. Gordon West, "The short-term careers of serious thieves," *Canadian Journal of Criminology* 20(1978), pp. 169–190. These findings are supported by ethnographic research in three neighborhoods of Brooklyn, New York. See Mercer L. Sullivan, *"Getting Paid"* (Ithaca, N.Y.: Cornell University Press, 1989).

9. Mercer L. Sullivan, *"Getting Paid"* (Ithaca, N.Y.: Cornell University Press, 1989), p. 207.

10. Clifford R. Shaw, *The Jack Roller* (Chicago: University of Chicago Press, 1930).

11. Stanley's adult years, however, were not free of turmoil and difficulty. He spent a short period of time in a state mental hospital, struggled with habitual gambling, and was prone to interpersonal quarrels and fighting. See The Jack-Roller and Jon Snodgrass, *The Jack-Roller at Seventy* (Lexington, Mass.: D. C. Heath, 1982).

12. Criminal careers vary on many dimensions, including the age when they begin, whether or not they are interspersed with periods of nonoffending, and whether or not they show escalation in the seriousness of offending. They also

vary by the rate or intensity of crime commission. Some offenders commit many offenses each month, and others do so infrequently. There has been a spirited intellectual debate over the utility of the criminal-career construct and these dimensions. See, for example, Michael Gottfredson and Travis Hirschi, "The true value of lambda would appear to be zero: An essay on career criminals, criminal careers, selective incapacitation, cohort studies, and related topics," *Criminology* 24(1986), pp. 213–234; Alfred Blumstein, Jacqueline Cohen, and David P. Farrington, "Criminal career research: Its value for criminology," *Criminology* 26(1988), pp. 1–35; Michael Gottfredson and Travis Hirschi, "Science, public policy, and the career paradigm," *Criminology* 26(1988), pp. 37–55; and Alfred Blumstein, Jacqueline Cohen, and David P. Farrington, "Longitudinal and criminal career research: Further clarifications," *Criminology* 26(1988), pp. 57–73.

13. John Bartlow Martin, *My Life in Crime* (New York: Harper & Brothers, 1952), pp. 182–183.

14. For interesting research on this process, see Richard Wright, Robert H. Logie, and Scott H. Decker, "Criminal expertise and offender decision making: An experimental study of the target-selection process in residential burglary," *Journal of Research in Crime and Delinquency* 32(1995), pp. 39–54.

15. For a definition and discussion of the importance of perceptual templates for understanding criminal decisionmaking, see Paul J. Brantingham and Patricia L. Brantingham, *Patterns in Crime* (New York: Macmillan, 1984).

16. David Luckenbill and Joel Best, "Careers in deviance and respectability: The analogy's limitation," *Social Problems* 29(1981), pp. 197–206.

17. Michael Gottfredson and Travis Hirschi, "The true value of lambda would appear to be zero: An essay on career criminals, criminal careers, selective incapacitation, cohort studies, and related topics," *Criminology* 24(1986), p. 218.

18. See, for example, Joan Petersilia, Peter W. Greenwood, and Marvin Lavin, *Criminal Careers of Habitual Felons* (Washington, D.C.: U.S. Department of Justice, National Institute of Law Enforcement and Criminal Justice, 1978), p. 27.

19. John Irwin, *The Felon* (Berkeley: University of California Press, 1987), p. 176.

20. Thomas Gabor et al., *Armed Robbery* (Springfield, Ill.: Charles C. Thomas, 1987), p. 203.

21. Nearly three years later, this man was found shot to death in a Chicago alley. One of his lifelong friends, also a thief, characterized the shooting to me as "execution-style."

22. John A. Mack and Kerner Hans-Jurgen, *The Crime Industry* (Lexington, Mass.: Heath, Lexington Books, 1975).

23. Mercer L. Sullivan, *"Getting Paid"* (Ithaca, N.Y.: Cornell University Press, 1989), p. 143. A similar practice of using young adults to fill the riskiest roles in drug-sales organizations in Detroit is reported in Thomas Mieczkowski, "Geeking up and throwing down: Heroin street life in Detroit," *Criminology* 24(1986), pp. 645–666.

24. Darrell J. Steffensmeier, *The Fence* (Totowa, N.J.: Rowman & Littlefield, 1986), p. 60.

25. Joseph D. Lohman, Lloyd E. Ohlin, and Dietrich C. Reitzes, "Description of Convicted Felons as a Manpower Resource in a National Emergency" (Springfield, Ill.: Illinois Division of Corrections, undated).

26. Dietrich C. Reitzes, "The effect of social environment upon former felons," *Journal of Criminal Law, Criminology, and Police Science* 46(1955), p. 231.

27. Daniel Glaser, *The Effectiveness of a Prison and Parole System* (Indianapolis: Bobbs-Merrill, 1964), p. 489.

28. Thomas Meisenhelder, "An exploratory study of exiting from criminal careers," *Criminology* 15(1977), p. 319.

29. Thomas Meisenhelder, "An exploratory study of exiting from criminal careers," *Criminology* 15(1977), p. 327. Interviews with 60 California parolees produced similar findings. See Rosemary Erickson, Wayman J. Crow, Louis A. Zurcher, and Archie V. Connett, *Paroled but Not Free* (New York: Behavioral Publications, 1973).

30. The Gluecks compared 500 institutionalized juvenile delinquents from Boston, Massachusetts, with 500 Boston youths with no known record of significant delinquency who were matched with the delinquents by age, I.Q., national origin, and type of neighborhood. A variety of data on members of the two groups were collected in the period 1939–1948. See Sheldon Glueck and Eleanor Glueck, *Unraveling Juvenile Delinquency* (New York: The Commonwealth Fund, 1950).

31. Robert J. Sampson and John H. Laub, *Crime in the Making* (Cambridge, Mass.: Harvard University Press, 1993), p. 248.

32. See also Irwin Waller, *Men Released from Prison* (Toronto: University of Toronto Press, 1974), p. 176; and Thomas Gabor et al., *Armed Robbery* (Springfield, Ill.: Charles C. Thomas, 1987), p. 204.

33. Donald Pollock, *Call Me a Good Thief* (London: Howard Baker, 1976).

34. Given a choice, few would decline employment as a tenured full professor at a major research university.

35. Dannie M. Martin and Peter Y. Sussman, *Committing Journalism* (New York: W. W. Norton, 1993).

36. Julie Leibrich, *Straight to the Point* (Dunedin, New Zealand: University of Otago Press, 1993).

37. Harold Finestone, "Reformation and recidivism among Italian and Polish criminal offenders," *American Journal of Sociology* 72(1967), p. 580.

38. Ros Burnett, "The Dynamics of Recidivism" (Oxford: University of Oxford, Centre for Criminological Research, 1992). Analysis of survey data collected in the Desistance Project likewise shows that desire to avoid disappointing or causing embarrassment and shame for others influences their decisionmaking.

39. A detailed and insightful description of some of these relationships can be found in Eleanor Miller, *Street Woman* (Philadelphia: Temple University Press, 1986).

40. For an excellent treatment of the difficulties encountered by men trying to reverse their criminal careers, see Robert A. Stebbins, *Commitment to Deviance* (Westport, Conn.: Greenwood, 1971).

41. Walter R. Gove, "The effect of age and gender on deviant behavior: A biopsychosocial perspective," in *Gender and the Life Course*, edited by Alice S. Rossi (New York: Aldine, 1985); and Rosemary Gartner and Irving Piliavin, "The aging offender and the aged offender," in *Life-Span Development and Behavior*, vol. 9, edited by P. B. Baltes, D. L. Featherman, and R. M. Lerner (Hillsdale, N.J.: Lawrence Erlbaum Associates, 1988).

42. Ros Burnett, "The Dynamics of Recidivism" (Oxford: University of Oxford, Centre for Criminological Research, 1992), p. 10.

43. Neal Shover, *Aging Criminals* (Beverly Hills, Calif.: Sage, 1985).

44. Brian Wilson, *Nor Iron Bars a Cage* (London: William Kimber, 1964), p. 118.

45. Thomas N. Meisenhelder, "An exploratory study of exiting from criminal careers," *Criminology* 15(1977), pp. 319–334.

46. John Bartlow Martin, *My Life in Crime* (New York: Harper & Brothers, 1952), pp. 277–278.

47. In the parlance of some residents of the District of Columbia, committing crime is known as "throwing bricks at the penitentiary." Committing high-visibility confrontational crimes is known as "throwing the *big* brick."

48. Bruce Jackson, *A Thief's Primer* (New York: Macmillan, 1969), p. 235.

49. Bernice L. Neugarten, "Adult personality: Toward a psychology of the life cycle," in *Middle Age and Aging: A Reader in Social Psychology,* edited by Bernice L. Neugarten (Chicago: University of Chicago Press, 1968).

50. Daniel J. Levinson, *The Seasons of a Man's Life* (New York: Alfred A. Knopf, 1978).

51. Paul Warren, *Next Time Is for Life* (New York: Dell, 1953), pp. 28–29. The fact that thieves understandably are interested in forms of theft that appear foolproof frequently causes them to prey upon one another or on others who have made money illegally. One reason is the belief these victims would not report to the police. Fences are a favorite target. Thus, an English thief counted among the lessons he learned as a youngster the insight "that fences' houses are good places to screw; they can't very well scream about losing something they know is stolen." Tony Parker and Robert Allerton, *The Courage of His Convictions* (London: Hutchinson, 1962), p. 78. A former heroin addict commented that "we used to stick up numbers joints because . . . that's where the money was." Stuart L. Hills and Ron Santiago, *Tragic Magic* (Chicago: Nelson-Hall, 1992), p. 75. In contemporary urban America, drug dealers are prime targets for victimization by thieves and hustlers.

52. Ernest Booth, *Stealing Through Life* (New York: Alfred A. Knopf, 1929), p. 132.

53. John Allen, *Assault with a Deadly Weapon,* edited by D. H. Kelly and P. Heymann (New York: Pantheon, 1977), pp. 106–107.

54. Malcolm Braly, *False Starts* (New York: Penguin, 1976).

55. Sharon Sopher, *Up from the Walking Dead,* as told by Charles McGregor (Garden City, N.Y.: Doubleday, 1978), p. 368.

56. Harry King, *Box Man,* as told to and edited by Bill Chambliss (New York: Harper Torchbooks, 1972), p. 158.

57. Andreas Schroeder, *Shaking It Rough* (Toronto: Doubleday, 1976), p. 59.

58. Thorsten Sellin, "Recidivism and maturation," *National Probation and Parole Association Journal* 4(1958), pp. 241–250; Barbara Wooton, *Social Science and Social Pathology* (London: Allen & Unwin, 1959), p. 164.

59. Walter R. Gove, "The effect of age and gender on deviant behavior: A biopsychosocial perspective," in *Gender and the Life Course,* edited by Alice S. Ross (New York: Aldine, 1985).

60. Dermot Walsh, *Heavy Business* (London: Routledge & Kegan Paul, 1986), p. 150.

61. Neal Shover, "The social organization of burglary," *Social Problems* 20(1973), pp. 499–514.

62. In the words of one thief, too late they realize that "it is not what a man steals, but what he saves that count." Hutchins Hapgood, *Autobiography of a Thief* (New York: Fox, Duffield, 1903), p. 179.

63. Dermot Walsh, *Break-Ins* (London: Constable, 1980).

64. Sylvester Monroe and Peter Goldman, *Brothers* (New York: William Morrow, 1988), p. 266.

65. Joan Petersilia, Peter W. Greenwood, and Marvin Lavin, *Criminal Careers of Habitual Felons* (Washington, D.C.: U.S. Department of Justice, National Institute of Law Enforcement and Criminal Justice, 1978), p. 70.

66. Pedro R. David, editor, *The World of the Burglar* (Albuquerque: University of New Mexico Press, 1974), p. 42.

67. Thomas Gabor et al., *Armed Robbery* (Springfield, Ill.: Charles C. Thomas, 1987), p. 204.

68. Mike Maguire, in collaboration with Trevor Bennett, *Burglary in a Dwelling* (London: Heinemann, 1982), p. 89.

69. W. Gordon West, "The short-term careers of serious thieves," *Canadian Journal of Criminology* 20(1978), pp. 169–190; Barry Glassner, M. Ksander, B. Berg, and Bruce D. Johnson, "A note on the deterrent effect of juvenile vs. adult jurisdiction," *Social Problems* 31(1983), pp. 219–221.

70. Maurice Cusson and Pierre Pinsonneault, "The decision to give up crime," in *The Reasoning Criminal*, edited by Derek B. Cornish and Ronald V. Clarke (New York: Springer-Verlag, 1986), p. 76.

71. Thomas N. Meisenhelder, "An exploratory study of exiting from criminal careers," *Criminology* 15(1977), p. 322.

72. Paul F. Cromwell, James N. Olson, and D'Aunn Wester Avary, *Breaking and Entering* (Newbury Park, Calif.: Sage, 1991), p. 83.

73. Ros Burnett, "The Dynamics of Recidivism" (Oxford: University of Oxford, Centre for Criminological Research, 1992), p. 21.

74. Ros Burnett, "The Dynamics of Recidivism" (Oxford: University of Oxford, Centre for Criminological Research, 1992), p. 15.

75. John Irwin, *The Felon* (Berkeley: University of California Press, 1987), p. 202.

76. Eugene Delorme, *Chief*, edited by Inez Cardozo-Freeman (Lincoln: University of Nebraska Press, 1994), p. 191.

77. Peter Crookston, *Villain* (London: Jonathan Cape, 1967), p. 155.

78. Harry King, *Box Man*, as told to and edited by Bill Chambliss (New York: Harper Torchbooks, 1972).

79. Malcolm Braly, *False Starts* (New York: Penguin, 1976), p. 118.

80. Brian Wilson, *Nor Iron Bars a Cage* (London: Wm. Kimber, 1964), p. 118.

81. John Irwin, *The Felon* (Berkeley: University of California Press, 1987), p. viii. A recent portrayal of the lives of street offenders is consistent with this picture. See Mark S. Fleisher, *Beggars and Thieves* (Madison: University of Wisconsin Press, 1995).

6

Threats, Decisions, and Confinement

It was not until public discourse about crime and crime control began moving in the direction of choice-and-punishment that social scientists deigned to examine carefully the merits of key assumptions underlying the change. Chief among these is the belief that the threat of arrest and confinement deters individuals from committing street crime and that the experience of imprisonment prevents a repeat of past mistakes by those who fail to heed the warning. At the aggregate level, this means that we would expect states with low rates of street crime also to be states in which those who commit these crimes are more likely to be arrested, prosecuted, and punished than their counterparts in states with less effective police, less determined prosecutors, and proportionately fewer deterrence-minded judges. If Minnesota has a lower armed robbery rate than South Carolina, how much confidence can we have concluding that it is produced in part by the latter's "no nonsense" criminal justice system? In a word, it is extremely difficult to know.[1] Besides the difference in their rates of robbery and punishment for robbers, South Carolina and Minnesota differ in so many other ways that one is reluctant to argue confidently the relationship is causal. That said, evidence from studies of the statistical link between the *certainty* of punishment and the rate of common crimes generally points to an inverse but weak relationship. Evidence from research on the impact of punishment *severity* is less clear even than evidence about the effects of variation in punishment certainty.

The ambiguous findings from aggregate-level research are one reason that a panel of the National Academy of Sciences called in 1978 for studies of decisionmaking by criminal offenders.[2] The call has not gone unheeded. In the years since, an increasing number of investigators have explored how offenders assess and weigh options, including criminal ones, and how they make crime-commission and target-selection decisions. The policy rationale for this development is straightforward and compelling: "There can be no more critical element in understanding and ultimately preventing crime than understanding the criminal's perceptions of the opportunities and risks associated with [criminal activities]."[3] In this chapter I examine these matters. I begin by reviewing how persistent thieves, prime targets of those who demand ever harsher responses to crime, make decisions. I then turn to an examination of imprisonment and focus on unintended consequences of the experience that erode its aversiveness while making some inmates bitter and determined to even the score when they are released.

Decisionmaking

An understanding of how decisions to commit serious crime are made and the factors that influence this process are critical in determining the likely impact of crime-control policies that provide for quick, certain, and severe punishment. Although the bulk of research on criminal decisionmaking is of limited value for those interested in the behavior of persistent thieves, the corpus of studies suitable for our purposes is substantial nonetheless. This is not to say the studies are methodologically rigorous. The research designs employed to examine crime-commission decisionmaking in particular are weak, the number of studies is rather small, and the bulk of evidence comes from interviews with imprisoned thieves. One of the principal shortcomings of using this type of sample is that offenders' descriptions are not collected in real-life decisionmaking situations. The target-selection process, by contrast, has been explored in a greater number and diversity of studies, including collection of data from offenders as they screened and weighed the desirability of potential targets. Some investigators have used photographs or videotape recordings of potential targets as a means of presenting offenders with hypothetical victims. Others have collected data from active, unincarcerated thieves and hustlers, including visiting with offenders places they previously victimized in order to reconstruct their decisionmaking. Although these studies are a marked improvement over those conducted on imprisoned offenders, even research on active offenders is not free entirely from design shortcomings that may bias their findings. It is remarkable, for example, how even the most inept and unsuccessful thieves cannot resist puffing themselves up a bit on occasion, particularly when they are under scrutiny by social scientists.

Crime Commission

The occurrence of a criminal act is the product of at least two analytically distinct decisions: a decision to commit crime and a decision to exploit a specific target. We can distinguish, therefore, crimes in which some time passes between the first and the second decisions, even if it is no more than an hour or so, and crimes in which the two are made nearly simultaneously. When offenders commit the first type of crime, they first decide to steal and then set out to locate a suitable target or to exploit one already in mind. In the latter case, they need only work out a plan of attack. In the case of robbery, this means either a "selective raid," in which the target is chosen at least an hour or so in advance, or a "planned job," in which case the target may have been chosen days or weeks earlier.[4] Spontaneous crimes, by contrast, are those in which the decision to commit a crime and the decision to victimize a specific place or person are made simultaneously. This occurs, for example, when persons with little or no prior intention to offend chance upon a situation they judge to be too enticing to pass up. Interviews with 45 street robbers in London, England, found that "over a third . . . reported just happening upon the victim and deciding then and there to do a robbery."[5] Information provided by convicted California robbers likewise shows that "a number had not even started out to commit a robbery."[6] Interviews with residential burglars have shown that one of the most common situations of the type that facilitate a decision to commit crime is when they chance to see individuals exiting a residence. As burglars see it, the dwelling will be unoccupied for some period of time, which makes it an inviting target.[7]

More often than not, the crime-commission and target-selection decisions are made serially. At one extreme, a crime may be planned for weeks before it is attempted. An informant described a burglary of this type:

A: We used a wrecker [truck] and pulled two safes through the building.
Q: How long did you plan this crime in advance?
A: Three months.
Q: What did you do during that three months to get ready for the crime? Watch the place?
A: Well, that and find me a wrecker to get and somewhere to take [the safes] to after we got them, torches and stuff to cut them open.
Q: Did you feel like you had everything set and ready to go?
A: Yeah. Didn't plan on the wrecker turning over, though. . . . The safes was hanging on the wrecker's boom, the double boom. We pulled the safes all the way through the front of the building—it should have collapsed the building when they come through the front of it—[then] we went around and come off of Jackson Pike and started to turn left and the safes were so heavy they swung out and just turned the wrecker over.

Protracted and detailed planning of this type by thieves and hustlers is extremely uncommon; generally, their planning is hasty and haphazard.[8] In the Rand Corporation's three-state survey of jail and prison inmates, subjects were questioned about how they committed crimes in the period before their arrest and confinement. Forty-seven percent of those accused or convicted of robbery, burglary, theft, or auto theft said they "never" or only "sometimes" "worked out a plan" before they went out to do crimes.[9] Asked how much time they usually spent planning their crimes, 46.7 percent of the thieves in the University of Massachusetts survey responded they did not plan their crimes "at all."[10] Interviews with 113 men convicted of robbery or an offense related to robbery revealed that "over half . . . reported no planning at all."[11] Far more common than crimes committed after a lengthy planning period, in fact, are crimes in which no more than an hour or two elapse before offenders bent on "doing wrong" find a victim to their liking:

> We was wanting to get high. That was the main reason for [it], you know, wanting to get high and everything, you know. And we just, well, started talking about it. And the jones [physical craving or need for heroin] came, you know. "We're gonna have to try to do something, you know, to satisfy jones." . . . So we went out to try to make some money. . . . We was just, like I said, riding, thinking about making some money, wanting some cocaine, you know. . . . We went by that bank and we saw . . . people tramping in and out, you know. They had a lot of money and everything [and] we was wanting money and everything real bad, too. . . . We went to try to snatch some or whatever, you know.
> Q: Tell me about the actual, doing the snatching. Did it take place in the bank or outside the bank?
> A: Well, it took place outside the bank.   ·
> Q: Had you gone in and seen the person, or how did you all choose the person to hit?
> A: Uh, uh. We was standing around the corner there, see, and, uh, letting them come out the bank there. And he come around the bank there and he had a big money bag on his arm, you know. And we know it's got a lot of money in it, you know.

There is no question that a great deal of the crime committed by persistent thieves is opportunistic and spontaneous in nature, albeit much of it is committed by men who are searching actively for a target at the time:

> I was going down the street and . . . I just stopped and I seen this house. . . . I stopped and looked at it. And most of the time I can always determine whether anyone is at home or not.
> Q: How can you tell that?
> A: Well you can always look in the garage or you can look at the house or you can stand and listen and if anybody is there you'll hear movement. If you go up to the house and knock and somebody comes to the door then,

quite naturally, you can always say you made a mistake or you thought someone else lived there.

Q: So after you saw the house, how much time went by before you went up to the front door?

A: It wasn't long, you know. I was just high enough to just go right on, you know. I just went right on up there and knocked on the door. And didn't nobody come. And I went around the side to try the window, you know. Most of the time . . . you just take a rock and hit it right there and knock it out.

[One day] we were just walking up First Street and [one of my companions] said as we were approaching Rhode Island Avenue, "let's go in here and rob this drug store." Went in there, the soda fountain was filled up, . . . robbed everybody on the stools. Went back in the post office, stole money orders and stamps and stuff, took the cash box. And we turned our backs on everybody in the store, going out! We didn't know whether the proprietor had a gun or what, but it just so happened that he didn't. But that's just the atmosphere in which, you know, that took place.

Robberies like this one, dubbed "ambushes" by one investigator,[12] can be very different from offenses that are preceded by at least some planning.

Just as a distinction can be drawn between planned and spontaneous crimes, so too can individuals who normally plan their crimes be distinguished from those who usually operate spontaneously. It is a distinction that should not be overdrawn. The fact is that even those who usually plan their crimes also commit opportunistic crimes on occasion. Similarly, thieves who normally commit opportunistic crimes may plan, particularly if the exigencies and pressures of their lifestyles permit it. An obvious difference between these groups is their access to motor vehicles. Planners are somewhat more likely than opportunists to have automobiles; the mobility this provides gives them access to a much larger number and variety of targets. Because of their finely tuned sensitivity to signs of vulnerability, it is not uncommon for thieves and hustlers who have motor vehicles to note potentially worthwhile targets whenever they are out driving. These are stored in memory as places or persons worthy at least of further scrutiny. An example is provided by an informant who worked with another man stealing appliances from under-construction housing subdivisions:

We went and rented a truck, and about 3:00 o'clock we went by where Andy was staying, . . . 'cause he had been wanting to go out and make a little extra money, you know. . . . We went to ride and . . . we went to all kinda different places, you know, just looking at things. . . . We [would] stop at these houses and look, you know, see what was there, and make a mental note of it to go back and pick it up. . . . We bought some real good pot and we smoked two or three joints of that. Then we rode around, you know, 'til it got dark.

Those without access to an automobile generally must travel to and from their targets on foot or by public transportation. Not surprisingly, they are more likely than motorized thieves to commit crimes close to their home neighborhood.[13]

One of the most striking aspects of the crime-commission decisionmaking of persistent thieves and hustlers is that a substantial proportion seem to give little or no thought to the possibility of arrest and confinement when deciding whether to commit crime:

Q: Did you think about . . . getting caught?
A: No.
Q: [H]ow did you manage to put that out of your mind?
A: [It] never did come into it.
Q: Never did come into it?
A: Never did, you know. It didn't bother me.

Q: Were you thinking about bad things that might happen to you?
A: None whatsoever.
Q: No?
A: I wasn't worried about getting caught or anything, you know. I was a positive thinker through everything, you know. I didn't have no negative thoughts about it whatsoever.

Even many who do think about the possibility of arrest manage to dismiss it easily and to carry through with their plans:

Q: Did you worry much about getting caught? On a scale of one to ten, how would you rank your degree of worry that day?
A: [T]he worry was probably a one, you know what I mean? The worry was probably one. I didn't think about the consequences, you know. I know it's stupidity, but it didn't—that [I] might go to jail, I mean—it crossed my mind but it didn't make much difference.

Q: As you thought about doing that [armed robbery], were there things that you were worried about?
A: Well, the only thing that I was worried about was—getting arrested didn't even cross my mind—just worrying about getting killed is the only thing, you know, getting shot. That's the only thing. . . . But, you know, . . . you'd have to be really crazy not to think about that . . . you

could possibly get in trouble. It crossed my mind, but I didn't worry about it all that much.

Certainly one reason many thieves do not calculate carefully is that they consciously and intentionally put out of mind all thoughts of possible arrest when deciding to commit a crime. Interview and observational data collected on 105 active residential burglars showed that they deliberately employed decisionmaking techniques that allowed them to neutralize fear of sanction. "The most common involved a steadfast refusal to dwell on the possibility of being apprehended."[14] Ethnographic interview data collected from formerly imprisoned persistent thieves paint a similar picture:

Q: Did you think about [the possibility of getting caught] very much that night?
A: I didn't think about it that much, you know. . . . It comes but, you know, you can wipe it away.
Q: How do you wipe it away?
A: You just blank it out. You blank it out.

Another informant said simply that "I try to put that [thought of arrest] the farthest thing from my mind that I can."

One of the principal rationales for this approach is the belief that thieves who are preoccupied with the risk of arrest are more likely to act suspiciously, to draw the attention and interest of anyone who chances to see them, and to make mistakes:

When I went out to steal, I didn't think about the negative things. 'Cause if you think negative, negative things are going to happen. And that's the way I looked at it. . . . I done it just like it was a job or something. Go out and do it, don't think about getting caught, 'cause that would make you jumpy, edgy, nervous. If you looked like you were doing something wrong, then something wrong is gonna happen to you . . . you just, you just put that out of your mind, you know.

The result of suppressing fear of arrest, in the words of another informant, is that when they make decisions to commit crime, some persistent thieves and hustlers "think about going to prison about like [they] think about dying."

There is considerable and consistent research support for this picture. A study of 83 imprisoned burglars revealed that 49 percent did not think about the chances of getting caught for any particular offense during their last period of offending. Although 37 percent of them did think about it, most thought there was little or no chance it would happen.[15] Interviews with 113 convicted robbers revealed that "over 60 percent . . . said they had not even thought about getting caught." Another 17 percent said they had thought about the possibility but "did not believe it to be a problem."[16] Analysis of prison interviews with 77 robbers and 45 burglars likewise revealed their "general obliviousness toward the consequences [of their crimes] and no thought of being caught."[17] As part of the University of Massachusetts survey, prisoners were asked how often they "personally thought about" the possibility "that [they] might get caught when [they] were getting ready to do a crime." Of the 1,038 men who were serving a prison sentence for armed robbery, burglary, auto theft, theft, or any combination of these offenses, 53 percent answered "often" or "regularly."[18] Asked specifically about the crime for which they were serving time, 72 percent said they were not worried about getting caught at the time they committed it.[19] As one informant put it, "you don't think about getting caught, you think about how in hell you're going to do it *not* to get caught, you know." These comments were echoed by another informant: "The only thing you're thinking about is looking and acting and trying *not* to get caught." This does not mean that offenders are completely indifferent to the fear of failure: "I wasn't afraid of getting caught, but I was cautious, you know. Like I said, I was thinking only in the way to prevent me from getting caught."

Instead of paying close attention to the potential legal consequences of their actions and planning carefully to avoid arrest, offenders generally focus their thoughts and their talk on the money that committing a crime may yield and how they plan to use it when the crime is behind them. In 1976, the Rand Corporation surveyed 624 prisoners in five California prisons. One of the main objectives was to identify factors that explain respondents' rate of offending prior to imprisonment (i.e., the number of crimes they committed each month). After analyzing data on prisoners' perceptions of the likely costs and rewards of criminal participation, the investigators concluded: "[R]espondents who were most certain in reporting that they would be arrested or otherwise suffer for crime did not report committing fewer crimes. Rather, . . . individual offense rates are related only to offenders' perceptions of the benefits to be derived from crime."[20] Others also have shown that the amount of gain offenders expect to receive is "the most important dimension" in their decisionmaking, whereas the certainty of punishment is the least important of the four dimensions on which subjects assessed crime opportunities.[21] Released prisoners who were interviewed during the Desistance Project similarly said they focused on the expected gains from their crimes:

I didn't think about nothing but what I was going to do when I got that money, how I was going to spend it, what I was going to do with it, you know.

See, you're not thinking about those things [possibility of being arrested]. You're thinking about that big paycheck at the end of thirty to forty-five minutes worth of work.

[A]t the time [that you commit crime], you throw all your instincts out the window. . . . Because you're just thinking about money, and money only. That's all that's on your mind, because you want that money. And you throw, you block everything off until you get the money.

I noted in Chapter 5 that the presence of co-offenders can increase the tendency to take risks and engage in reckless behavior.[22] Support for the facilitative effects of others is provided by evidence that those who work in groups may have a higher incidence of offending than solo thieves and that crime sprees are far more common for groups as well.[23] The willingness of individuals to submerge their identity in the group and to take part in risky action even when they harbor deep misgivings about the wisdom of it is well known:

[What began as a] lark had turned into the more serious business of highway robbery . . . Over the engine's rumbling I could distinctly hear the footsteps of some approaching couple. My head was whirling—I gripped the steering wheel and clenched my teeth. I tried to see the faces of Red and Fred, and though they were but dim white blurs, I could sense that they too were not so nonchalant as they would have liked me to believe. . . . It was the ancient herd-instinct that buoyed us up; forced us to continue though we separately did not wish to.[24]

Nor are co-offender effects limited to momentary situations in which decisions are made. Crime partners who realize short-term success in their joint endeavors may experience a bond that both sustains them and increases the odds they will continue their teamwork as crime partners:

[M]y life changed dramatically [when] I met up with four or five guys that were heavy into robbery on almost a daily basis. . . . We worked in a sort of loose, unstructured way. Each one of us finding places to hit; casing the layout; setting the job up. . . . And when our group . . . were planning a caper, we *belonged*. We worked together like machined parts, we respected each other's abilities and talents, and we accepted each other to such an extent we would die for a brother if need be. For almost two years Izzy and I and Fred and Alan were like that. In a strange, perverted sense it was almost like love; not sexual, but *being tight* together.[25]

The record of systematic research on group effects in crime commission is very limited. Almost nothing is known particularly about group processes in decisionmaking when the use of alcohol or other drugs is added to the interactional mix, as often they are. Nevertheless, there is little reason to believe that the presence of co-offenders *increases* the likelihood that men will weigh carefully the options and risks before them when deciding whether or not to commit crime. A man who traveled with his crime partner to other cities to steal was asked if the two of them ever talked about the chances of being caught:

> No, we never, we rarely ever talked about getting caught. We didn't, we didn't feel like—unless they just happened to slip up on us, you know—that we'd ever get caught. . . . I mean they'd have to be right there and see you do it or set up a roadblock or something and catch you with the stuff on you. . . . It'd just be almost impossible for them to catch you doing it unless they caught you in the act.
> Q: So then you weren't all that worried about getting caught? Or am I wrong in saying that?
> A: No. Well, you know, the thought is always there but it wasn't something we sat around and discussed, you know—"what if we get caught?" There's no "what if you get caught." If you get caught you go to jail!
> Q: You all didn't say "what if we get caught?"
> A: No, we knew what happened, what would happen if we got caught so we didn't discuss it.

Similar comments were made by another informant who was asked what he and his two crime partners talked about while they rode around looking for suitable criminal opportunities:

> Q: Did you all talk about any negative things that you thought could happen to you?
> A: Well, no, you wouldn't, you know. You wouldn't talk about getting caught because the main thing is, because you don't want to get caught, you know, you more or less don't want to talk about it or think about it.

Persistent thieves' avoidance of careful and articulated deliberation is similar to the way blue-collar males cope with risk in their legitimate work. Ironworkers, for example, are fully aware of the hazards of working high in the air, but they do not dwell on the bodily carnage that would result from a fall.[26] To do so would be pointless. Those who cannot push risk to the background when working on "high iron," simply give up earning a living in this way. For those who continue the work, all thought and action are devoted to ensuring that mistakes do not happen. It is thus with most forms of edgework.[27] That persistent thieves and hustlers approach crime in the same way may be an important experiential effect of criminal participation. This concept refers to the ways, largely uncataloged, that offenders are changed by participation in crime and by firsthand experience with the criminal justice process. There is reason to believe, for example, that repeated successful participation in crime may cause offenders to lower their estimates of the likelihood of being arrested for such activity.[28]

Target Selection

Although thieves and hustlers tend to be remarkably casual about the risk of arrest when deciding to commit crime, their attention becomes more systematic and focused when they move to consideration of specific targets. How do they decide when and which targets to exploit? On the surface, there appears to be considerable variation in the process. Because burglary and robbery are very different crimes, the factors assessed when choosing robbery victims are not those considered when selecting residences to burglarize. Burglars generally wish to avoid their victims, and a decisionmaking process that increases the odds of doing so is commonplace among them. In the perceptual templates[29] they employ when assessing potential targets, burglars pay close attention to whether or not a residence is occupied and also to how easily potential entry points can be seen by neighbors or passersby.[30] Consequently, in the hours when they are unoccupied, houses and businesses that are not visible easily to neighbors or passersby are at risk of being victimized. Multiunit dwellings without access security, corner houses or those located adjacent to parks or other open spaces, structures surrounded by view-obstructing foliage, and those located distant from other structures are more likely to be victimized than structures without these environmental liabilities. And, not surprisingly, suburban homes without burglar alarms are at somewhat higher risk of victimization than those that are alarm-protected.[31]

It is clear that target selection varies with offenders' age, means of transportation, available resources or weapons, and the urgency of their economic needs. Further complicating the picture, victim selection is influenced by the presence of co-offenders; individuals and groups often do not behave alike. The joint influence of co-offenders and age is instructive. Young thieves and hustlers often operate in groups, and numbers change robbers' decisionmaking. What they may lack in weaponry is compensated for by numbers. "If [an offender] needs money urgently, has no firearms or car and is alone, he may see no option to attacking a convenient target even though it may be well secured relative to others."[32]

Street robbers generally do not plan their offenses carefully or in detail beforehand. "More than a quarter" of 45 London street robbers reported that they left home for the purpose of doing a robbery on the day they committed the offense."[33] In contrast to robbers whose crimes were committed spontaneously, these offenders tended to rob alone, "to have chosen the offense venue, [to] have a reason for offending at that time of day, to wait at the scene until a suitable victim came along, and to have planned their escape route."[34] When street robbers are "on the stroll," they prefer victims who are perceived as unlikely to resist and likely to yield an acceptable payoff.[35] The London street robbers indicated that persons they encountered who appeared wealthy or had property visible, such as jewelry, a watch, or a bag, were more likely than others to be victimized.[36] On the basis of interviews with 67 imprisoned robbers, another investigator concluded that "in considering whom to rob, the offender usually considers the amount of money available, the vulnerability of the victim, the risk he faces during the robbery, and the likelihood that the victim will resist."[37] Interviews with convicted bank robbers revealed that the three most important considerations in choosing banks to rob are location, the absence of a guard, and small size.[38] The location of a bank determines how quickly and unobtrusively robbers can get away from the crime scene, and large size both increases the difficulty of monitoring the scene and controlling persons in the bank.

There is no doubt that the presence of others can increase arousal and thereby distort the decisionmaking process, but the net effect of co-offenders on target-selection decisions is unclear. In street robbery, where numbers are strength, the presence of co-offenders decreases concern with potential victim resistance. As a result, groups can behave brazenly.[39] Balancing somewhat the increased arousal caused by the presence of co-offenders is the fact that residential burglars become more adept at spotting problems with specific potential targets. This makes them less likely to choose risky targets.[40]

Notwithstanding variation in target selection by type of crime, age, and the number of offenders, it is equally clear that street-level persistent thieves are sensitive to the risk of failure. They behave purposefully and even rationally. It would be a mistake, however, to infer from this that they are aware of and sensitive even to substantial variation or changes in the schedule of threatened punishments. Most often they are not. And although it is true that the confinement experience increases their understanding and awareness of these matters, often it fails to convince them that misfortune and further incarceration are inevitable if they return to committing crime.

The Prison Experience

Although it is tempting to imagine that many men who commit direct-contact property crimes go unarrested and unpunished, in crime as in other forms of gambling, misfortune looms for those who "take the bucket to the well" repeatedly. More than 25 years ago, Edwin Lemert suggested that "[w]hether significant numbers of criminals in the open still lead lives uncomplicated by contacts with law enforcement agencies and large-scale correctional institutions is highly dubious."[41] There was little reason to doubt his assessment at the time, and there is even less reason to do so today. Consider that the ensuing years have brought the development and adoption by many police departments of vastly improved communications and records-keeping technology as well as programs aimed specifically at repeat offenders. Certainly no one would claim these developments have made it *easier* for persistent thieves and hustlers to evade arrest and imprisonment.

Given the high probability of arrest for thieves who steal repeatedly, much of what transpired during the short life of the "Stanford County Jail" probably heartens promoters of imprisonment as an effective crime-control strategy. "Inmates" appeared to experience confinement as an extremely negative, aversive experience that they tried to withdraw from as quickly as possible. From this observation it is but a short inferential leap to the assumption that those who have suffered as real-life prisoners will think carefully about the pains of imprisonment before choosing to commit crime again. But if we want to understand imprisonment and its potential as a deterrent, we must examine how men reared in the working class experience it.

As I pointed out in Chapter 2, many real-life prison inmates have had extensive experience as subordinates whose wishes and views are treated as unimportant or insignificant. These men are drawn from class and family backgrounds in which demands that persons surrender their autonomy and submit to direction of others are veneered but thinly.[42] They have a firm grounding in regimentation and its demands, some as a result of prior military service.[43] Others have served time in juvenile institutions. This was true of 25.1 percent of the 1,199 thieves in the 1978 Rand three-state survey of jail and prison inmates.[44] By the time they reach the penitentiary, they already know a thing or two about punishment and the world of total institutions.

Concern about the potential criminogenic consequences of confinement probably are as old as the prison itself. Certainly, one of the main reasons training schools and prisons periodically are criticized is because of the belief that inmates only expand their criminal contacts and acquire new criminal skills while there. As an adult, Malcolm Braly reflected on his juvenile confinement in California's Preston School of Industry:

> The most serious and persistent charge leveled against institutions like Preston is that they function as crime schools where young naive boys are tutored in criminal techniques by the more experienced. . . . The [charge] . . . bears some examination. It isn't, I think, information one gets here. I heard many accounts of how to hotwire cars to bypass the ignition so they could be stolen without the key, but this technique never became clear to me,

and I've never used it. . . . What one learns to want in a "crime school" is the respect of one's peers. This is the danger. The naive will be drawn into competing for status in a system of values that honors and glorifies antisocial behavior.[45]

Because virtually no one disputes the indictment of prisons as places that too often have a worsening influence on inmates, we sometimes lose sight of the possibility that other aspects of the confinement experience also may increase the odds of criminal persistence, at least for some prisoners.

Rationalization of Crime

As advocates of deterrence-based crime control see it, a taste of "the joint" surely reduces the odds that released prisoners will choose to commit crime again. It does so in large part because exposure to a measured dose of confinement as a response to specific criminal acts is meant to nurture the *rationalization of crime.* This is the process by which persons develop and employ in decisionmaking a more precise calculus and metric of crime and punishment. By contributing to this process, imprisonment replaces an emotion-laden and impulsive decisionmaking process with a more careful and prudent one.

To the external observer, crimes committed by juveniles and by young adults do not seem very rational. And it is true that many youths become involved in stealing without having developed an autonomous and rationalized set of criminal motives. Questioned retrospectively about their criminal motives when they were juveniles, 49 imprisoned armed robbers reported using little or no sophistication in planning the offenses they committed.[46] Juveniles often commit offenses for "expressive" reasons such as hostility, revenge, thrills, or peer influence.[47] The result is that the potential repercussions of crime to some extent are blunted. Juveniles neither possess nor bring to bear a precise, consistent metric for assessing the potential consequences of delinquent episodes. They fail to see or to calculate carefully their potential losses if apprehended. For many youths, crime is a risk-taking activity in which the risks are only dimly appreciated or calculated.

Imprisonment is one of the most important accelerants of the rationalization of crime, the process by which offenders transform it into a somewhat more calculated affair than it is for most juveniles. Imprisonment promotes criminal rationalization because, in clarifying previously inestimable variables in the offender's criminal calculus, it also transforms it. By familiarizing offenders with the definitions and penalty tables at the heart of the criminal code, imprisonment promotes a keener awareness of the potential costs of criminal behavior and a more clearly articulated understanding of the price of crime. Generally this process begins in jail and then continues in prison:

Q: Did you know of the penalties [for crime]?
A: Well, once you get to prison you learn. . . . You learn a lot of things in prison. What other people was doing and got caught at and stuff like that.

Q: How did you come to know about [the] penalties?
A: [From] a combination of friends being arrested . . . and then by me being arrested, you know. When you're in jail you learn a lot of things, you know. You've got guys—everybody has got their own problems and everybody is trying to tell you, you know, "you've got your problems, but I'm trying to tell you how I got busted and why I got busted" and what, you know, I should do. And we're exchanging views. You're tell[ing] me, "well man, here's all they can do to you is this, that, and the other. Here's what they did to me on the same thing."

Vicariously, in the recounted experiences of fellow prisoners, they learn the range of sentences and the "going rate" for common crimes. They learn to think of the criminal code as a table of specific *threats* to which specific, calculable punishments are attached. Never mind that the entire criminal justice apparatus is clumsy and seemingly nonrational in *operation;* the claim of rationality that underpins and justifies it is not lost on the prisoner. In causing men to see more clearly that criminal definitions and crime control are rational matters, confinement improves their ability to calculate before acting.

Another way that imprisonment promotes the rationalization of crime is by helping elevate *money,* the most calculable of payoffs, to the forefront of criminal motives. Prison conversations are laced with depictions of criminal acts as a means of acquiring money, perhaps even "big money." This talk is not without effect. Money increasingly assumes more importance as a criminal objective. Prisoners learn the importance of assessing and committing crimes on the basis of an increasingly narrow and precise metric of potential benefits and costs. After serving a term in the National Training School, an informant and his friends began robbing gamblers and bootleggers. I asked him,

Q: Did the desire for excitement play any part in those crimes?
A: No, I think the desire for excitement had left. It was, we recognized that it was a dangerous mission then, because we knew that gamblers and bootleggers carried guns and things like that. And it was for, you know, just for the money.

An ex-thief expressed a similar matter-of-fact view:

> When I first began stealing I had but a dim realization of its wrong. I accepted it as the thing to do because it was done by the people I was with; besides, it was adventurous and thrilling. Later it became an everyday, cold-blooded business, and while I went about it methodically . . . I was fully aware of the gravity of my offenses.[48]

This development was described by another informant also: "Whatever started me in crime is one thing, but at some point I know that I'm in crime for the money. There's no emotional reason for me being into crime."

The prison world is filled with talk of crime as a rational pursuit, some of it pushed by administrators and some of it by prisoners' peers. Men who are abject failures at crime talk as if they were successful and well-informed professionals. To those who do not know better, prison conversation makes criminal success seem easily attainable so long as offenders plan and execute better. Friends and other inmates generally admonish them to use their head and commit crime in ways that tip the odds in their favor—in short, to be rational about it.

Crime, young prisoners come to believe, can be both a lucrative and a low-risk enterprise so long as one is "careful." The prison experience seduces them into believing that they can avoid arrest. Those who return to stealing often do so with confidence because they now plan marginally better than in their adolescent years:

> I didn't worry too much about getting caught because, like I said, I put a lot of planning and forethought into it. . . . The potential gain that I saw increased substantially. The risk diminished because I was a lot more aware of my capabilities.

> I was aware of what could happen now, if I get busted again, how much time that I could receive in prison by me being locked up and incarcerated that first time. . . . I learned about different type crimes that would get you the most time. . . . I'd always weigh my chances of being captured, being caught, and I'd always have an escape plan. [I approached crime] as a professional.

Forty-nine imprisoned armed robbers said that during their young adult years they developed a new confidence in their ability to avoid arrest for their crimes; their concern about it declined significantly.[49]

The truth, in fact as in their fantasies, is that the odds of being arrested for any specific criminal act are in their favor.[50] Whether it is because they know this, sense it, or simply refuse even to think about getting caught, these men analyze past offenses to develop more perfect criminal techniques for success as if there is a finite, manageable number of ways a criminal act can fail. An interview with a British thief reveals this reasoning process:

Q: When you're arrested, what are your reactions at that moment?
A: I think the first thing's annoyance . . . with myself. How could I be so stupid as to get nicked? What's gone wrong, what have I forgotten, where have I made the mistake?[51]

Once the full array of errors and "mistakes" is learned, men like him are confident, prison is a thing of the past:

Every person who ever did time can tell you what he did wrong to get caught. Every one feels that all he has to do is rectify that one mental error and he's on his way. I knew what had gone wrong in the McDonald's stickup. We hadn't planned carefully. I *knew* I could do it right this time.[52]

Malcolm Braly observed, "Whenever I began to steal it was always with the rationale I wouldn't make the mistakes I had made before." Years would pass before he would realize "there were literally thousands of ways I could get caught."[53] As Braly did in his youth, those who continue to commit crimes after their first incarceration think about the possibility of legal sanction more than in the past but show only marginally improved planning in crime commission.[54]

If the rationalization of crime was the only consequence of imprisonment, it arguably could be counted successful. The experiential consequences of imprisonment, however, go beyond those envisioned by most advocates of crime as choice. Given life in state programs and entrusted to bureaucracies, crime-control policies often produce unplanned or unintended consequences that diminish their effectiveness. That is the case with imprisonment; even as it makes offenders more rational about crime, it causes some to believe either that the odds of being captured may not be great or that the pain of penalty is not excessive in any case. How does this happen?

Reassurance

Despite the fact that many offenders have previous experience with confinement as juveniles and in jail, nearly all men approach their first prison sentence with trepidation. Their image of the world they are about to enter has been formed by old movies, sensationalized media reports, and jail conversations with inmates who have prison experience under their belt. Those on their way to prison for the first time see it as a test of their mettle, one they understand must be endured "like a man." Although many are confident, others fear involuntary segregation from the outside world and the violence and exploitation related in jail stories. Impending imprisonment is never experienced with greater apprehension than by the uninitiated.

Penitentiary confinement tends to polarize prisoners. Some recoil from it and resolve never again to do anything that would put them back in a similar situation. Those who can count on strong interpersonal support and respectable, well-paid employment may avoid returning to it, particularly if they lack identification with crime as a way of life. For other prisoners, however, the reaction is different. They adapt and grow acclimated to their surroundings as they learn about prison sentences, prison lifestyles, and the ins and outs of the correctional system (e.g., sentence reduction for "good and honor time"). Many are reassured by learning they will not have to serve their maximum sentence:

Q: When I asked you how much time you did, you said "nothing, 18 months." Did that not seem like much time to you?

A: I always thought it wasn't nothing because I went and did it and come on back here. But it really wasn't 18 months, it was 13 months and something. See, they give me 18 months . . . [but] they give me so much off for good behavior. Just like this time I'm doing now. To you 15 years would be a lot of time because you don't quite understand it. But after you get into the system here, then they give you so many points for this and so many points for that, . . . and when you get through looking at that you really don't have to stay as long as you might think.

John Irwin described how inmates new to the jail environment undergo several forms of adaptation.[55] Jail confinement erodes their conventional sensibilities, teaches them how to cope successfully with a depriving and dangerous environment, and acclimates them to deviant norms, adaptations, and others. This experience increases their detachment from conventional others and relationships even as it prepares them for future jail time. What is true of the jail and its impact is true of the prison as well. Experience with it may undermine its value as a deterrent to future criminal conduct. Simply put, one learns to do time, in part by learning coping strategies. One that many of the imprisoned try at one time or another is exhibiting irrational behavior in response to unusual or unwelcome stimuli or overtures: A prisoner explained:

Craziness. . . , like strength, provides some personal security. Nobody bothers the crazies or the psychos or the weirdos—they are the untouchables in prison. . . , [g]uys . . . who are not to be messed with and seldom are.[56]

Reflecting on the time he spent in prison, an informant echoed the words of most men who have been confined, saying that the "first year was the hardest part." One of the principal reasons for this was the unsettling effects of visits from family members or friends:[57]

> I think that people visiting was very upsetting. I'd get hyped up for a week before I knew they were coming, you know, and then two or three days afterwards, you know, I'd be depressed as hell. It was just upsetting to my routine.

Eventually, however, most prisoners become acclimated to the boredom and monotony of prison life:

> I used to, I could get off my job on Friday afternoon, go to the chow hall, go to the gym, come back and sleep, and just get up to go to the gym and eat, all weekend. And I could sleep the rest of the time, you know. I mean, it was just, I could lay down and sleep, just like a dog, you know. It lays down and sleeps, you know. It's just unconscious, it doesn't realize, you know, there's anything else to do. I just lost all concept, I guess, of even being there, you know, of time passing. Just the sameness. I had a friend that I worked with there [and] one of the games that we played was that we'd try to remember what we had for lunch, . . . like at three or four o'clock in the afternoon. And more days than not, we couldn't remember what we'd eaten for lunch.

Conservative commentators and political leaders are quick to say that imprisonment is not meant to be a pleasant experience. And it is not, at least for the overwhelming majority of those who suffer it. Even for those who have spent more than one stint in prison, it can be "a terrible thing to have to put up with."[58] But those who discover that they can survive satisfactorily or even thrive in the prison world are changed by this realization. Surviving in prison teaches the important lesson that one can "handle it."[59] Coping successfully with confinement reassures its survivors by allaying doubts and uncertainties. They now know they can bear up under the harshest penalties that the state can impose on anyone. The new reassurance can lessen the perceived threat of prison life:

> Q: Prison must not be much of a threat to you?
> A: It's not. Prison wasn't what I thought it was.
> Q: What do you mean by that?
> A: When I went in, . . . well, at that point in time it was kind of an awful thing to go to prison. That's what I had always heard. But when I got there and then found out that "well, hell, look who is here. . . . I didn't know he was here, or they was here" . . . Then I seen that I'm a man just like they are and I can make it.

> Q: What kind of effect did that first time you were incarcerated have on you?

A: I was 17 years old, and they sent me to a men's prison, you know. And I went down there, and I made it, you know. I survived it. And I come out, I thought, a man. . . . It just showed me that what, you know, what I had been afraid of happening wasn't nothing to be afraid of.

The harshness of prison is diminished not only by the realization that they can do time but also by the presence in prison of friends from the streets or acquaintances from other institutions. For too many of those who pass through prison once, the experience will leave them less fearful of and better prepared for a second trip if that should happen:

Q: Did you, did you actually think at [the time you passed forged checks] that, "hey, I could go to jail for this?"
A: I think I thought about it, but I didn't care if I went to jail. Jail was just, I was used to jail. Jail wasn't a threat to me.

Q: Before you went to prison the first time in your life, was it a threat to you?
A: Yeah, it was, the first time was. It was a change.
Q: Was prison something that you were kind of scared of?
A: *Scared of!* I was even scared for the first year that I was in prison. Because I knew nothing about the lifestyle. But now I do know about the lifestyle, and it doesn't scare me. I would rather not be locked up. I'd rather get out and get my head screwed on right, . . . but I'm not able to do that.

The new self-confidence of persistent thieves proves both illusory and self-defeating, however. The vast majority exaggerate their ability to rationalize crimes and to commit them successfully. A former thief remarked, "Whenever I began to steal it was always with the rationale I wouldn't make the mistakes I had made before. . . . It didn't occur to me there were literally thousands of ways I could get caught."[60] The repercussions from decisions they made, frequently years earlier, and their lifestyles eventually defeat whatever rationalization they undertake. To be rational about any undertaking inevitably means one must pay attention to planning, schedules, and timing, processes that are in fundamental conflict with the way thieves and hustlers choose to live their lives.[61] Consequently, despite their dreams of criminal success and faith that they can attain it by being "more careful," few who return to committing robbery, burglary, and theft after a stint in prison are equipped with the personal qualities, the connections, or the statistically improbable good luck needed if they are to reverse their past criminal fortunes.[62]

Notes

1. Alfred Blumstein, Jacqueline Cohen, and Daniel Nagin, editors, *Deterrence and Incapacitation* (Washington, D.C.: National Academy of Sciences, 1978).

2. Charles F. Manski, "Prospects for inference on deterrence through empirical analysis of individual criminal behavior," in *Deterrence and Incapacitation,* edited by Alfred Blumstein, Jacqueline Cohen, and Daniel Nagin (Washington, D.C.: National Academy of Sciences, 1978).

3. George Rengert and John Wasilchick, "Space, Time, and Crime: Ethnographic Insights into Residential Burglary" (final report to the National Institute of Justice, U.S. Department of Justice, 1989), p. 1.

4. Werner J. Einstadter, "The social organization of armed robbery," *Social Problems* 17(1969), pp. 64–83.

5. Mary Barker, Jane Geraghty, Barry Webb, and Tom Key, *The Prevention of Street Robbery* (London: Home Office, Police Research Group, 1993), p. 18.

6. Floyd Feeney and Adrianne Weir, "The prevention and control of robbery," *Criminology* 13(1975), p. 105.

7. Richard T. Wright and Scott H. Decker, *Burglars on the Job* (Boston: Northeastern University Press, 1994), p. 100.

8. On the basis of interviews with a sample of armed robbers in Montreal, Canada, investigators concluded that "very few armed robberies involve detailed planning. [Robbers'] selection of targets is often based on chance or is otherwise fairly spontaneous." Thomas Gabor et al., *Armed Robbery* (Springfield, Ill.: Charles C. Thomas, 1987), p. 201.

9. Mark Peterson, Jan Chaiken, and Patricia Ebener, *Survey of Jail and Prison Inmates,* 1978 (Ann Arbor, Mich.: Inter-University Consortium for Political and Social Research, 1984), p. 105. My analysis. See the Appendix for a description of this study.

10. James Wright and Peter Rossi, *Armed Criminals in America* (Ann Arbor, Mich.: Inter-University Consortium for Political and Social Research, 1985), p. 95. My analysis. See the Appendix for a description of this study.

11. Floyd Feeney and Adrianne Weir, "The prevention and control of robbery," *Criminology* 13(1975), p. 105.

12. Werner J. Einstadter, "The social organization of armed robbery," *Social Problems* 17(1969), pp. 54–83.

13. The distance offenders travel from home to the places they usually commit crime is less in some areas than others. One of the principal reasons some offenders move far away from their home neighborhoods is to avoid informal social controls and also residents' condemnation of victimizing one's own. For a discussion of this, see Mercer L. Sullivan, *"Getting Paid"* (Ithaca, N.Y.: Cornell University Press, 1989).

14. Richard T. Wright and Scott Decker, *Burglars on the Job* (Boston: Northeastern University Press, 1994), p. 127.

15. Trevor Bennett and Richard Wright, *Burglars on Burglary* (Aldershot, U.K.: Gower, 1984), Table A14.

16. Floyd Feeney, "Robbers as decision makers," in *The Reasoning Criminal,* edited by Derek B. Cornish and Ronald V. Clarke (New York: Springer-Verlag, 1986), pp. 59–60.

17. Dermot Walsh, *Heavy Business* (London: Routledge & Kegan Paul, 1986), p. 157.

18. For a description of the study, the wording of questions, and frequency counts for the entire sample, see James Wright and Peter Rossi, *Armed Criminals in*

America (Ann Arbor, Mich.: Inter-University Consortium for Political and Social Research, 1985), p. 96.

19. James Wright and Peter Rossi, *Armed Criminals in America* (Ann Arbor, Mich.: Inter-University Consortium for Political and Social Research, 1985), p. 55.

20. Mark A. Peterson and Harriet B. Braiker, with Suzanne M. Polich, *Who Commits Crimes?* (Cambridge, Mass.: Oelgeschlager, Gunn & Hain, 1981), p. xxvi.

21. John S. Carroll, "Committing a crime: The offender's decision," in *The Criminal Justice System*, edited by J. Konecni and E. B. Ebbesen (San Francisco: W. H. Freeman, 1982).

22. Dermot Walsh, *Heavy Business* (London: Routledge & Kegan Paul, 1986), p. 104.

23. Paul Cromwell, James N. Olson, and D'Aunn Wester Avary, *Breaking and Entering* (Newbury Park, Calif.: Sage, 1991), p. 70.

24. Ernest Booth, *Stealing Through Life* (New York: Alfred A. Knopf, 1929), pp. 72–73.

25. Richard J. Rettig, Manual J. Torres, and Gerald R. Garrett, *Manny* (Boston: Houghton Mifflin, 1977), pp. 57–59.

26. Mike Cherry, *On High Steel* (New York: Ballantine, 1975).

27. Stephen Lyng, "Edgework: A social-psychological analysis of voluntary risk taking," *American Journal of Sociology* 95(1990), pp. 851–886.

28. See, for example, Daniel S. Claster, "Comparison of risk perception between delinquents and nondelinquents." *Journal of Criminal Law, Criminology, and Police Science* 58(1967), pp. 80–86; and Scott Decker, Richard Wright, and Robert Logie, "Perceptual deterrence among active residential burglars: A research note," *Criminology* 31(1993), pp. 135–147.

29. Paul J. Brantingham and Patricia L. Brantingham, *Patterns in Crime* (New York: Macmillan, 1984).

30. See, for example, Stuart Winchester and Hilary Jackson, *Residential Burglary* (London: H. M. Stationery Office, 1982).

31. Simon Hakim and Andrew Buck, *Residential Security* (Bethesda, Md.: National Burglar and Fire Alarm Association, 1991).

32. Thomas Gabor et al., *Armed Robbery* (Springfield, Ill.: Charles C. Thomas, 1987), p. 210.

33. Mary Barker, Jane Geraghty, Barry Webb, and Tom Key, *The Prevention of Street Robbery* (London: Home Office, Police Research Group, 1993), p. 18.

34. Mary Barker, Jane Geraghty, Barry Webb, and Tom Key, *The Prevention of Street Robbery* (London: Home Office Police Research Group, 1993), p. 18.

35. Robert LeJeune, "The management of a mugging," *Urban Life* 6(1977), pp. 123–148.

36. Mary Barker, Jane Geraghty, Barry Webb, and Tom Key, *The Prevention of Street Robbery* (London: Home Office Police Research Group, 1993), pp. 22–23.

37. John E. Conklin, *Robbery and the Criminal Justice System* (Philadelphia: J. B. Lippincott, 1972), p. 88.

38. George Mallery Camp, "Nothing to Lose: A Study of Bank Robbery in America" (Ph.D. dissertation, Department of Sociology, Yale University, 1968), p. 110.

39. Mary Barker, Jane Geraghty, Barry Webb, and Tom Key, *The Prevention of Street Robbery* (London: Home Office Police Research Group, 1993).

40. Paul Cromwell, James N. Olson, and D'Aunn Wester Avary, *Breaking and Entering* (Newbury Park, Calif.: Sage, 1991), pp. 67–70; Richard T. Wright and Scott H. Decker, *Burglars on the Job* (Boston: Northeastern University Press, 1994).

41. Edwin M. Lemert, Review of *Hustlers, Beats and Others*, by Ned Polsky, *American Journal of Sociology* 73(1968), pp. 649–650.

42. Investigators have documented, and routinely castigated, the use of corporal punishment disproportionately in working-class and underclass families. For one discussion of some possible effects of this for criminal participation, see Mark Colvin and John Pauley, "A critique of criminology: Toward an integrated structural-Marxist theory of delinquency production," *American Journal of Sociology* 89(1983), pp. 513–551.

43. For a discussion of the importance of military service in the lives of street-corner African American males, see Elijah Anderson, *A Place on the Corner* (Chicago: University of Chicago Press, 1978), especially pp. 129–178.

44. Mark Peterson, Jan Chaiken, and Patricia Ebener, *Survey of Jail and Prison Inmates, 1978* (Ann Arbor, Mich.: Inter-University Consortium for Political and Social Research, 1984), p. 105. My analysis. See the Appendix for a description of this study.

45. Malcolm Braly, *False Starts* (New York: Penguin, 1976), pp. 51–52.

46. Joan Petersilia, Peter W. Greenwood, and Marvin Lavin, *Criminal Careers of Habitual Felons* (Washington, D.C.: U.S. Department of Justice, National Institute of Law Enforcement and Criminal Justice, 1978), pp. 60–65.

47. Joan Petersilia, Peter W. Greenwood, and Marvin Lavin, *Criminal Careers of Habitual Felons* (Washington, D.C.: U.S. Department of Justice, National Institute of Law Enforcement and Criminal Justice, 1978), p. 76.

48. Jack Black, *You Can't Win* (New York: A. L. Burt, 1926), p. 254.

49. Joan Petersilia, Peter W. Greenwood, and Marvin Lavin, *Criminal Careers of Habitual Felons* (Washington, D.C.: U.S. Department of Justice, National Institute of Law Enforcement and Criminal Justice, 1978), pp. 69–70.

50. Marcus Felson, *Crime and Everyday Life* (Thousand Oaks, Calif.: Pine Forge, 1994).

51. Tony Parker and Robert Allerton, *The Courage of His Convictions* (London: Hutchinson, 1962), p. 149.

52. Nathan McCall, *Makes Me Wanna Holler* (New York: Random House, 1994), p. 22.

53. Malcolm Braly, *False Starts* (New York: Penguin, 1976), p. 65.

54. Joan Petersilia, Peter W. Greenwood, and Marvin Lavin, *Criminal Careers of Habitual Felons* (Washington, D.C.: U.S. Department of Justice, National Institute of Law Enforcement and Criminal Justice, 1978), p. 60.

55. John Irwin, *The Jail* (Berkeley: University of California Press, 1985).

56. Arthur Hamilton, Jr., and William Banks, *Father Behind Bars* (Waco, Texas: WRS Publishing, 1993), p. 79. Compare Andreas Schroeder, *Shaking It Rough* (Toronto: Doubleday, 1976), p. 23.

57. An outstanding description of the psychic turmoil caused by visits is Andreas Schroeder, *Shaking It Rough* (Toronto: Doubleday, 1976), pp. 135–141.

58. Peter Crookston, *Villain* (London: Jonathan Cape, 1967), p. 96.

59. Dannie M. Martin and Peter Y. Sussman, *Committing Journalism* (New York: W. W. Norton, 1993), p. 23.

60. Malcolm Braly, *False Starts* (New York: Penguin, 1976), p. 65.

61. Mike Maguire, in collaboration with Trevor Bennett, *Burglary in a Dwelling* (London: Heinemann, 1982).

62. For an excellent autobiographical example of how good "connections" can increase substantially the financial success from crime, see Frank Hohimer, *The Home Invaders* (Chicago: Chicago Review Press, 1975).

7

Crime Control and Persistent Thieves

During most of America's current war on crime, political leaders have claimed that the greatest promise for effective street-crime management lies in escalating the threat and the empirical odds of punishment for offenders. Along with development of an array of aggressive and tough criminal justice policies and practices, both increased significantly in the years after 1975.[1] Training school, jail, and prison populations, for example, have climbed to historically unprecedented levels, surpassing all predictions of just a few years earlier.[2] At a time when public schools in many regions of the United States are under severe budgetary constraints, the nation's infrastructure is decaying, and millions of citizens cannot secure quality health care, expenditure of public revenues for crime control has skyrocketed. And there is more of everything. Onto traditional criminal justice programs, legislators and administrators have grafted new ones, including intensive probation and electronic monitoring. The sentencing reform movement that swept the nation has left in its wake dramatically refashioned criminal sentencing codes, including provisions for "three strikes and you're out."[3] A typical statutory incarnation mandates a life sentence for anyone convicted of his or her third felony. Most of these changes are predicated on the belief that the threat of punishment deters and that imprisonment, if it accomplishes nothing else, at least incapacitates those confined. As advocates of the choice-and-punishment approach to crime and criminal justice sometimes say in justification of their preferred approach: "When I see a hot stove, I know better than to touch it. Because I know it will burn me." In this concluding chapter I explore some policymaking implications of the materials presented in Chapters 1 through 6.

One of the first lessons learned by investigators who deign to examine offenders' lives, their calculus, and their decisions is that the hot-stove analogy provides little more than a directional heading for understanding matters that are more complex. Most of what is known about persistent thieves and stealing admittedly is derived from studies of known offenders, and there is no way to know how widely their experiences can be generalized. It is unclear whether there is anything peculiar about their makeup that not only explains their lawbreaking but also limits application of what is learned about them.[4] Lessons about crime and crime control drawn from the experiences of persistently apprehended offenders may have limited application to others precisely because of the former's demonstrated willingness and propensity to commit crime and their apparent lack of success doing so. It is possible that crime-control policies that are ineffective with persistent thieves might work well in restraining the conduct of most adults. In addition to the confounding effect of past willingness to commit crime, it is impossible to determine how much decisionmaking and responses to imprisonment by persistent thieves reflect the effects of past experience and success committing crime and avoiding arrest. The great majority of them have gotten away with many more acts of theft than resulted in arrest. Given these problems, caution and modesty clearly are more than justified as we explore some implications of the preceding chapters.

Class and Choice

Academics and political leaders who employ the language of choice to explain criminal participation typically live orderly, comfortable lives constructed painstakingly in a calculated fashion. From an early age, they have had apparent to them respectable if not always well-paying career options and unambiguous pathways to achieving these. Their entire bourgeois world is wrapped in a rationality familiar to accountants. The metrics they employ are clear-cut, unidimensional, and in many cases calibrated precisely, often in monetary units. At virtually every stage of their lives, they are able to see the relationship between the law-abiding or virtuous behavior of yesterday and the payoffs of today. Economically secure and respectable citizens, they can visualize and calculate easily the losses in reputation and wealth that would follow from misconduct or detection. And if they need any reminder, the risks of crime are brought home by media coverage when someone like them falls from grace. The transgressions and humiliation of men and women who "ought to know better" are newsworthy stuff.[5]

How different things are for lower-class women and men, whose cultural capital severely constrains their awareness of and preparation to take advantage of countless legitimate opportunities. Consequently, the most important choices in their lives typically are made in an option-barren landscape. A great many 17-year-old lower-class boys and girls, for example, have no more attractive option and no higher ambition than enlisting in the military. Their limited options are one reason that alternative, deviant identities and lifestyles can be appealing to them.

The fact that a high proportion of persistent direct-contact stealing is done by men from the lower reaches of the working class cannot be ignored. Inequality in any form, whether it is based on race, gender, or class, plays an important part in structuring many of the correlates of crime.[6] If it does nothing else, this fact challenges policymakers to imagine the impact of their policies not through the eyes of successful men and women but instead through the clouded lenses of the economically marginal and despised. The fact that the war on crime was launched and gained momentum with rather little interest in this perspective or in how offenders live and make choices must be ranked as one of its more remarkable aspects.

Identity, Context, and Mood

The challenge of constructing crime-control policies grounded in notions of crime as choice would be less difficult if there was not substantial personal and contextual variation in the meaning of and attention paid to legal threats and punishment. This variation and its implications have received little recognition or attention from crime analysts or from advocates of crime-and-punishment.

> [The] situational nature of sanction properties has escaped the scales and indicators employed in official record and self-report survey research. In this body of research an arrest and a year in prison are generally assumed to have the same meaning for all persons and across all situations. The situational grounding of sanction properties suggests [,however,] that we look beyond official definitions of sanctions and the attitudinal structure of individuals to the properties of situations.[7]

Men and women who choose deviant identities and lifestyles are decisionmaking but distant kin to members of the local Rotary Club, and their metrics and calculus must be seen and interpreted through their eyes and with some awareness of the circumstances of their lives. As Dermot Walsh noted, the former's "definitions of costs and rewards seem to be at variance with society's estimates of them."[8] This does not mean that thieves' decisionmaking is uninterpretable in the language and theory of crime as choice, but it does highlight some of the complexities of a process that is neither irrational nor simple. Offenders do calculate in some manner, but the process is constrained severely by their prior choices of identity and lifestyle. Consequently, although they may calculate potential benefits and costs, they do so differently from what is sketched in decisionmaking models. It should come as little surprise, therefore, to learn that an investigation of 589 incarcerated property offenders concluded that the subjects apparently do not utilize "a sensible cost-benefit analysis" when weighing the utilities of crime.[9] As the investigators noted, thieves "substantially underestimate the risk of arrest for most crimes, routinely overestimate the monetary benefit they expect, and seem to have grossly inaccurate perceptions of the costs and benefits associated with property crime."[10] In choosing life as party, its celebrants elevate to unrivaled place in their attention subterranean values.[11] These values are in conflict or opposition with other publicly proclaimed values, but they also are accepted by many. They include the search for excitement or "thrills," disdain for work, the desire to acquire large sums of money quickly and easily, and the readiness to employ violence as proof of manhood.

Identity and character projects are imbued with utilities more ephemeral and less calculable in conventional metrics even than crimes committed during party pursuits. Use of crime as a vehicle to establish respect or character gives to it and to the calculus of choice distinctive qualities. In these circumstances, values are not experienced as the neat and continuous variables envisioned by bourgeois academics and policymakers. The fact that an option or act is risky, for example, can increase its attractiveness to men for whom character and respect are reckoned as *everything*. Like "prize fighters and a good many saloon fighters" many persistent thieves may "die in the gutter," but they "have moments of glory unknown to accountants."[12]

In some respects, responses to situations perceived as pregnant with criminal opportunity are like responses to overtures of interest by members of the opposite sex. Context and identity can be all-important. The same is true of mood. Men who commit street-level stealing typically do so not only while in the company of others and under the influence of drugs but often as well in moments of desperation, arrogance, or self-righteousness. These considerations complicate significantly the challenge of influencing their choices. The chances that sexual overtures will meet with indifference or rebuff are greatest when this is seen as virtue and when conventional significant others are present. This is a long way from the kind of situations in which thieves characteristically choose to commit crime. Contexts populated almost exclusively by young, drug-using males simply are not the kind in which decisionmakers pay close attention to threat and virtue.

Life Course and Calculation

Nor are identity, context, and mood the only factors that condition the effectiveness of threat. We know also that the meaning of crime and the calculus of stealing are not invariant over the life course.[13] Young offenders know little and care less about the schedule of penalties; whether the law threatens 5 years or 25 years is inconsequential for them. For the most part, they simply fail to give it serious thought. And the penalties do not seem all that severe in any case. Even the passage of time scarcely is noticed. Juveniles and young adults often have little awareness or appreciation of the legal and personal repercussions of their criminality. This is true especially of their perceptions of time spent in institutions such as training schools and prisons:

> I've seen the time in my life, man, where it might seem foolish, 'cause it seems foolish to me now. When I was in the street, hustling, I'd say, "if I get knocked off and don't get but a nickel"—five years—I said, "hell with it," you know. The only thing would be in my mind, if I got busted could I hang around, try to have my lawyer try to get me some kind of plea or something so I wouldn't get but a nickel. 'Cause I knew I could knock five years out.

Another informant echoed these remarks, saying that when he was young,

> I don't know, man, I just didn't give a fuck, you know. I was young, simple, man. I didn't care, you know. Shit, doing time, you know, I didn't know what doing time was all about. Doing time to me was nothing, you know.

With a prison stint behind them, offenders are much more knowledgeable about the law and its threats, but they are confident they will not be caught.

Clearly, both the ability and the inclination to calculate carefully before commiting crime change over the life course. Those who ordinarily are models of thoughtful, prudent decisionmaking may have moments when they behave very differently. Likewise, individuals who behave naively or impulsively at one stage of life often look back on these moments with disbelief over their poor judgment. There also are distinct age-related changes in the likelihood that the estimated risks of committing crime will outweigh the possible gains.

In many states, as matters stand today, the heaviest penalties fall at the point when many offenders are on the verge of desisting or shifting to less serious forms of crime. Heavy prison sentences can exact such a toll from offenders that they miss all timetables for achieving success legitimately. The remarks of an informant who was interviewed in prison are instructive. He had served several lengthy previous sentences but had failed to desist from serious crime:

> A lot of the guys here tell me, say "man, why don't you straighten up?" I tell them all the same thing: "Why? *Why!* If I work every day of my goddamned life from now on, I'll never have nothing. Only way I'm going to get what I

want is to steal it. . . . I'll be 47 when I get out of here, and there's no way possible for me to ever get ahead now. It's too late in life. A guy's got to start
about 21 or 22 like you probably did. I'm just too old now. I'm not going to
have nothing.

When I asked him what he saw in the future, he replied, "If I can get out
of here, and make it [working], . . . make good enough money to live off
of, I'll make it. But if I don't, [I'll] put a gun in my hand again or a check-
book or something."

This informant is not alone. Consider the remarks of a man who spent
17 years in various Washington state institutions. He found himself, at age
51, unemployed, addicted to alcohol, and in bad health.

[W]hat am I supposed to be doing? Keep asking for help? Be down at the
mission with the rest of them bums? It ain't gonna happen. I guarantee it
ain't gonna happen to me. There's one way out, one way or the other: go back
to prison . . . and let them take care of me for the rest of my life. You know,
like the oldtimers in the movies? . . . Go for the last big one. You either make
it or you break it. . . . If I lose, I go back to prison. Federal prison this time,
because they got more money.[14]

This man subsequently spent additional time in institutions, including jail
and a state hospital.

Unintended Consequences of Harshness

Before its displacement by the theory of crime as choice, labeling theory
was the dominant perspective in criminology. Labeling theory placed
squarely on the shoulders of the state and its social control apparatus part
of the responsibility for individual persistence in deviance and criminality. Proponents of labeling theory took seriously the fact that official processing is not meant to be and is not a neutral process. Formal processing
by agencies such as the police and courts, the theory predicted, exacerbates the problems offenders encounter when they try to make a clean
break with their past. They often experience consequential changes in
opportunities, reputation, and patterns of association as a result. The U.S.
Army, for example, looks differently on choir boys and convicted armed
robbers. The latter may discover in addition that former friends now turn
away while ones of a less wholesome nature seem drawn to them. They
also begin to see themselves and their environment differently. An example of this process is provided in the ex-convict Malcolm Braly's description of how he was changed by his punishment for attempted escape from
California's Preston School of Industry:

I was assigned to A Company. A Company was ... a disciplinary unit, reserved for hardheads and stone fuck-ups. ... [C]ompany life was designed to be stern. We went everywhere at quick-step march, double the usual tempo. We were never given At Ease. We stood at rigid attention. We maintained constant silence. For the slightest infraction ... the fuck-ups [stood] in front of the Man's desk with their arms held parallel to the floor. ... We stood for hours. ... I liked A Company. I liked knowing it was as bad as it could get and nothing was being held back to be awarded if you were quiet and cooperative. Sucking the Man's ass bought you nothing. We were denied the hope of small mitigations and I discovered I didn't care. ... I gained [reputationally] by managing to stand firm with the hard asses ... but I also learned there were things more important than the hope of comfort.[15]

For those formerly naive about crime and criminal opportunities, arrest and confinement can change their perceptual templates to the point they can see little else.

And this does not exhaust the potential deleterious impacts of punishment. When persistent thieves are incarcerated, the results sometimes are different from those intended by advocates of punishment. Perceptions of its harshness are undermined by experience with imprisonment, particularly reassurance that it can be endured. Persistent thieves rationalize crime and believe they can perfect criminal techniques and become successful. It can be argued, of course, that if prison conditions generally were more austere and regimented, surely fewer thieves would react to the experience in this way. If confinement does not put sufficient fear into inmates, perhaps it is because the regimen is too easy and an increase in unpleasantness is needed.

No one can say confidently what the net result of such a development would be, but it is useful to note that enduring extremely harsh or brutal treatment can reassure some prisoners even as it kindles dangerous emotions. I refer specifically to embitterment, anger, and the desire to wreak revenge. This reaction can crystallize and strengthen a conception of oneself as a person who has been treated unfairly by authorities. Advocates and supporters of America's return to harsh crime-control policies have paid scant attention to the emotional consequences of the programs spun off of them. We must look to an earlier generation of ex-convict writers for the best glimpse of this process. An informant who devoted most of his adult life to stealing told of the period he spent in a state industrial school during the 1920s. The institutional regimen was austere and harsh: "Now, you see, at a tender age ... you can build up a pretty good well of hate from being mishandled and abused. ... And I'll guarantee you, when you came out of there, you would either never steal again or you didn't fear God himself."[16] Instead of deflecting him from a criminal pathway, this experience toughened and made him resolute. His experience is not unique:

> I am glad now, and I was glad then, that they lashed me. It did me good. Not in the way it was intended to, of course, but in a better way. I went away from the tripod with fresh confidence. . . . I had taken everything they had in the way of violence and could take it again. Instead of going away in fear, I found my fear removed. *The whipping post is a strange place to gather fresh confidence and courage, yet that's what it gave me, and in that dark cell I left behind many fears and misgivings.*[17]

We should not lose sight of the fact that harshness angers and embitters at least some who are subjected to it and leaves them with strengthened resolve never to submit or, should they ever get the chance, to take revenge:

> While robbing other people's houses, I was perfectly conscious of the wrong I was doing, quite as much as of the great risks which I was running of getting caught or killed. Indeed, my own common sense told me that I could not keep up this kind of work indefinitely and that, sooner or later, I was bound to be sent back to prison. . . . What was the motive behind it all? What made it worth while to me? The answer to these questions is that I strongly wanted to get even with society for the wrong which I felt it had done me. This spirit of revenge, instilled in me by the years of suffering and ill-treatment behind prison walls, pervaded my whole nature.[18]

In the depths of the Great Depression, when the U.S. government opened Alcatraz penitentiary, it was touted as just what was needed to control violent and dangerous career criminals. As an "end-of-the-line" prison, it was meant to be tough. A former Alcatraz prisoner once told me that he interpreted his transfer there as a sign that he never would be released from confinement. Instead of being cowed by his plight, he strengthened his resistance to prison officials. As he put it, "I was defiant, even to the warden, and I said 'If I have to die, I'm gonna die just like I am.' I said, 'nobody's gonna change me.'" Despite their anecdotal nature, reports like this suggest we must not assume that the effects of policies that increase the risk of and the pain imposed on offenders are entirely one-sided. For several years after Alcatraz was closed, U.S. government officials considered whether to designate another prison to serve the functions it once served. Eventually they did so and settled on the U.S. penitentiary at Marion, Illinois. Just a few years later, as the nation's prison population began increasing and the prison construction boom got under way, both the federal and state governments invested costly resources in these so-called super-max prisons for inmates who they argued could not be controlled elsewhere. Exemplified by Pelican Bay in California, the

new high-security end-of-the-line prisons are places of extreme deprivation and suffering. Typically, inmates are confined to one-person cells for
23 hours a day, cut off from all contact with other human beings. We must
not be so blind or pig-headed as to ignore the possibility that confinement
of this type drives some men deeper into confusion, disorientation, or
rage. John Irwin and James Austin warned, for example, that "we should
be concerned by the fact that [these prisons] are spewing out damaged
human material, [some of whom] will violently lash out, perhaps mur-
dering or raping someone."[19] The number of offenders who are so affected
may not be large, but the price they exact from victims and the community at large may be substantial. There is reason, then, for caution and
humility in constructing excessively punitive crime-control policies justified by an ideology of crime as choice.

Offenders who are not hardened by gratuitous, excessive punishment
in the name of crime control may be depleted by the experience and left
dependent. Working-class culture, like all human cultures, "can be visu-
alized, if only in part, as a kind of theater in which certain contrary ten-
dencies are played out."[20] For every prisoner who assists official control
by exaggerated displays of independence, there is at least one other who
opts for *dependence*. Describing the appeal of incarceration, Brian Biluszek
said that in prison, "I can kick back if I want. I can do as much as I feel
comfortable doing, or as little as I want to do. They're still gonna feed me
and they're still gonna give me a warm place to sleep. I can get institutionalized real easy. It's comfortable."

Like Brian, many who are forced to accommodate themselves to subordination and dependency manage to create from the experience some
aspects of it that are satisfying. If nothing else, enforced subordination
frees one of the responsibilities and obligations of self-direction. A 65-
year-old man who was interviewed in prison expressed ambivalence
about returning to the free world:

> In a way, I'm looking forward to getting out, and another way it don't much
> matter to me. . . . I know everybody here. . . . I do almost like I want. I go to
> early chow. [Earlier today] I went down to the law library and used their
> copying machine. I can do fairly well what I want to do without anybody
> buggin' me about it, 'cause all the officials know me.

Despite the normative call of independence and autonomy, men of working-class background adapt easily to hierarchical supervision. Surveying
his options, which he acknowledged were bleak, a middle-aged persistent
offender acknowledged his dependence:

> I don't care much about being in the free world. Too tough, too tough for me.
> I'm too institutionalized, been in prison too much, been taken care of too

much as a youngster and as an adult by the state and it kind of gets into your system. . . . See, I do fine when I'm in institutions. . . . Can't get a better guy. I help cook, I help do this, I help do that, but you let me out on my own, I won't do a goddam thing for myself.[21]

The challenge of minimizing noncompliance with law shares some qualities with the challenge of minimizing the harmful consequences of sexual attraction between human beings. Every "solution" carries its price. The lesson this teaches is how important timing can be in application of sanctions most likely to be effective and efficient. One-size-fits-all crime-control policies not only run the risk of increasing secondary deviation but cost an enormous sum of money at a time when it surely could be spent better elsewhere.

At this time of pessimism about career criminals and the threat they pose, it may be instructive to recall the life of Robert Timmons, a man whose many years of confinement included stays in some of America's harshest prisons. In my first interview with Robert, he commented on changes in himself that occurred as he got older:

Practically all my life, I was in some kind of an institution. . . . And they called me *"incorrigible."* I laugh at it now—"incorrigible." I couldn't be changed.
Q: Why do you laugh at it now?
A: Because they're *"experts,"* they're experts. And they're supposed to be able to analyze a person and come up with the exact answer. There was nothing that could be done with me, I would never change. I *have* changed!

Changes like these, as noted in Chapter 5, are not uncommon.

Robert Timmons's experience is matched by that of Reginald Perkins, an informant who brought to our interview a scrapbook. It opened with the front page of a yellowed newspaper. Under a headline proclaiming "Terrorists Captured," the report detailed the victimization of a tourist couple who were abducted near the Washington, D.C., train station, pistol-whipped, and robbed. Next to a photograph of four young predators who were arrested soon after the incident was a picture of the beaten and bruised husband, taken in his hospital bed. Then 18 years old, Reginald Perkins was one of the young men arrested and pictured.[22] As he looked at the picture of his victims 35 years later, his eyes filled with tears. Following his arrest, Reginald spent several years in a state mental hospital, feigning mental illness in order to beat the criminal charges detailed in the newspaper story. Subsequently, he returned to committing crime, was convicted of several armed robberies, and served a prison sentence at Lorton. While there he took advantage of the few opportunities available, attended school, and eventually received his baccalaureate degree. A statistician and planner today, Reginald and his spouse are suburban homeowners. It is unfortunate that many of the pretenders described in this book take so long to learn the lesson he eventually learned. Many learn too late.

Intelligent Sanctioning

The principal crime-control lesson to be drawn from the life and experiences of Reginald Perkins and men who grow old "swaggering in defiance of a machine that isn't paying the slightest attention"[23] is that the appeal of harshness must be tempered by realization that the impact of all programs is mixed; no approach to crime control yields only benefits. Moreover, all policies and the programs that give life to them cost money. Some cost a great deal more than others, but in crime control as in other areas of public expenditure, there are no free lunches. This fundamental insight, which many advocates of choice-and-punishment apply instinctively to other areas of public expenditure, is no less true of crime control. Nothing said here is meant to imply that legal threats have no deterrent effect, but tinkering with them on the assumption offenders are aware of and behaviorally sensitive to the changes at best is naive and at worst is disingenuous. Offenders, who are largely ignorant about the arcane details of the law and who tend to be inattentive to risk when making criminal choices in any case, likely will not be marginally deterred by an escalation of the threatened penalty of, say, armed robbery from five to seven years. We must be extremely wary of crime-control proposals that promise significant reductions in street crime for marginal increases in threat and repression. The possibility that a little punishment might be a good thing is hardly justification for assuming that its benefits continue increasing as its use and its harshness are stepped up. The complexities of decisionmaking by persistent thieves in no way contradict that stealing is volitional or that punishment may serve positive social functions independent of its effectiveness reducing crime, but they certainly justify a call for greater modesty by supporters of choice-and-punishment.

In closing this description and discussion of persistent thieves, I cannot help noting that crime-control policies constructed on the notion of crime as choice are aimed almost exclusively at increasing the risk of criminal participation. This ignores the theoretically obvious: Offenders' behavior can be changed not only by manipulating threat but also by increasing legitimate opportunities and by decreasing illicit ones. Increasing legitimate opportunities extends the choices available to men who otherwise choose criminal ones. It is poor science and poor public policy theoretically to ignore the fact that disadvantage, disrepute, and the cultural capital they spawn limit options. It is foolish and misleading to expect men and women this describes to make their way in life with the same confidence and outcome as peers who do not share their handicaps. Those who manage to exploit successfully legitimate opportunity are less likely to be interested in crime and to find that the estimated risk of breaking the law increases as well. In failing to acknowledge and explore this, most discussions of crime-deterrence processes are grounded inadequately in theory and, more important, fail to present policymakers with the full range of options, some of which surely are more efficient than others.

Notes

1. See, for example, Patrick A. Langan, "America's soaring prison population," *Science* 251(March 29, 1991), pp. 1568–1573.

2. Barry Kreisberg, Robert DeComo, and Norma C. Herrera, *National Juvenile Custody Trends 1978–1989* (Washington, D.C.: U.S. Department of Justice, Office of Juvenile Justice and Delinquency Prevention, 1992); Bureau of Justice Statistics, *Correctional Populations in the United States, 1990* (Washington, D.C.: U.S. Department of Justice, 1992); John Irwin and James Austin, *It's About Time* (Belmont, Calif.: Wadsworth, 1994).

3. For an insightful discussion of these developments, see Nils Christie, *Crime Control as Industry*, 2d and enlarged edition (London: Routledge, 1994).

4. Michael R. Gottfredson and Travis Hirschi, *A General Theory of Crime* (Stanford, Calif.: Stanford University Press, 1990); Daniel S. Nagin and Raymond Paternoster, "On the relationship of past to future participation in delinquency," *Criminology* 29(1991), pp. 163–189.

5. Few of the robberies and virtually none of the burglaries committed by persistent thieves receive any mention by the media. Put simply, when unemployed, drug-using lower-class males are arrested for these crimes, it is not "news"; no one is surprised.

6. For an outstanding discussion of the importance and the meaning of inequality, see John Braithwaite, *Crime, Shame and Reintegration* (Cambridge, U.K.: Cambridge University Press, 1989); and John Brathwaite "Poverty, power, white-collar crime, and the paradoxes of criminological theory," *Australian–New Zealand Journal of Criminology* 24(1991), pp. 40–58.

7. Sheldon Ekland-Olson, John Lieb, and Louis Zurcher, "The paradoxical impact of criminal sanctions: Some microstructural findings" *Law and Society Review* 18(1984), p. 174.

8. Dermot Walsh, *Break-Ins* (London: Constable, 1980), p. 141.

9. Figgie International, *The Figgie Report Part VI—The Business of Crime* (Richmond, Va.: Figgie International, 1988), p. 25.

10. Figgie International, *The Figgie Report Part VI—The Business of Crime* (Richmond, Va.: Figgie International, 1988), p. 81.

11. The classic statement of these subterranean values is David Matza and Gresham Sykes, "Juvenile delinquency and subterranean values," *American Sociological Review* 26(1961), pp. 712–719.

12. Nathan Glazer and Daniel Patrick Moynihan, *Beyond the Melting Pot* (Cambridge, Mass.: MIT Press, 1963), pp. 261–262.

13. Robert J. Sampson and John H. Laub, "Crime and deviance in the life course," *Annual Review of Sociology* 18(1992), pp. 63–84.

14. Eugene Delorme, *Chief*, edited by Inez Cardozo-Freeman (Lincoln: University of Nebraska Press, 1994), p. 187.

15. Malcolm Braly, *False Starts* (New York: Penguin, 1976), pp. 59–60.

16. This man, a burglar for much of his adult life, spent a total of nine years in confinement but earned well from crime. By the reckoning of his peers, he was a reasonably successful thief.

17. Jack Black, *You Can't Win* (New York: A. L. Burt, 1926), pp. 270, 278.

18. A Burglar, *In the Clutch of Circumstance* (New York: D. Appleton, 1922), pp. 147–148.

19. John Irwin and James Austin, *It's About Time* (Belmont, Calif.: Wadsworth, 1994), p. 110.

20. Kai T. Erikson, *Everything in Its Path* (New York: Simon and Schuster, 1976), p. 82.

21. Eugene Delorme, *Chief*, edited by Inez Cardozo-Freeman (Lincoln: University of Nebraska Press, 1994), pp. 179–181.

22. According to Reginald, one of the others later died in Alcatraz following "disciplinary action" by prison staff.

23. Andreas Schroeder, *Shaking It Rough* (Toronto: Doubleday, 1976), p. 59.

Appendix: Materials and Methods

Besides drawing heavily from social science research on street offenders, the analysis in *Great Pretenders* makes use of data from my ethnographic studies of thieves. Data for an initial study,[1] a description and interpretation of the activities and careers of burglars, were collected during 1969 and 1970 in interviews with and surveys completed by men incarcerated for burglary in the Illinois State Penitentiary system. In those halcyon days before informed consent, the process of securing official approval for research and the task of data collection were facilitated by the contacts I had among prison sociologists. The survey I administered to inmates at Joliet and other Illinois prisons included self-report measures of past criminal participation, background and criminal history information, and estimates of the formal risk of various types of criminal behavior. A second study,[2] conducted during 1980 and 1981 while I was a Visiting Fellow at the National Institute of Justice, explored the process of crime desistance through retrospective ethnographic interviews with 50 men who were incarcerated for property crimes once or more during their earlier years. The tape-recorded interviews with ex-offenders that resulted from this study largely focused on the subjects' criminal histories, interpersonal and social-psychological changes they experienced as they got older, and the relationships between these changes and the subjects' criminal participation.

Data collection for a third study, the Desistance Project, also was supported by the National Institute of Justice and carried out during 1987 and 1988.[3] The principal research objective was an enhanced understanding of crime desistance by serious repetitive property offenders. From the population of all men incarcerated in Tennessee state prisons during 1987, a sample was selected of 60 male recidivists with a demonstrated preference for property crimes who also were nearing release from confinement. Fifty-eight of the men had served at least one prior prison sentence, and the remaining two had served one or more jail sentences, primarily for armed robbery, burglary, or theft. Every member of the sample was interviewed approximately one month prior to release from prison and also completed a self-administered survey about his social and criminal background, self-reported past participation in a variety of crimes, and estimates of the potential gains and losses of any future criminal participation following release. Seven to 10 months after their release from prison, 46 of the men were successfully traced, contacted, and interviewed. The semistructured ethnographic interviews included questions about their activities, living arrangements, and means of support following release and the context of reinvolvement in crime. The subjects also completed a self-administered survey instrument that included self-report questions about postrelease criminal participation. Part of the interviews produced detailed descriptions of the most recent, easily recalled property crime that each subject had committed in the free world prior to the interview. All interviews were audio tape recorded, transcribed, and analyzed. The crime descriptions specifically were analyzed using *The Ethnograph,* a software package for use on text-based data.[4] David Honaker and Kenneth Tunnell, research assistants on this project, conducted nearly all the interviews and also completed graduate theses using data they collected.[5]

Autobiographies of offenders and ex-offenders, published both in North America and Britain, were another source of data for this analysis of persistent thieves. I began examining and using for research purposes this constantly growing corpus of materials more than 25 years ago. I have read dozens of these works, and I have coded and stored for retrieval the contents of many. The desire to convert their life story into a book is extremely common among thieves and former thieves, and it is surprising how many do so. Although at one time I tried to identify and maintain a complete list of these materials, I have discovered this is an impossible task. Offender autobiographies are a dime a dozen. Consequently, I no longer am surprised on learning about ones I was unaware of, often issued by small regional publishers.[6] For whatever reason, a great many former offenders believe their life history would make an entertaining and perhaps useful contribution to understanding crime and those who commit it. When this belief is nurtured or reinforced by straight persons who happen to meet or befriend them, the result occasionally is an autobiographical account with rich interpretive and theoretically useful observations. Products of collaboration with academicians[7] or other accomplished writers, these works generally are significant as data sources far beyond their numbers.[8]

It is tempting to dismiss offenders' life histories as biased and therefore of little value for purposes of social science research. Those who would make use of them as research data must be able, however, to see beyond the potential and real short-comings of these data. Rather than dwell on reasons why these sources are not perfect, I prefer to emphasize their positive value for understanding offenders and their criminal careers. The promise and potential payoff are evident in two areas. First, the life histories and interpretations contained in published accounts in many cases profit from the extended length of time the subjects have invested in sorting out and making sense of their lives. Men who spend years in prison characteristically devote hours to examining their pasts, the forces that shaped them, and significant contingencies in their lives. Published autobiographies are storehouses of these interpretations and other materials. *My Life in Crime* and *False Starts* are two examples that come to mind immediately. Unlike responses to face-to-face questions, which are given without time for reflection, the insights and interpretations presented in these materials were not developed hastily. Consequently, they often contain sharper and more impressive descriptions and interpretations.[9] Second, when they are used in combination with other data sources, offenders' life histories can be extremely useful in generating, disconfirming, or refining interpretations and generalizations grounded in other kinds of data. If nothing else, use of them increases the number and range of subjects whose experiences can be analyzed.[10]

More important, it is not at all clear a priori that the biographical accounts of street-level persistent thieves are any less trustworthy than the published memoirs of, say, Richard Nixon, Henry Kissinger, or Robert McNamara, all persons surely motivated less to render accurate history than to present carefully edited accounts of themselves and their activities. This in no way denies that one must approach with caution the autobiographies of thieves. Unquestionably, some are written by men who use their accounts only to exaggerate or romanticize their criminal exploits or to impress with the depth of their suffering. It is equally clear, however, that most are written by men sincerely motivated to confront and to understand their mistakes and the pathways they have traveled.

Many published life histories, however, contain little that is useful for those intent upon gaining an understanding of their subjects' perspectives and lives. Given their authors' varied abilities and the varied circumstances in which they were written, this shortcoming is not surprising; most were written with little or no assistance from others,[11] whereas some authors benefited from the knowledge and expertise of accomplished writers.[12] The authors of some were excellent writers in their own right.[13] Although a few were written at a time when the authors had little or no intention of abandoning crime,[14] most were published while they were in the midst of what they hoped would be a permanent transition to noncriminal life or some years after the final break with crime.[15] Although this body of work includes many shallow and uninformative life histories,[16] it also contains more than a handful of extremely perceptive, insightful, and well-written works that more than compensate for the large volume of dross that must be processed locating them.[17]

At a number of places in *Great Pretenders*, I present secondary analyses of survey data collected in studies supported by the National Institute of Justice. A 1976 survey by the Rand Corporation of 624 men incarcerated in five California prisons was the first.[18] This was followed by the Rand Inmate Survey, a 1978 study of jail and prison inmates in California, Texas, and Michigan[19] and a subsequent follow-up study of the prison inmates.[20] I also report further descriptive analysis of data from the University of Massachusetts survey of 1,874 felons imprisoned in ten states.[21] Analyses reported here are limited, however, to the 1,038 men who were serving time for robbery, burglary, auto theft, or theft at the time they completed the survey.

My background and experiences, I assume, provide a context for whatever biases may be evident in the foregoing materials. I was reared in a blue-collar household in that time of post–World War II prosperity dubbed by C. Wright Mills the "American celebration." My father earned a good hourly wage as a carpenter, but the seasonal nature of his work and the presence of nine children gave to things a somewhat precarious quality. My mother was unsurpassed at managing scarce resources and moderating the effects of sometimes severe fluctuations in family income. Bounded intellectually by *Reader's Digest* and my father's monthly union magazine, this narrow world still taught important lessons. Their "bedrock [was the] notion . . . that a man's place was among those who worked and struggled, not with the wealthy and the powerful."[22] Growing up, I performed passably in the racially diverse inner-city public schools attended by children from largely blue-collar backgrounds. None of the work I did before the prospect of becoming an academic took root in my consciousness bears even a remote resemblance to how I earn a living today.

For inexplicable reasons, I have long had an interest in the first-person accounts and perspectives of criminals and prisoners. This interest took shape during my undergraduate years, at a time when the individual treatment model and indeterminate sentence reigned unchallenged in the theories of intellectuals and in the policies of elected representatives. Through his use of first-person reading materials, Dr. Samuel P. Daykin further stimulated development of an interest in the offender's perspective; I specifically recall, for example, reading Willard Motley's *Knock on Any Door*.[23] During a summer internship in a federal reformatory, I was astounded and puzzled to discover that the inmates, many of whom were serving sentences of 60 days to 6 years under terms of the Federal Youth Corrections Act, generally detested indeterminate sentences. This experience marked my realization that those who are the objects of criminal justice theory and practice sometimes have a view of these matters that differs dramatically from the official line. Once this is acknowledged, it is only common sense that offenders' perspectives must be understood and taken account of in any endeavor aimed at changing their behavior or controlling them in any fashion.

This belief was strengthened during nearly three years employment at the Illinois State Penitentiary where, together with several other prison sociologists, the bulk of my time was spent preparing classification reports, parole progress reports, and reports summarizing official contacts with inmates. These various reports routinely were distributed to an array of officials, filed, and so far as I could determine, completely ignored unless some extraordinary occurrence brought external public scrutiny; until the bureaucratic schedule required that a new one be written; or until some official called on its verbiage for justification of an action he planned or already had taken. Although this occurred during what is known as "the era of individual treatment," white-collar treatment personnel daily had to contend with blue-collar custodial staff who were quite happy ideologically living in the nineteenth century. The prison riots that swept the United States during the 1952–1954 period left these worthies securely in control of their institutions. Consequently, at Joliet and at prisons throughout America, treatment danced to custody's tune.[24] For this reason and many others as well, it was clear that individual treatment in practice was little more than an ideological patina on moral and bureaucratic dynamics constrained by very different assumptions.

During graduate studies in sociology at the University of Illinois, I acquired an understanding and appreciation of ethnographic methods that merged easily with my already acquired interest in offenders' perspectives. Norman Denzin's instruction and example from this time stand out as particularly significant. During a one-year stint at the University of Akron, I continued and expanded the ethnographic research begun initially for my doctoral thesis. In their homes and in the bars and taverns frequented by offenders and ex-offenders, I spent some time getting to know and interviewing thieves. I regularly moved between my academic office, my home, and a series of bars and lounges. In addition to my participation and casual observation in these settings, I completed tape-recorded interviews with persons as diverse as students who flirted with crime via an occasional burglary to men who had spent much of their adult lives stealing and paying the consequences for doing so.[25] During this period, I also met and spent considerable time talking with "Jack Noble," a successful burglar.

After moving to the University of Tennessee, I spent the 1980–1981 academic year in Washington, D.C., interviewing men who were imprisoned earlier in their lives. During part of the study, I was assisted by Michael Preston, one of the men described in Chapter 1. A former street-level thief and hustler, Michael spent more than fourteen years in various jails and penitentiaries and, at age 61, continues to use heroin recreationally even though his crime years are well behind him. He has been arrested only once since 1980, that following a dispute of some kind with his former partner. He spent one night in jail. I first met Michael through his niece, who then was working in a federal office where colleagues and I were doing research on regulation of surface coal mining.[26] She described Michael to me and I later called him. After we met and began working together, Michael and I spent many hours visiting on D.C. street corners, making contact with men he knew from years of street-level hustling and imprisonment. Some of these men I then interviewed. With further help from "Jack Noble," I contacted and interviewed several thieves and former thieves, principally in northern Ohio. I also interviewed six men in federal prisons and, with the aid of probation records, several men on federal parole in east Tennessee. Day-to-day experiences occasionally bring me into contact still with ex-prisoners or other characters of sometimes uncertain compliance with all proscriptions of the criminal code. The analysis in *Great Pretenders* also draws from hours of conversation and some tape-recorded interviews with these friends and acquaintances.

Every research effort, in both design and style, exposes its users to a more or less distinctive complex of problems, and ethnographic research on criminal offenders is no different. Its challenges and contingencies largely are alien to investigators who perform statistical analyses on government data or who administer surveys to samples of more conventional and reputable persons. Anyone who has spent time in the free community with offenders or ex-offenders accumulates in the process a range of interesting and sometimes unconventional experiences. Late-night calls for personal assistance, requests for cash loans, and the occasional request that one intercede with legal authorities, usually to no effect, or arbitrate disputes with their partners are examples that come to mind quickly, but the list is a long one.[27]

Certainly research of this type is not for those who must be able to contact the subjects of their studies quickly and easily, who assume that their subjects will come to the investigator's office, will be on time, and will be in shape to behave as responsible subjects. Ethnographic research on thieves and hustlers can be very different, not only because it often requires the investigator to leave his or her office to locate and contact the subjects of interest but also because once located they may be drunk, high, hungover, or in jail.

Not all the problems of ethnographic research with offenders are so benign, however. To spend time in the company of offenders or former offenders, particularly if it is spent in the social settings that comprise their daily rounds, is to encounter a wide range of characters, to acquire knowledge of wrongdoing, and to become involved in unpredictable group dynamics. The cast of characters may include snitches, braggarts, and aggressive bullies. This mix of characters and guilty knowledge puts a premium on self-aware sensitivity both to the underlying normative structure of these settings and to relationship work. The ability to keep one's mouth shut and simply listen can be an important virtue and research asset in these circumstances, but it is not easy to set down hard and fast rules for negotiating them successfully.

I am reminded of my relationship with the Bankston brothers, two men whose life trajectories intersected mine several years ago. Willie was a working man who supplemented his wages with a variety of small-time hustles worked out of the back door of the large tire shop where he was employed. His efforts were facilitated enormously by its weak security and haphazard inventory procedures. Junior was a lighthearted but unpredictably violent man who seemingly took from others much of what he needed to get by and cared not if his victims were humiliated in the process. Many people avoided him. He did not work. Adding to his reputation as a violent person were reports that he was a U.S. Marine combat veteran of Vietnam who never ran from and occasionally started barroom fights. Junior often appeared publicly wearing martial arts attire at unusual times and places, which fed the rumor that he either taught or was learning karate. A year or so after I met the Bankstons, in the middle of the night an unindentified person tipped into Junior's small apartment, which was located above a bar, and buried an ax in his head. Although the assault did not kill him, I was told that it did make a new man of Junior, and soon he was shipped off for long-term care to a V.A. hospital. I thought Willie Bankston perhaps had reason for the assault on his brother, particularly in light of Junior's very public shenanigans with Willie's spouse. I recall asking matter-of-factly of Willie Bankston if he had done it. Not surprisingly, he said "no." If the situation had been reversed and it was Willie who was assaulted, I certainly would not have been as cheeky questioning Junior. It is possible that interactional experience in all-male working-class worlds is useful when observing blue-collar males on the margins of society, but common sense and a measure of luck do not hurt things one bit.

Further complicating the process of research in which one gets close to and interacts with offenders in diverse settings is the high likelihood that at some point she or he will come under scrutiny by law enforcement personnel and agencies. This can be a hassle under the best of circumstances, but managing it successfully is facilitated immeasurably if one is culpable of nothing that truly interests them.

Notes

1. Neal Shover, "Burglary as an Occupation" (Ph.D. thesis, Department of Sociology, University of Illinois, Urbana-Champaign, 1971).

2. Neal Shover, *Aging Criminals* (Beverly Hills, Calif.: Sage, 1985).

3. Neal Shover and David Honaker, "The socially bounded decision making of persistent property offenders," *Howard Journal of Criminal Justice* 31(1992), pp. 276–294.

4. J. V. Seidel, R. Kjolseth, and E. Seymour, *The Ethnograph* (Littleton, Colo.: Qualis Research Associates, 1988).

5. Kenneth D. Tunnell, *Choosing Crime* (Chicago: Nelson-Hall, 1992); and David Willis Honaker, "Aging, Peers, and the Propensity for Crime: A Contextual Analysis of Criminal Decision Making" (M.A. thesis, Department of Sociology, University of Tennessee, Knoxville, 1992).

6. Examples include Horace Woodroof, *Stone Wall College* (Nashville, Tenn.: Aurora, 1970); and Frank Watson, *Been There and Back* (Winston-Salem, N.C.: J.F. Blair, 1976).

7. Beginning with Charles L. Clarke and Earle Eubank, *Lockstep and Corridor* (Cincinnati: University of Cincinnati Press, 1927), a list of some of the best-known works of this type includes Edwin H. Sutherland, *The Professional Thief* (Chicago: University of Chicago Press, 1937); Bruce Jackson, *A Thief's Primer* (New York: Macmillan, 1969); Bruce Jackson, *In the Life* (New York: Holt, Rinehart and Winston, 1972); Harry King, *Boxman*, as told to and edited by Bill Chambliss (New York: Harper and Row, 1972); Richard P. Rettig, Manual J. Torres, and Gerald R. Garrett, *Manny* (Boston: Houghton Mifflin, 1977); John Allen, *Assault with a Deadly Weapon*, edited by Dianne Hall Kelly and Phillip Heymann (New York: Pantheon Books, 1977); Darrell J. Steffensmeier, *The Fence* (Totowa, N.J.: Rowman & Littlefield, 1986); Stuart L. Hills and Ron Santiago, *Tragic Magic* (Chicago: Nelson-Hall, 1992); and Eugene P. Delorme, *Chief,* edited by Inez Cardozo-Freeman (Lincoln: University of Nebraska Press, 1994).

8. Among the best-known and useful works of this type are John Bartlow Martin, *My Life in Crime* (New York: Harper & Brothers, 1952); Tony Parker and Robert Allerton, *The Courage of His Convictions* (London: Hutchinson, 1962); Tony Parker, *The Unknown Citizen* (London: Hutchinson, 1963); and James Willwerth, *Jones* (New York: M. Evans and Co., 1974).

9. See the excellent discussion in Jack Katz, *Seductions of Crime* (New York: Basic Books, 1988), p. 11.

10. The fact that I use materials from these and other autobiographies very selectively inevitably raises in some minds the question of whether they were chosen and quoted simply to make a point and therefore are not representative. My response is that they were chosen because they illustrate clearly something discussed by me. At the same time, they represent others that could have been chosen as well as materials elicited during interviews with persistent thieves.

11. Examples include Jack Black, *You Can't Win* (New York: A. L. Burt, 1926); Paul Warren, *Next Time Is for Life* (New York: Dell, 1953); John McVicar, *McVicar, by Himself* (London: Hutchinson, 1974); James Carr, *Bad,* edited by Dan Hammer and Isaac Cronin (New York: Herman Graf Associates, 1975); and Kody Scott, *Monster* (New York: Atlantic Monthly Press, 1993).

12. Examples include Marlene Webber and Tony McGilvary, *Square John* (Toronto: University of Toronto Press, 1988); and Henry Williamson, *Hustler,* edited by R. Lincoln Keiser (New York: Avon Books, 1965). After his autobiography was published, "Henry Williamson" was shot while trying to make his getaway from an armed robbery. Left a paraplegic and confined to a wheelchair, a few months later he entered the Illinois State Penitentiary where I was then employed.

13. See, for example, Malcolm Braly, *False Starts* (New York: Penguin, 1976); and Nathan McCall, *Makes Me Wanna Holler* (New York: Random House, 1994).

14. Tony Parker and Robert Allerton, *The Courage of His Convictions* (London: Hutchinson, 1962).

15. The Jack-Roller and Jon Snodgrass, *The Jack-Roller at Seventy* (Lexington, Mass.: D. C. Heath, 1982).

16. See, for example, Red Rudensky, *The Gonif* (Blue Earth, Minn.: Piper Company, 1970).

17. See, for example, Malcolm Braly, *False Starts* (New York: Penguin, 1976); and Nathan McCall, *Makes Me Wanna Holler* (New York: Random House, 1994).

18. Mark A. Peterson and Harriet B. Braiker, *Who Commits Crime?* (Cambridge, Mass.: Oelgeschlager, Gunn & Hain, 1981).

19. Mark Peterson, Jan Chaiken, Patricia Ebener, and Paul Honig, *Survey of Prison and Jail Inmates* (Santa Monica, Calif.: Rand Corporation, 1982).

20. Steven P. Klein and Michael N. Caggiano, *The Prevalence, Predictability, and Policy Implications of Recidivism* (Santa Monica, Calif.: Rand Corporation, 1986).

21. James D. Wright and Peter H. Rossi, *Armed and Considered Dangerous* (New York: Aldine de Gruyter, 1986).

22. Tom Wicker, *A Time to Die* (New York: Ballantine, 1975), p. 210.

23. Willard Motley, *Knock on Any Door* (New York: D. Appleton-Century, 1947).

24. I have an enduring memory of waiting to be passed through a locked gate while the guard who controlled the gate pretended not to notice my presence.

25. Some of these materials were included in Neal Shover, "The social organization of burglary," *Social Problems* 20(1973), pp. 499–514.

26. Neal Shover, Donald A. Clelland, and John P. Lynxwiler, *Enforcement or Negotiation?* (Albany: State University of New York Press, 1986).

27. For a discussion of some of these contingencies and problems, see Richard T. Wright, Scott H. Decker, Allison K. Redfern, and Dietrich L. Smith, "A snowball's chance in hell: Doing fieldwork with active residential burglars," *Journal of Research in Crime and Delinquency* 29(1992), pp. 148–161. See also Eloise Dunlap et al., "Studying crack users and their criminal careers," *Contemporary Drug Problems* 17(1990), pp. 121–144.

Bibliography

Abbott, Jack Henry, *In the Belly of the Beast*. New York: Random House, 1981.

Akerstrom, Malin, *Crooks and Squares: Lifestyles of Thieves and Addicts in Comparison to Conventional People*. New Brunswick, N.J.: Transaction Books, 1985.

Albanese, Jay S., "Tomorrow's thieves." *The Futurist* 22(September-October 1988):24–28.

Allen, John, *Assault with a Deadly Weapon*, edited by D. H. Kelly and P. Heymann. New York: Pantheon, 1977.

Anderson, Elijah, *A Place on the Corner*. Chicago: University of Chicago Press, 1978.

_____, *Streetwise: Race, Class, and Change in an Urban Community*. Chicago: University of Chicago Press, 1990.

Armbrister, Trevor, *Act of Vengeance*. New York: Saturday Review Press, 1975.

Auletta, Ken, *The Underclass*. New York: Random House, 1982.

Baker, Russell, *Growing Up*. New York: Congdon and Weed, 1982.

Ball, J. C., J. W. Shaffer, and D. N. Nurco, "The day-to-day criminality of heroin addicts in Baltimore: A study in the continuity of offense rates." *Drug and Alcohol Dependence* 12(1983):119–142.

Barker, Mary, Jane Geraghy, Barry Webb, and Tom Key, *The Prevention of Street Robbery*. London: British Home Office, 1993.

Beaver, Patricia Duane, *Rural Community in the Appalachian South*. Lexington: University Press of Kentucky, 1986.

Becker, Gary, "Crime and punishment: An economic approach." *Journal of Political Economy* 76(1968):169–217.

Bennett, Trevor, and Richard Wright, *Burglars on Burglary*. Hampshire, U.K.: Gower, 1984.

Benson, Michael L., "Denying the guilty mind: Accounting for involvement in a white-collar crime." *Criminology* 23(1985):583–607.

Benton, Peggie, *Peterman*. London: Arthur Barker, 1966.

Biernacki, Patrick, *Pathways from Heroin Addiction: Recovery Without Treatment*. Philadelphia: Temple University Press, 1986.

Billboard, "RIAA domestic anti-piracy plan is paying off." March 27, 1993.

Black, Donald, "Crime as social control." *American Sociological Review* 48(1983):34–45.

Black, Jack, *You Can't Win*. New York: A. L. Burt, 1926.

Blumstein, Alfred, Jacqueline Cohen, and David P. Farrington, "Criminal career research: Its value for criminology." *Criminology* 26(1988):1–35.

_____, "Longitudinal and criminal career research: Further clarifications." *Criminology* 26(1988):57–73.

Blumstein, Alfred, Jacqueline Cohen, and Daniel Nagin, editors, *Deterrence and Incapacitation: Estimating the Effects of Criminal Sanctions on Crime Rates.* Washington, D.C.: National Academy of Sciences, 1978.

Blumstein, Alfred, David P. Farrington, and Soumyo Moitra, "Delinquency careers: Innocents, desisters, and persisters." In Michael Tonry and Norval Morris, editors, *Crime and Justice: An Annual Review of Research,* vol. 6. Chicago: University of Chicago Press, 1985.

Booth, Ernest, *Stealing Through Life.* New York: Alfred A. Knopf, 1929.

Bordieu, Pierre, *Outline of a Theory of Practice.* Cambridge, U.K.: Cambridge University Press, 1977.

Bordieu, Pierre, and Passeron, Jean-Claude, *Reproduction in Education, Society, and Culture.* Newbury Park, Calif.: Sage, 1977.

Braithwaite, John, *Crime, Shame, and Reintegration.* Cambridge, U.K.: Cambridge University Press, 1989.

_____, "Poverty, power, white-collar crime, and the paradoxes of criminological theory." *Australian–New Zealand Journal of Criminology* 24(1991):40–58.

Braly, Malcolm, *On the Yard.* Boston: Little, Brown, 1967.

_____, *False Starts.* New York: Penguin, 1976.

Brantingham, Paul J., and Patricia L. Brantingham, *Patterns in Crime.* New York: Macmillan, 1984.

Bureau of Justice Statistics, *Electronic Fund Transfer Fraud.* Washington, D.C.: U.S. Department of Justice, 1985.

_____, *Household Burglary.* Washington, D.C.: U.S. Government Printing Office, 1985.

_____, *Robbery Victims.* Washington, D.C.: U.S. Department of Justice, 1987.

_____, *White Collar Crime.* Washington, D.C.: U.S. Department of Justice, 1987.

_____, *Correctional Populations in the United States, 1990.* Washington, D.C.: U.S. Department of Justice, 1992.

_____, *Drugs, Crime, and the Justice System.* Washington, D.C.: U.S. Department of Justice, 1992.

_____, *Forgery and Fraud-Related Offenses in 6 States, 1983–88.* Washington, D.C.: U.S. Department of Justice, 1992.

_____, *Felony Sentences in State Courts, 1990.* Washington, D.C.: U.S. Department of Justice, 1993.

_____, *Sourcebook of Criminal Justice Statistics, 1992.* Washington, D.C.: U.S. Government Printing Office, 1993.

_____, *Survey of State Prison Inmates, 1991.* Washington, D.C.: U.S. Department of Justice, 1993.

_____, *Criminal Victimization in the United States, 1992.* Washington, D.C.: U.S. Government Printing Office, 1994.

Burglar, A, *In the Clutch of Circumstance.* New York: D. Appleton, 1922.

Burnett, Ros, "The Dynamics of Recidivism: Summary Report." Oxford, U.K.: University of Oxford, Centre for Criminological Research, 1992.

Camp, George Mallery, "Nothing to Lose: A Study of Bank Robbery in America." Ph.D. thesis, Department of Sociology, Yale University, 1968.

Carr, James, *Bad.* New York: Herman Graf Associates, 1975.

Carroll, John S., "A psychological approach to deterrence: The evaluation of crime opportunities." *Journal of Personality and Social Psychology* 36(1978):1512–1520.

_____, "Committing a crime: The offender's decision." In J. Konecni and E. B. Ebbesen, editors, *The Criminal Justice System: A Social-Psychological Analysis*. San Francisco: W. H. Freeman, 1982.

Chaiken, Jan M., and Marcia R. Chaiken, *Varieties of Criminal Behavior*. Santa Monica, Calif.: Rand Corporation, 1982.

Chaiken, Marcia R., and Bruce D. Johnson, *Characteristics of Different Types of Drug-Involved Offenders*. Washington, D.C.: National Institute of Justice, 1988.

Cherry, Mike, *On High Steel: The Education of an Ironworker*. New York: Ballantine, 1975.

Cheung, Yuet W., Patricia G. Erickson, and Tammy C. Landau, "Experience of crack use: Findings from a community-based sample in Toronto." *Journal of Drug Issues* 21(1991):121–140.

Christie, Nils, *Crime Control as Industry* (2d and enlarged edition). London: Routledge, 1994.

Clarke, Charles L., and Earle Eubank, *Lockstep and Corridor*. Cincinnati: University of Cincinnati Press, 1927.

Clarke, Michael, "Insurance fraud." *British Journal of Criminology* 29(1989):1–20.

_____, *Mortgage Fraud*. London: Chapman & Hall, 1991.

Clarke, Ronald V., and Derek B. Cornish, "Modeling offenders' decisions: A framework for research and policy." In Michael Tonry and Norval Morris, editors, *Crime and Justice: A Review of Research*, vol. 6. Chicago: University of Chicago Press, 1985.

Claster, Daniel S., "Comparison of risk perception between delinquents and nondelinquents." *Journal of Criminal Law, Criminology, and Police Science* 58(1967):80–86.

Cohen, Lawrence E., and Marcus Felson, "Social change and crime rate trends: A routine activity approach." *American Sociological Review* 44(1979):588–608.

Colvin, Mark, and John Pauley, "A critique of criminology: Toward an integrated structural-Marxist theory of delinquency production." *American Journal of Sociology* 89(1983):513–551.

Conklin, John E., *Robbery and the Criminal Justice System*. Philadelphia: J. B. Lippincott, 1972.

Cook, Philip J., "Robbery violence." *Journal of Criminal Law and Criminology* 78(1987):357–376.

Cordilia, Ann T., *The Making of an Inmate: Prison as a Way of Life*. Cambridge, Mass.: Schenkman, 1983.

_____, "Alcohol and property crime: Exploring the causal nexus." *Journal of Studies on Alcohol* 46(1985):161–171.

_____, "Robbery arising out of a group drinking context." In Anne Campbell and John J. Gibbs, editors, *Violent Transactions*. New York: Blackwell, 1986.

Cromwell, Paul F., James N. Olson, and D'Aunn Wester Avary, *Breaking and Entering: An Ethnographic Analysis of Burglary*. Newbury Park, Calif.: Sage, 1991.

Crookston, Peter, *Villain*. London: Jonathan Cape, 1967.

Croteau, David, *Politics and the Class Divide*. Philadelphia: Temple University Press, 1995.

Currie, Elliott, *Reckoning: Drugs, the Cities, and the American Future*. New York: Hill and Wang, 1993.

Cusson, Maurice, and Pierre Pinsonneault, "The decision to give up crime." In D. B. Cornish and R. V. Clarke, editors, *The Reasoning Criminal*. New York: Springer-Verlag, 1986.

David, Pedro R., editor, *The World of the Burglar: Five Criminal Lives*. Albuquerque: University of New Mexico Press, 1974.

Davis, Clyde B., *The Rebellion of Leo McGuire*. New York: Farrar and Rinehart, 1944.

Decker, Scott, Richard Wright, and Robert Logie, "Perceptual deterrence among active residential burglars: A research note." *Criminology* 31(1993):135–147.

Decker, Scott, Richard Wright, Allison Redfern, and Dietrich Smith, "A woman's place is in the home: Females and residential burglary." *Justice Quarterly* 10(1993):143–162.

Delorme, Eugene P., *Chief: The Life History of Eugene Delorme, Imprisoned Santee Sioux*, edited by Inez Cardozo-Freeman. Lincoln: University of Nebraska Press, 1994.

Deschenes, Elizabeth Piper, M. Douglas Anglin, and George Speckart, "Narcotic addiction: Related criminal careers, social and economic costs." *Journal of Drug Issues* 21(1991):383–411.

Dionne, E. J. Jr., *Why Americans Hate Politics*. New York: Simon & Schuster, 1991.

Duncan, Lee, *Over the Wall*. New York: E. P. Dutton, 1936.

Duneier, Mitchell, *Slim's Table*. Chicago: University of Chicago Press, 1992.

Dunlap, Eloise, Bruce Johnson, Harry Sanabria, Elbert Holliday, Vicki Lipsey, Maurice Barnett, William Hopkins, Ira Sobel, Doris Randolph, and Ko-Lin Chin, "Studying crack users and their criminal careers." *Contemporary Drug Problems* 17(1990):121–144.

Earley, Pete, *The Hot House: Life Inside Leavenworth Prison*. New York: Bantam Books, 1992.

Eck, John E., *Solving Crimes: The Investigation of Burglary and Robbery*. Washington, D.C.: U.S. Department of Justice, National Institute of Justice, 1983.

Edwards, Ed, *Metamorphosis of a Criminal*. New York: Hart, 1972.

Einstadter, Werner J., "The social organization of armed robbery." *Social Problems* 17(1969):54–83.

Ekland-Olson, Sheldon, John Lieb, and Louis Zurcher, "The paradoxical impact of criminal sanctions: Some microstructural findings." *Law and Society Review* 18(1984):159–178.

Erickson, Rosemary, Wayman J. Crow, Louis A. Zurcher, and Archie V. Connett, *Paroled but Not Free*. New York: Behavioral Publications, 1973.

Erikson, Kai T., *Everything in Its Path: Destruction of Community in the Buffalo Creek Flood*. New York: Simon and Schuster, 1976.

Ewen, Lynda Ann, "All God's children ain't got shoes: A comparison of West Virginia and the urban 'underclass.'" *Humanity and Society* 13(1989):145–164.

Farrington, David P., "Age and crime." In Michael Tonry and Norval Morris, editors, *Crime and Justice: A Review of Research*, vol. 7. Chicago: University of Chicago Press, 1986.

Faupel, Charles E., and Carl B. Klockars, "Drugs-crime connections: Elaborations from the life histories of hard-core heroin addicts." *Social Problems* 34(1987):54–68.

Federal Bureau of Investigation, *Crime in the United States: Uniform Crime Reports, 1963*. Washington, D.C.: U.S. Government Printing Office, 1964.

_____, *Crime in the United States: Uniform Crime Reports, 1964*. Washington, D.C.: U.S. Government Printing Office, 1965.

_____, *Crime in the United States: Uniform Crime Reports, 1983*. Washington, D.C.: U.S. Government Printing Office, 1984.

_____, *Crime in the United States: Uniform Crime Reports, 1990*. Washington, D.C.: U.S. Government Printing Office, 1991.

_____, *Crime in the United States: Uniform Crime Reports, 1992*. Washington, D.C.: U.S. Government Printing Office, 1993.

_____, *Crime in the United States: Uniform Crime Reports, 1993*. Washington, D.C.: U.S. Government Printing Office, 1994.

Federal Deposit Insurance Corporation, Financial Reporting Section, *Data Book*. Washington, D.C.: U.S. Government Printing Office, 1992.

Feeney, Floyd, "Robbers as decision-makers." In Derek B. Cornish and Ronald V. Clarke, editors, *The Reasoning Criminal: Rational Choice Perspectives on Offending*. New York: Springer-Verlag, 1986.

Feeney, Floyd, and Adrianne Weir, "Prevention and control of armed robbery." *Criminology* 13(1975):102–105.

Felson, Marcus, *Crime and Everyday Life*. Thousand Oaks, Calif.: Pine Forge, 1994.

Figgie International, *The Figgie Report Part VI—The Business of Crime: The Criminal Perspective*. Richmond, Va: Figgie International Inc., 1988.

Finestone, Harold, "Cats, kicks, and color." In Howard S. Becker, editor, *The Other Side*. New York: Free Press, 1964.

_____, "Reformation and recidivism among Italian and Polish criminal offenders." *American Journal of Sociology* 72(1967):575–588.

Fleisher, Mark S., *Beggars and Thieves: Lives of Urban Street Criminals*. Madison: University of Wisconsin Press, 1995.

Franklin, H. Bruce, *The Victim as Criminal and Artist: Literature from the American Prison*. New York: Oxford University Press, 1978.

Frazier, Charles E., and Thomas N. Meisenhelder, "Criminality and emotional ambivalence: Exploratory notes on an overlooked dimension." *Qualitative Sociology* 8(1985):266–284.

Gabor, Thomas, Micheline Baril, Maurice Cusson, Daniel Elie, Marc LeBlanc, and Andre Normandeau, *Armed Robbery: Cops, Robbers, and Victims*. Springfield, Ill.: Charles C. Thomas, 1987.

Gans, Herbert J., *Urban Villagers: Group and Class in the Life of Italian-Americans*. New York: Free Press, 1962.

Garland, David, *Punishment and Modern Society*. Chicago: University of Chicago Press, 1990.

Gartner, Rosemary, and Irving Piliavin, "The aging offender and the aged offender." In P. B. Baltes, D. L. Featherman, and R. M. Lerner, editors, *Life-Span Development and Behavior*, vol. 9. Hillsdale, N.J.: Lawrence Erlbaum Associates, 1988.

Gibbs, John J., and Peggy L. Shelley, "Life in the fast lane: A retrospective view by commercial thieves." *Journal of Research in Crime and Delinquency* 19(1982):299–330.

Glaser, Daniel, *The Effectivness of a Prison and Parole System*. Indianapolis, Ind.: Bobbs-Merrill, 1964.

_____, *Adult Crime and Social Policy*. Englewood Cliffs, N.J.: Prentice-Hall, 1971.

Glazer, Nathan, and Daniel Patrick Moynihan, *Beyond the Melting Pot*. Cambridge, Mass.: MIT Press, 1963.

Glassner, Barry, M. Ksander, B. Berg, and Bruce D. Johnson, "A note on the deterrent effect of juvenile vs. adult jurisdiction." *Social Problems* 31(1983):219–234.

Glueck, Sheldon, and Eleanor Glueck, *Unraveling Juvenile Delinquency*. New York: The Commonwealth Fund, 1950.

Goffman, Erving, *Interaction Ritual*. Garden City, N.Y.: Anchor, 1967.

Gordon, Diana R., *The Justice Juggernaut: Fighting Street Crime, Controlling Citizens*. New Brunswick, N.J.: Rutgers University Press, 1990.

Gottfredson, Michael R., and Travis Hirschi, "The true value of lambda would appear to be zero: An essay on career criminals, criminal careers, selective incapacitation, cohort studies, and related topics." *Criminology* 24(1986):213–234.

_____, "Science, public policy, and the career paradigm." *Criminology* 26(1988):37–55.

_____, *A General Theory of Crime*. Stanford, Calif.: Stanford University Press, 1990.

Gould, Leroy, "Crime as a Profession." Report to the President's Commission on Law Enforcement and Criminal Justice. New Haven, Conn.: Department of Sociology, Yale University, 1967, photocopy.

Gove, Walter R., "The effect of age and gender on deviant behavior: A biopsychosocial perspective." In Alice S. Rossi, editor, *Gender and the Life Course*. New York: Aldine, 1985.

Greenberg, Norman, *The Man with a Steel Guitar*. Hanover, N.H.: University Press of New England, 1980.

Hagedorn, John, *People and Folks: Gangs, Crime, and the Underclass in a Rustbelt City*. Chicago: Lake View Press, 1988.

Hakim, Simon, and Andrew Buck, *Residential Security*. Bethesda, Md.: National Burglar and Fire Alarm Association, 1991.

Halberstam, David, *The Fifties*. New York: Villard, 1993.

Hamilton, Arthur, Jr., and William Banks, *Father Behind Bars*. Waco, Texas: WRS Publishing, 1993.

Hannerz, Ulf, *Soulside: Inquiries into Ghetto Culture and Community*. New York: Columbia University Press, 1969.

Hapgood, Hutchins, *Autobiography of a Thief*. New York: Fox, Duffield, 1903.

Haran, James F., "The Loser's Game: A Sociological Profile of 500 Armed Bank Robbers." Ph.D. dissertation, Department of Sociology, Fordham University, 1982.

Harris, Jean, *Stranger in Two Worlds*. New York: Macmillan, 1986.

Heineke, John M., editor, *Economic Models of Criminal Behavior*. Amsterdam, N.Y.: North-Holland, 1978.

Henry, Stuart, *The Hidden Economy: The Context and Control of Borderline Crime*. London: Martin Robertson, 1978.

Hills, Stuart L., and Ron Santiago, *Tragic Magic: The Life and Crimes of a Heroin Addict*. Chicago: Nelson-Hall, 1992.

Hobbs, Dick, editor, *Professional Criminals*. Aldershot, U.K.: Dartmouth, 1995.

Hohimer, Frank, *The Home Invaders: Confessions of a Cat Burglar*. Chicago: Chicago Review Press, 1975.

Honaker, David Willis, "Aging, Peers, and the Propensity for Crime: A Contextual Analysis of Criminal Decision Making." M.A. thesis, Department of Sociology, University of Tennessee, Knoxville, 1992.

Howell, Joseph T., *Hard Living on Clay Street: Portraits of Blue-Collar Families*. New York: Anchor, 1973.

Hughes, Everett C., "Good people and dirty work." In Everett C. Hughes, editor, *The Sociological Eye*, vol. 1. Chicago: Aldine Atherton, 1971.

Inciardi, James A., "Vocational crime." In Daniel Glaser, editor, *Handbook of Criminology*. Chicago: Rand McNally, 1974.

_____, *Careers in Crime*. Chicago: Rand McNally, 1975.

Inciardi, James A., and Anne E. Pottieger, "Crack-cocaine use and street crime." *Journal of Drug Issues* 24(1994):273–292.

Irwin, John, *The Felon* (originally published in 1970). Berkeley: University of California Press, 1987.

_____, *The Jail*. Berkeley: University of California Press, 1985.

Irwin, John, and James Austin, *It's About Time: America's Imprisonment Binge*. Belmont, Calif.: Wadsworth, 1994.

Irwin, John, and Donald R. Cressey, "Thieves, convicts, and the inmate subculture." *Social Problems* 10(1962):142–155.

Jack-Roller, The, and Jon Snodgrass, *The Jack-Roller at Seventy*. Lexington, Mass.: D. C. Heath, 1982.

Jackson, Bruce, *A Thief's Primer*. New York: Macmillan, 1969.

_____, *In the Life: Versions of the Criminal Experience*. New York: Holt, Rinehart and Winston, 1972.

Jackson, Jerome, "Fieldwork as a methodology to examine economic law-violators: The case of the fraud master." Presented at the annual meeting of the American Society of Criminology, New Orleans, November 1992.

Jansyn, Leon R., Jr., "Solidarity and delinquency in a street corner group." *American Sociological Review* 31(1966):600–614.

Jesilow, Paul, Henry N. Pontell, and Gilbert Geis, *Prescription for Profit: How Doctors Defraud Medicaid*. Berkeley: University of California Press, 1993.

Johnson, Bruce D., Paul J. Goldstein, Edward Preble, James Schmeidler, Douglas S. Lipton, Barry Spunt, and Thomas Miller, *Taking Care of Business: The Economics of Crime by Heroin Addicts*. Lexington, Mass.: D. C. Heath, 1985.

Johnson, Bruce D., E. Wish, and K. Anderson, "A day in the life of 105 drug abusers: Crimes committed and how the money was spent." *Sociology and Social Research* 72(1988):185–191.

Katz, Jack, *Seductions of Crime: Moral and Sensual Attractions in Doing Evil*. New York: Basic Books, 1988.

_____, "The motivation of persistent robbers." In Michael Tonry, editor, *Crime and Justice: An Annual Review of Research*, vol. 14. Chicago: University of Chicago Press, 1991.

King, Harry, *Box Man*, as told to and edited by Bill Chambliss. New York: Harper Torchbooks, 1972.

Klein, Steven P., and Michael N. Caggiano, *The Prevalence, Predictability, and Policy Implications of Recidivism*. Santa Monica, Calif.: Rand Corporation, 1986.

Knoxville News-Sentinel, "Fraud ring gets rich by raiding trash bins." October 13, 1995, p. A13.

Kreisberg, Barry, Robert DeComo, and Norma C. Herrera, *National Juvenile Custody Trends 1978–1989*. Washington, D.C.: U.S. Department of Justice, Office of Juvenile Justice and Delinquency Prevention, 1992.

Landesco, John, "The life history of a member of the '42' gang." *Journal of Criminal Law, Criminology, and Police Science* 23(1933):964–998.

Langan, Patrick A., "America's soaring prison population." *Science* 251(March 29, 1991):1568–1573.

Leibrich, Julie, *Straight to the Point: Angles on Giving Up Crime*. Dunedin, New Zealand: University of Otago Press, 1993.

Lejeune, Robert, "The management of a mugging." *Urban Life* 6(1977):123–148.

LeMasters, E. E., *Blue-Collar Aristocrats: Life-styles at a Working-class Tavern*. Madison: University of Wisconsin Press, 1975.

Lemert, Edwin, "An isolation and closure theory of naive check forgery." In Marshall B. Clinard and Richard Quinney, editors, *Criminal Behavior Systems: A Typology*. New York: Holt, Rinehart and Winston, 1967.

_____, Review of *Hustlers, Beats, and Others*, by Ned Polsky. *American Journal of Sociology* 73(1968):649–650.

Leopold, Nathan F., Jr., *Life Plus 99 Years*. New York: Doubleday, 1958.

Letkemann, Peter, *Crime as Work*. Englewood Cliffs, N.J.: Prentice-Hall, 1973.

Levi, Michael, *Regulating Fraud*. London: Tavistock, 1987.

_____, "The victims of fraud." Paper presented at the second Liverpool Conference on Fraud, Corruption, and Business Crime, University of Liverpool, 1991.

Levi, Michael, Paul Bissell, and Tony Richardson, *The Prevention of Cheque and Credit Card Fraud*. Crime Prevention Unit paper no. 26. London: Home Office, 1991.

Levinson, Daniel J., *The Seasons of a Man's Life*. New York: Alfred A. Knopf, 1978.

Liebow, Eliot, *Tally's Corner*. Boston: Little, Brown, 1966.

Lindquist, John H., *Misdemeanor Crime: Trivial Criminal Pursuits*. Newbury Park, Calif.: Sage, 1988.

Lohman, Joseph D., Lloyd E. Ohlin, and Dietrich C. Reitzes, "Description of Convicted Felons as a Manpower Resource in a National Emergency." Springfield, Ill.: Illinois Division of Corrections, undated.

Luckenbill, David F., "Generating compliance: The case of robbery." *Urban Life* 10(1981):25–46.

Luckenbill, David F., and Joel Best, "Careers in deviance and respectability: The analogy's limitations." *Social Problems* 29(1981):197–206.

Luckenbill, David F., and Daniel P. Doyle, "Structural position and violence: Developing a cultural explanation." *Criminology* 27(1989):419–436.

Lyng, Stephen, "Edgework: A social-psychological analysis of voluntary risk taking." *American Journal of Sociology* 95(1990):851–886.

MacIsaac, John, *Half the Fun Was Getting There*. Englewood Cliffs, N.J.: Prentice-Hall, 1968.

Mack, John A., "The able criminal." *British Journal of Criminology* 12(1972):44–54.

Mack, John A., and Kerner Hans-Jurgen, *The Crime Industry*. Lexington, Mass.: Heath, Lexington Books, 1975.

MacLeod, Jay, *Ain't No Makin' It*. Boulder, Colo.: Westview, 1987.

Maguire, Kathleen, Ann L. Pastore, and Timothy J. Flanagan, *Sourcebook of Criminal Justice Statistics, 1992*. Washington, D.C.: U.S. Government Printing Office, 1993.

Maguire, Mike, in collaboration with Trevor Bennett, *Burglary in a Dwelling*. London: Heinemann, 1982.

Majors, Richard, and Janet Mancini Billson, *Cool Pose: The Dilemmas of Black Manhood in America*. Lexington, Mass.: Lexington, 1992.

Malcolm X, with the assistance of Alex Haley, *Autobiography of Malcolm X*. New York: Grove, 1965.

Manski, Charles F., "Prospects for inference on deterrence through empirical analysis of individual criminal behavior." In Alfred Blumstein, Jacqueline Cohen, and Daniel Nagin, editors, *Deterrence and Incapacitation: Estimating the Effects of Criminal Sanctions on Crime Rates*. Washington, D.C.: National Academy of Sciences, 1978.

Marks, Carole, "The urban underclass." *Annual Review of Sociology* 17(1991):445–466.

Martin, Dannie M., and Peter Y. Sussman, *Committing Journalism: The Prison Writings of Red Hog*. New York: W. W. Norton, 1993.

Martin, John Bartlow, *My Life in Crime*. New York: Harper & Brothers, 1952.

Massey, Dennis, *Doing Time in American Prisons: A Study of Modern Novels*. New York: Greenwood Press, 1989.

Matza, David, and Gresham Sykes, "Juvenile delinquency and subterranean values." *American Sociological Review* 26(1961):712–719.

McCaghy, Charles H., and R. Serge Denisoff, "Record piracy." In Leonard D. Savitz and Norman Johnston, editors, *Crime in Society*. New York: John Wiley & Sons, 1978.

McCall, George, and J. L. Simmons, *Identities and Interactions*. New York: Free Press, 1966.

McCall, Nathan, *Makes Me Wanna Holler*. New York: Random House, 1994.

McVicar, John, *McVicar, by Himself*. London: Hutchinson, 1974.

Meisenhelder, Thomas N., "An exploratory study of exiting from criminal careers." *Criminology* 15(1977):319–334.

Messerschmidt, James W., *Masculinities and Crime*. Lanham, Md.: Rowman & Littlefield, 1993.

Mieczkowski, Thomas, "Geeking up and throwing down: Heroin street life in Detroit." *Criminology* 24(1986):645–664.

Miller, Billie, and David Helwig, *A Book About Billie*. Ottawa: Oberon Press, 1972.

Miller, Eleanor, *Street Woman*. Philadelphia: Temple University Press, 1986.

Miller, Walter B., "Lower-class culture as a generating milieu of gang delinquency." *Journal of Social Issues* 14(1958):5–19.

Mills, Barbara Kleban, "Up Front." *People* 15(January 19, 1981):30–33.

Monroe, Sylvester, and Peter Goldman, *Brothers: Black and Poor—A True Story of Courage and Survival*. New York: William Morrow, 1988.

Morton, James (Big Jim), with D. Wittels, "I was king of the thieves." *Saturday Evening Post* (August 5, 12, and 19, 1950):17–19, 78–81; 28, 92, 94–96; 30, 126, 128, 130–132.

Motley, Willard, *Knock on Any Door*. New York: D. Appleton-Century, 1947.

Nagin, Daniel S., David P. Farrington, and Terrie E. Moffitt, "Life-course trajectories of different types of offenders." *Criminology* 33(1995):111–140.

Nagin, Daniel S., and Kenneth C. Land, "Age, criminal careers, and population heterogeneity: Specification and estimation of a nonparametric, mixed Poisson model." *Criminology* 31(1993):327–362.

Nagin, Daniel S., and Raymond Paternoster, "The preventive effects of the perceived risk of arrest: Testing an expanded conception of deterrence." *Criminology* 29(1991):561–587.

_____, "On the relationship of past to future participation in delinquency." *Criminology* 29(1991):163–189.

National Association of Convenience Stores, *1992 Convenience Store Industry Factbook*. Washington, D. C.: Congressional Information Service, 1992.

Neugarten, Bernice L., "Adult personality: Toward a psychology of the life cycle." In Bernice L. Neugarten, editor, *Middle Age and Aging: A Reader in Social Psychology*. Chicago: University of Chicago Press, 1968.

New York Times, "Authorities search a home of suspect." December 10, 1980, p. 21.

_____, "One less thing to believe in: High-tech fraud at an ATM." May 13, 1993, pp. A1, A9.

Pappas, Gregory, *The Magic City: Unemployment in a Working-Class Community*. Ithaca, N.Y.: Cornell University Press, 1989.

Parker, Tony, *The Unknown Citizen*. London: Hutchinson, 1963.

Parker, Tony, and Robert Allerton, *The Courage of His Convictions*. London: Hutchinson, 1962.

Parton, Dolly, *Dolly: My Life and Other Unfinished Business*. New York: Harper-Collins, 1994.

Paternoster, Raymond, "The deterrent effect of the perceived certainty and severity of punishment: A review of the evidence and issues." *Justice Quarterly* 4(1987):173–217.

Persson, M., "Time-perspectives amongst criminals." *Acta Sociologica* 24(1981):149–165.

Petersilia, Joan, Peter W. Greenwood, and Marvin Lavin, *Criminal Careers of Habitual Felons*. Washington, D.C.: U.S. Department of Justice, National Institute of Law Enforcement and Criminal Justice, 1978.

Peterson, Mark, Jan Chaiken, Patricia Ebener, and Paul Honig, *Survey of Prison and Jail Inmates*. Santa Monica, Calif.: Rand Corporation, 1982.

Peterson, Mark, Jan Chaiken, and Patricia Ebener, *Survey of Jail and Prison Inmates, 1978: California, Michigan, Texas*. Ann Arbor, Mich.: Inter-University Consortium for Political and Social Research, 1984.

Peterson, Mark, and Harriet B. Braiker, with Suzanne M. Polich, *Who Commits Crime? A Survey of Prison Inmates*. Cambridge, Mass.: Oelgeschlager, Gunn & Hain, 1981.

Phelan, James Leo, *Criminals in Real Life*. London: Burke, 1956.

Pileggi, Nicholas, *Wiseguy*. New York: Simon and Schuster, 1985.

Piliavin, Irving, Rosemary Gartner, and Ross Matsueda, "Crime, deterrence, and rational choice." *American Sociological Review* 51(1986):101–119.

Pollock, Donald, *Call Me a Good Thief*. London: Howard Baker, 1976.

Preble, Edward, and John J. Casey, Jr., "Taking care of business: The heroin user's life on the street." *International Journal of the Addictions* 4(1969):1–24.

Rainwater, Lee, *Behind Ghetto Walls: Black Families in a Federal Slum.* Chicago: Aldine, 1970.

Recording Industry Association of America, *News.* February 27, 1994.

Reiss, Albert J., Jr., "Co-offending and criminal careers." In Michael Tonry and Norval Morris, editors, *Crime and Justice: An Annual Review of Research,* vol. 10. Chicago: University of Chicago Press, 1991.

Reitzes, Dietrich C., "The effect of social environment upon former felons." *Journal of Criminal Law, Criminology, and Police Science* 46(1955):226–231.

Rengert, George F., and John Wasilchick, *Suburban Burglary.* Springfield, Ill.: Charles C. Thomas, 1985.

_____, "Space, Time, and Crime: Ethnographic Insights into Residential Burglary." Final report submitted to the National Institute of Justice, U.S. Department of Justice, 1989.

Repetto, Thomas A., *Residential Crime.* Cambridge, Mass.: Ballinger, 1974.

Rettig, Richard P., Manual J. Torres, and Gerald R. Garrett, *Manny: A Criminal Addict's Story.* Boston: Houghton Mifflin, 1977.

Reuter, Peter, *Disorganized Crime.* Cambridge, Mass.: MIT Press, 1983.

Reuter, Peter, Robert MacCoun, and Patrick Murphy, *Money from Crime.* Santa Monica, Calif.: Rand Corporation, 1990.

Reynolds, Morgan O., *Crime by Choice: An Economic Analysis.* Dallas: Fisher Institute, 1985.

Roebuck, Julian, *Criminal Typology.* Springfield, Ill.: Charles C. Thomas, 1967.

Rose, Dan, *Black American Street Life: South Philadelphia, 1969–1971.* Philadelphia: University of Pennsylvania Press, 1987.

Roshier, Bob, *Controlling Crime: The Classical Perspective in Criminology.* Chicago: Lyceum, 1989.

Rowe, Alan R., and Charles R. Tittle, "Life cycle changes and criminal propensity." *Sociological Quarterly* 18(1977):223–236.

Rubin, Lillian Breslow, *Worlds of Pain: Life in the Working-Class Family.* New York: Basic Books, 1976.

_____, *Families on the Fault Line.* New York: HarperCollins, 1994.

Rudensky, Red, *The Gonif.* Blue Earth, Minn.: Piper Company, 1970.

Sampson, Robert J., and John H. Laub, "Crime and deviance in the life course." *Annual Review of Sociology* 18(1992):63–84.

_____, *Crime in the Making: Pathways and Turning Points Through Life.* Cambridge, Mass.: Harvard University Press, 1993.

Schroeder, Andreas, *Shaking It Rough: A Prison Memoir.* Toronto: Doubleday, 1976.

Schulz, David, *Coming Up Black.* Englewood Cliffs, N.J.: Prentice-Hall, 1969.

Schwendinger, Herman, and Julia Siegel Schwendinger, *Adolescent Subcultures and Delinquency,* research edition. New York: Praeger, 1985.

Scott, Kody, *Monster.* New York: Atlantic Monthly Press, 1993.

Seidel, John V., R. Kjolseth, and E. Seymour, *The Ethnograph: A User's Guide* (Version 3.0). Littleton, Colo.: Qualis Research Associates, 1988.

Sellin, Thorsten, "Recidivism and maturation." *National Probation and Parole Association Journal* 4(1958):241–250.

Sennett, Richard, and Jonathan Cobb, *The Hidden Injuries of Class*. New York: Alfred A. Knopf, 1972.

Shannon, Lyle, *Criminal Career Continuity: Its Social Context*. New York: Human Sciences Press, 1988.

Shapiro, Susan, *Wayward Capitalists*. New Haven, Conn.: Yale University Press, 1984.

Shaw, Clifford Robe, *The Jack Roller*. Chicago: University of Chicago Press, 1930.

Short, James F., and Fred Strodtbeck, *Group Process and Gang Delinquency*. Chicago: University of Chicago Press, 1965.

Shover, Neal, "Burglary as an Occupation." Unpublished Ph.D. thesis, Department of Sociology, University of Illinois, Urbana, 1971.

_____, "The social organization of burglary." *Social Problems* 20(1973):499–514.

_____, "Professional criminal: Major offender." In Sanford H. Kadish, editor, *Encyclopedia of Crime and Justice*. New York: Macmillan, 1983.

_____, *Aging Criminals*. Beverly Hills, Calif.: Sage, 1985.

Shover, Neal, Donald A. Clelland, and John P. Lynxwiler, *Enforcement or Negotiation? Constructing a Regulatory Bureaucracy*. Albany: State University of New York Press, 1986.

Shover, Neal, Greer Litton Fox, and Michael Mills, "Long-term consequences of victimization by white-collar crime." *Justice Quarterly* 11(March 1994):301–324.

Shover, Neal, and David Honaker, "The socially bounded decision making of persistent property offenders." *Howard Journal of Criminal Justice* 31(1992):276–294.

Sillitoe, Alan, *The Loneliness of the Long-Distance Runner*. New York: Signet, 1959.

Skolnick, Jerome H., *Justice Without Trial*. New York: John Wiley & Sons, 1966.

Smith, Joan, and William Fried, *The Uses of the American Prison: Political Theory and Penal Practice*. Lexington, Mass.: Lexington, 1974.

Sopher, Sharon, *Up from the Walking Dead*, as told by Charles McGregor. Garden City, N.Y.: Doubleday, 1978.

Stebbins, Robert A., *Commitment to Deviance*. Westport, Conn.: Greenwood, 1971.

Steffensmeier, Darrell J., "Organization properties and sex segregation in the underworld: Building a sociological theory of sex-differences in crime." *Social Forces* 61(1983):1010–1032.

_____, *The Fence: In the Shadow of Two Worlds*. Totowa, N.J.: Rowman & Littlefield, 1986.

Steffensmeier, Darrell J., and Robert M. Terry, "Institutional sexism in the underworld: A view from the inside." *Sociological Inquiry* 56(1986):304–323.

Stephens, Richard, and Stephen Levine, "The street-addict role: Implications for treatment." *Psychiatry* 34(1971):351–357.

Sullivan, Mercer L., *"Getting Paid": Youth Crime and Work in the Inner City*. Ithaca, N.Y.: Cornell University Press, 1989.

Sutherland, Edwin H., *The Professional Thief*. Chicago: University of Chicago Press, 1937.

Sykes, Gresham M., and Sheldon L. Messinger, "The inmate social system." In Richard A. Cloward, Donald R. Cressey, George H. Grosser, Richard McCleery, Lloyd E. Ohlin, Gresham M. Sykes, and Sheldon L. Messinger, editors, *Theoretical Studies in Social Organization of the Prison*. New York: Social Science Research Council, 1960.

Taylor, Carl S., *Dangerous Society*. East Lansing: Michigan State University Press, 1990.

Terkel, Studs, *Working: People Talk About What They Do All Day and How They Feel About What They Do*. New York: Pantheon, 1974.

_____, *Race: How Blacks and Whites Think and Feel About the American Obsession*. New York: Anchor Books, 1993.

Thackery, Ted, Jr., *The Thief*. Los Angeles: Nash Publishing, 1971.

Thomas, Piri, *Down These Mean Streets*. New York: Signet, 1968.

Tien, James M., Thomas F. Rich, and Michael F. Cahn, *Electronic Fund Transfer Systems Fraud*. Washington, D.C.: U.S. Department of Justice, Bureau of Justice Statistics, 1986.

Titus, Richard M., Fred Heinzelman, and John M. Boyle, "Victimization of persons by fraud." *Crime and Delinquency* 41(1995):54–72.

Toch, Hans, *Living in Prison: The Ecology of Survival*. New York: Free Press, 1977.

_____, *Coping, Maladaptation in Prison*. Rutgers, N.J.: Transaction, 1989.

Tracy, Paul E., Marvin E. Wolfgang, and Robert M. Figlio, *Delinquency Careers in Two Birth Cohorts*. New York: Plenum, 1990.

Tremblay, Pierre, Yvan Clermont, and Maurice Cusson, "Jockey and joyriders: Changing patterns in car theft opportunity structures." *British Journal of Criminology* 34(1994):307–321.

Tunnell, Kenneth D., *Choosing Crime: The Criminal Calculus of Property Offenders*. Chicago: Nelson-Hall, 1992.

U.S. Bureau of the Census, *Statistical Abstract of the United States, 1994*. Washington, D.C.: U.S. Government Printing Office, 1995.

U.S. Congress, House of Representatives, Joint Hearing before the Subcommittee on Regulation, Business Opportunities, and Energy of the Committee on Small Business, *Innovation in Telemarketing Frauds and Scams*. 102d Congress, 1st session. Washington, D.C.: U.S. Government Printing Office, 1991.

U.S. Congress, House of Representatives, Committee on Government Operations, *The Scourge of Telemarketing Fraud: What Can Be Done Against It?* 102d Congress, 1st session. Washington, D.C.: U.S. Government Printing Office, 1991.

U.S. Congress, Senate, Committee on Governmental Affairs, Hearing before the Permanent Subcommittee on Investigations of the Senate Committee on Governmental Affairs, *Professional Motor Vehicle Theft and Chop Shops, 1979*. 96th Congress, 1st session. Washington, D.C.: U.S. Government Printing Office, 1980.

U.S. Congress, Senate, Hearing before the Subcommittee on Consumer Affairs of the Committee on Banking, Housing, and Urban Affairs, *Credit Card Fraud*. 98th Congress, 1st session. Washington, D.C.: U.S. Government Printing Office, 1983.

U.S. Congress, Senate, *U.S. Government Efforts to Combat Fraud and Abuse in the Insurance Industry*. 102d Congress, 2d session. Washington, D.C.: U.S. Government Printing Office, 1992.

U.S. Congress, Senate, Hearing before the Subcommittee on Consumer Affairs of the Committee on Commerce, Science, and Transportation, *Telemarketing Fraud and S. 568, The Telemarketing and Consumer Fraud and Abuse Protection Act*. 103d Congress, 1st session. Washington, D.C.: U.S. Government Printing Office, 1993.

U.S. News and World Report, "Health care fraud." February 24, 1992, pp. 34–43.

Waldorf, Dan, Craig Reinarman, and Sheigla Murphy, *Cocaine Changes: The Experience of Using and Quitting.* Philadelphia: Temple University Press, 1991.

Waller, Irwin, *Men Released from Prison.* Toronto: University of Toronto Press, 1974.

Walsh, Dermot, *Break-Ins: Burglary from Private Houses.* London: Constable, 1980.

_____, *Heavy Business: Commercial Burglary and Robbery.* London: Routledge & Kegan Paul, 1986.

Walter, Ingo, *The Secret Money Market.* New York: Harper and Row, 1990.

Warren, Paul, *Next Time Is for Life.* New York: Dell, 1953.

Washington Post, "Intruder kills Dr. Halberstam." December 6, 1980, p. A1.

_____, "Welch convicted of murder, robbery, nine other counts." April 11, 1981, p. A1.

Watson, Frank, *Been There and Back.* Winston-Salem, N.C.: J. F. Blair, 1976.

Webber, Marlene, and Tony McGilvary, *Square John: A True Story.* Toronto: University of Toronto Press, 1988.

Weisburd, David, Stanton Wheeler, Elin Waring, and Nancy Bode, *Crimes of the Middle Classes.* New Haven, Conn.: Yale University Press, 1991.

Weller, Jack E., *Yesterday's People.* Lexington: University of Kentucky Press, 1965.

West, W. Gordon, "The short-term careers of serious thieves." *Canadian Journal of Criminology* 20(1978):169–190.

Wicker, Tom, *A Time to Die.* New York: Ballantine, 1975.

Wideman, John Edgar, *Brothers and Keepers.* New York: Holt, Rinehart and Winston, 1984.

Williams, Terry M., and William Kornblum, *Growing Up Poor.* Lexington, Mass.: D. C. Heath, 1985.

Williamson, Henry, *Hustler.* R. Lincoln Keiser, editor. New York: Avon, 1965.

Willis, Paul, *Learning to Labour: How Working-Class Kids Get Working-Class Jobs.* Farnborough, U.K.: Saxon House, 1977.

Willwerth, James, *Jones: Portrait of a Mugger.* New York: M. Evans, 1974.

Wilson, Brian, *Nor Iron Bars a Cage.* London: Wm. Kimber, 1964.

Wilson, James Q., *Thinking About Crime.* New York: Basic Books, 1975.

_____, "Drugs and crime." In Michael Tonry and James Q. Wilson, editors, *Crime and Justice.* Chicago: University of Chicago Press, 1990.

Wilson, William Julius, *The Truly Disadvantaged: The Inner City, the Underclass and Public Policy.* Chicago: University of Chicago Press, 1987.

Winchester, Stuart, and Hilary Jackson, *Residential Burglary.* Home Office Research Study no. 74. London: H. M. Stationery Office, 1982.

Wolfgang, Marvin, Robert M. Figlio, and Thorsten Sellin, *Delinquency in a Birth Cohort.* Chicago: University of Chicago Press, 1972.

Woodroof, Horace, *Stone Wall College.* Nashville, Tenn.: Aurora, 1970.

Wooton, Barbara, *Social Science and Social Pathology.* London: Allen & Unwin, 1959.

Wright, James D., and Peter H. Rossi, *Armed Criminals in America: A Survey of Incarcerated Felons, 1983.* Ann Arbor, Mich.: Inter-University Consortium for Political and Social Research, 1985.

_____, *Armed and Considered Dangerous.* Hawthorne, N.Y.: Aldine de Gruyter, 1986.

Wright, Richard T., and Scott Decker, *Burglars on the Job: Streetlife and Residential Break-ins.* Boston: Northeastern University Press, 1994.

Wright, Richard T., Scott H. Decker, Allison K. Redfern, and Dietrich L. Smith, "A snowball's chance in hell: Doing fieldwork with active residential burglars." *Journal of Research in Crime and Delinquency* 29(1992):148–161.

Wright, Richard, Robert H. Logie, and Scott H. Decker, "Criminal expertise and offender decision making: An experimental study of the target selection process in residential burglary." *Journal of Research in Crime and Delinquency* 32(1995):39–53.

Zablocki, Benjamin D., and Rosabeth Moss Kanter, "The differentiation of lifestyles." In Alex Inkeles, James Coleman, and Neil Smelser, editors, *Annual Review of Sociology*, vol. 2, pp. 269–298. Palo Alto, Calif.: Annual Reviews, 1976.

Zimbardo, Philip, "Pathology of imprisonment." *Society* 9(1972):6–8.

About the Book and Author

Persistent thieves—criminals who resume committing crimes of burglary, robbery, vehicle theft, and ordinary theft despite previous attempts to stop—are a main focal point of American criminology and criminal justice. Cast as "career criminals," they are also one of the principal targets of the "war on crime" that American governments have waged for more than two decades.

Building on a theoretical interpretation of crime as *choice*, crime-control policies and programs justified by notions of deterrence and incapacitation have proliferated. America's urban police departments now have "repeat offender units," and many of the new state sentencing codes mandate lengthy sentences for defendants with previous convictions.

Great Pretenders is based on the author's original studies and previously published research and on more than fifty autobiographies of persistent thieves. Shover uses a crime-as-choice framework and a life-course perspective to make sense of important decisions and changes in the lives of persistent thieves. He shows how the working-class origins of most persistent thieves produce both low legitimate and low criminal aspirations, even as those origins leave them ill-equipped to exploit comparatively safe, lucrative, and newer forms of criminal opportunity.

In this book Shover describes how many persistent thieves and hustlers identify with crime and pursue a lifestyle of *life as party* in which their choices are made alternately in contexts of drug-using hedonism or desperation. Their estimates of the likely payoffs from crime are severely distorted, and most give little thought to possible arrest. As they get older, however, persistent thieves make qualitative changes in the crimes they commit, and many eventually stop committing crimes altogether.

The author highlights some unintended consequences of harsh crime-control measures and raises critical questions about the "one-size-fits-all" approach to crime of recent decades.

Neal Shover is a professor in the Department of Sociology at the University of Tennessee in Knoxville.

Index